CRITICAL
FOR A WOM.

"*A Woman's World* is not just a book
for 'Everyman.' It shows how wo.
how the world relates to them." —*The New York Times*

"A rare pleasure." —*Travel & Leisure*

"Whether trekking through remote Bhutan, congregating at a well in
Cameroon, or piling into a minivan for an annual trip to an outlet mall
in Eastern Tennessee, women approach travel with a unique sense of
discovery and appreciation for other cultures." —*The Seattle Times*

"A wondrous journey into the heart of womanhood and a hard book
to put down. I felt a true sisterhood with the writers as they shared
their laughter and pain, and was awed by the adventures they chose to
tackle. More than entertaining, this moving collection of personal tales
is certain to encourage and inspire women in their search for the true
meaning of life." —*Shape Magazine*

"*A Woman's World* not only gives us a special sense of place and a
glimpse into the women traveling through it, but also insight into ourselves. The book is packed with stories of courage and confidence, independence and introspection; if they don't inspire you to pack your
bags and set out into the world, I cannot imagine what would."
—*Self Magazine*

"Women travel for all sorts of reasons, but in a way, they all seem to be
looking for a little magic. In *A Woman's World*...traveling seems to
reignite in many of the women dormant feelings of an earlier time,
when they seemed to know for certain that there was more that they
wanted, even if they weren't always sure how to find it. Some of them
finally have, and readers will delight in sharing their experiences."
—*San Francisco Chronicle*

"Women do travel differently from men, and as I read *A Woman's
World*, I found myself admiring their insight, their determination, and
their courage. Marybeth Bond has put together a wonderful collection
of stories that shape a fascinating perspective of women on the go and
the places they visit." —*The Miami Herald*

A WOMAN'S WORLD AGAIN

TRUE STORIES OF WORLD TRAVEL

Edited by

MARYBETH BOND

TRAVELERS' TALES
AN IMPRINT OF SOLAS HOUSE, INC.
PALO ALTO

Travelers' Tales and Solas House are trademarks of Solas House, Inc., 853 Alma
Street, Palo Alto, California 94301. www.travelerstales.com

Cover design: Stefan Gutermuth
Cover photograph: Jupiter Images
Page layout: Cynthia Lamb

Library of Congress Cataloging-in-Publication Data

A woman's world again : true stories of world travel / edited by Marybeth Bond.
— 1st ed.
    p. cm.
  ISBN 1-932361-52-9 (pbk.)
1. Women travelers—Anecdotes. 2. Voyages and travels—Anecdotes.
I. Bond, Marybeth.

G465.W649 2007
910.4092'2—dc22
                    2007027700

First Edition
Printed in the United States
10 9 8 7 6 5 4 3 2 1

I am developing a high opinion of myself as a traveler. I consider that I excel most masculine travelers, for I travel in all countries without arms to protect me, without Baedecker and Bradshaw to inform me, and without book companion or tobacco to console me.

—LILIAN LELAND
Traveling Alone: A Woman's Journey Around the World (1890)

Table of Contents

Introduction

My writing career began in a most unconventional way. After college and graduate school, I moved from one corporate job to another. I found myself building a career I did not really want. At twenty-nine I realized I was stuck in a successful but unsatisfying job in the high tech industry in San Francisco. I was living in a velvet coffin: cultivated life, tasteful possessions, and plenty of money. But I was bored, dissatisfied, and had no passion for my life. I dated but couldn't find a "Mr. Right." I wasn't ready to settle down to marriage, mortgage, and the white picket fence. I had to do something to get a new perspective on my life and to find the gusto I'd lost. But what? And how?

While visiting my parents in Ohio, I found a box of faded yellow *National Geographic* magazines in the attic. Leafing through issue after issue reminded me of a childhood dream of traveling around the world. My unfulfilled dream spurred me to action.

A year later, after much saving and planning, I quit my job, put my car, clothing, and career in storage, and bought a one way ticket to Bangkok. Why Bangkok? It sounded exotic. I took a sleeping pill on the flight because I was terrified of traveling alone. In fact, I had very little experience in being alone. I had never eaten in a restaurant or gone to a movie without a companion. While some friends thought (and told me) I was nuts, I traveled "single and solo" for two years around the world. It was during my travels that I discovered the "gutsy woman" within and rekindled my passion for life. I found a new purpose: to give women advice, support, and the courage to get out and see the world.

For two years I walked, hiked, climbed, cycled, swam, and kayaked my way through six continents and more than seventy countries, from the depths of the Flores Sea to the summit of Mt. Kilimanjaro, across the Himalayas and the Sahara Desert. I lived with nomads in the Thar Desert of India, Sherpa families in Nepal, the Black Thai hill tribes in Northeast Vietnam, Gamelan musicians in Bali, Gaelic dairy farmers on the Dingle Peninsula, and I even met my future husband, an American trekker, in Kathmandu.

When I got home, *Self* and *Outside* magazines interviewed me about my solo travels. *Outside* put me on the cover. My travels led me to a career in travel writing; from *City Sports*, ivillage.com, national newspapers and magazines to creating the books *A Woman's World* and *Gutsy Women*. These all helped me fulfill my need to encourage women to "just go."

The success of these books led to more books: *A Woman's Passion for Travel*, *A Woman's Europe*, *A Woman's Asia*, *A Mother's World*, and *Gutsy Mamas*. Each book reflected my changing life and travel experiences. *Gutsy Women* even led me to be a guest on *The Oprah Winfrey Show*.

After I married Gary, the American trekker I met in Kathmandu, a new chapter of my life began. I shared in the responsibility of parenting and mortgages. For several years my exotic travels gave way to domestic family vacations and business trips. As my books became more popular, I appeared on national television and spoke at international corporate conferences. I participated in literary festivals and presented to women's groups as an advocate for women's travel. Speaking to audiences of women stimulated me to write more books and to share stories and wisdom about life on the road.

Fortunately my family life didn't end my wanderlust and opportunities to travel. Instead we began to travel together. In the last decade, my husband and I have taken our girls to Indonesia, Thailand, Europe, Mexico, and camping across the United States. We survived the tsunami in Phuket, Thailand, "Euro-trekking" with backpacks and rail passes across Europe, and youth hostels in defunct lighthouses along the Pacific Coast. We have bunked down in remote villages in the homes of the Karen Tribe in Northern Thailand and camped with the Navajo on tribal lands in Arizona. We lived with and shared in the daily lives of two Mexican families (in Cuernavaca and San Miguel de Allende) while attending language school. Other families hosted us in their homes in Switzerland, Luxembourg, and France. What did we learn along the way? We discovered that language, culture, and age are not barriers to communication and new friendships.

Through an astounding range of encounters worldwide, I have witnessed that where women go, relationships follow. We move in and out of the lives of the people we meet along the way. The shared experience of nurturing creates a strong bond between us. For many women travelers, including myself, the most meaningful memories involved the people with whom we connected on the journey. Women— complete strangers— have reached out and helped me when I was lost, lonely, or unsure of myself, from Marrakech to Machu Picchu.

My books are a way for me to give back to all those generous women. *A Woman's World Again* is my attempt to reach out to female travelers with encouragement and inspiration, through my own stories and those of other bold, courageous women. There is still a great need for advice, support, and a nudge to go out and explore our beautiful planet.

My mother used to tell her three daughters, "Give the best you have to the world, and the best will come back to you." This collection of women's travel stories includes just a few of the best experiences women's travel has to offer. May these stories help you on your journey through life and on the road.

—MARYBETH BOND

SUSAN VAN ALLEN

⋆ * ⋆

Pulling the Trigger
on a Trip

How do you know when to say Yes?

"I USED TO BE THE KIND OF PERSON WHO COULD MAKE decisions," I tell my shrink as I stretch out on the stiff gray couch. "I mean shouldn't a woman in her forties be in a position to easily say 'yes' or 'no' to a pop-up ad for an airfare sale to Rome, instead of feeling tormented?" It's these little things that really drive home the fact that my life has become one big unsalvageable mess.

In the silence that follows my outburst, I know he's giving me time to look deep inside and answer that question myself. Ouch...the thought of leaving town and saving money on these excruciating weekly sessions—using it for something like a plane ticket—seems very appealing. The poor doctor would probably be relieved to have his Wednesday afternoons free of the monotonous saga of my life's holding patterns The dilemma of the moment is that of course I want to leap at this airfare sale, but my leaping mechanism is fouled up by a horrid condition I call Traveler's Block.

Has all that talk about the rising Euro and advice about how a woman in my age bracket should be focused on saving for retirement seeped in and put my Holly Golightly years behind me? No, it's more like the TB (Traveler's Block) is rooted in a slow-simmering "I don't know what's going to happen next" panic. As in, a freelance writer who doesn't know where her next paycheck is coming from cannot simply click-click and fly off to Italy…or can she?…or should she?

I could take my friend Mark's advice. "Buy a non-refundable ticket," is what he says to anyone "between jobs" in Los Angeles. According to Mark, who works as a freelance film editor, buying a non-refundable airplane ticket has gotten him work every time.

I call him from the car when I leave the shrink and he urges me to make the leap, rattling away in his bulldozing style: "Just make sure the ticket's absolutely non-refundable and comes with a fat penalty for changing dates. You've gotta treat the L.A. business as though it's a boyfriend who's not stepping up to the plate. The minute you make a commitment to date someone else—WHAM! Boyfriend Number One is on his knees begging you to come back with the proposal and the ring. Trust me, it's the only way."

I give him back some nice "uh-huhs" while thinking his non-refundable advice absolutely cuckoo. With a nearly maxed out credit card, I am in no position to play Mark's risky game or to even think about travel.

People who think about travel have life plans, steady incomes, dental plans that fully cover root canals. They have those solid jobs that come with vacation time. They're people like my friend Pam, who calls to tell me that she and two other couples have booked a villa in Provence for the spring vacation two years from now. I can't make a decision about what I'm doing in two days, never mind two years. At this point, I get sent into a spin when I'm at the supermarket and the cashier asks, "Paper or plastic?"

All I do know is I've got to stick around, write spec upon spec, keep my feelers out, check job-site after job-site on the internet.... Which is what I was doing when the ad zapped on to my screen. "DO NOT CLICK—DO NOT!" screamed my inner killjoy.

After sending out two pitch letters with clips, temptation took hold of my devilish right hand, which shot out to click open that ad. Why did they have to include the most beautiful photographs—the Spanish Steps blanketed by pale magenta azaleas in bloom, gushing fountains all lit up in the Piazza Navona? Why can't it be a bargain fare to any place else but Rome—*la citta eterna* that tugs at my heart—where on every visit that deep sense of home shoots through me the moment my plane touches down...Rome!

On the phone with my sister, who calls to offer her support through my down time, I joke about chucking it all and heading off to Italy. She finds the idea hysterical—married with children and no ups and downs in her financial department, my lifestyle offers her constant amusement. I blab away, "Yeah, like I'd just disappear for a

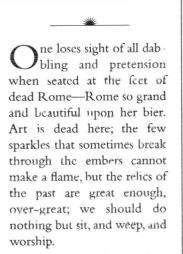

One loses sight of all dabbling and pretension when seated at the feet of dead Rome—Rome so grand and beautiful upon her bier. Art is dead here; the few sparkles that sometimes break through the embers cannot make a flame, but the relics of the past are great enough, over-great; we should do nothing but sit, and weep, and worship.

—Margaret Fuller Ossoli,
At Home and Abroad (1848)

while and get inspired by great art and beautiful people who don't care about plastic surgery—wouldn't that be just nuts?"

There's an edge to her laugh, as if she's holding back panic, imagining me showing up on her doorstep, destitute and begging to crash in her basement for the rest of my life.

I hang up and mutter defenses: "I mean, isn't traveling at the drop of a hat one of the perks of freelancing? Aren't these life-enriching experiences necessary for a writer?" Then I see sister's face before me: "Admit it, you're just trying to escape reality."

I need to do something with that damn ad. I forward it to my Italophile galfriend, Louise. She instantly e-mails back: "Are you going?" and comes up strong against what she calls my "lame-ass excuses" with: "If you don't spend the money on that it'll go to your teeth or your car. Years from now you think you'll regret it? You think you'll be sitting in some ratty dive when you're seventy-five eating cat food, complaining: *Oh, if I hadn't spent that money on that trip to Italy I'd be in much better financial shape now?*

Well, maybe if something drops out of the sky before the fare sale deadline on Friday, I could consider it.... I could get an assignment for a couple of months from now and then squeeze this trip in as a little celebratory gift to myself. Who knows what *could* happen?

Aaaghhh.... Why can't all of this *I shouldn't go/maybe I should/I can't/maybe I can* just resolve itself? I need some sure sign—a burst of a red light that will keep me confidently in L.A. or a green light that could allow me to move forward with absolute assurance to go ahead and buy that ticket.

Betsy, my old friend from San Francisco, calls while I'm back at the computer. As she fills me in on her latest money-making scheme, I multi-task. Just for a laugh, I get back on that airline site and punch in some departure and return dates. I stare at the screen as Betsy, who ran a mega-bucks dot com biz in the late 90s, jabbers on about her plan for a new project that's sure to revive her company, and somehow I'm zapped to a reservation form. I freeze until my session gets timed out. I get booted off as Betsy switches the topic to a friend of hers I've met a couple of times: "Kathy felt a lump…"

I cradle the phone with my shoulder and use both hands to reach under my shirt and do that exam I forget to do every month, as Betsy goes on about the horrors of chemo and shaky diagnoses. Everything feels okay.

Betsy finishes up with: "So you never know what's going to happen. And how are you?"

"I'm fine," I tell her. "In fact, I'm going to Italy in a couple of weeks."

The excitement and relief that rushes over me as I click "submit" is absolutely non-refundable.

Susan Van Allen is a Los Angeles-based writer who has written for National Public Radio's Savvy Traveler and Marketplace, CNN.com, newspapers, magazines, web sites, and the television show Everybody Loves Raymond. *She travels to Italy as often as possible, to visit relatives, eat and drink well, bike through the countryside, wander through museums, and enjoy the flirtations of those handsome Italian men.*

ABBIE KOZOLCHYK

⋆ ⁺ ⋆

Pretty, Please

An accidental interloper gets a makeover.

IT HAD ALL THE GRAVITY, PURPOSEFULNESS, AND URGENCY OF a situation room—and in fact *was* one, of sorts. Benita's Salon de Belleza, a cramped little lair hidden amidst the sprawl of the surrounding resort, housed a team of stone-faced, sweat-dappled women who worked dauntlessly toward a single goal: prepping every client therein for the looming party.

No mere fiesta was this. The official kickoff to the Fifth Annual Ritmo Social International Golf Invitational of the Dominican Republic promised to be the It event of the season for Dominican A-Listers, the vast majority of whom had just descended on the Puntacana Resort & Club in spectacular fashion. Nearly empty only a day earlier, the property was now awash in super-sized logos, industrial-strength cologne, and the kinds of cars that tend to come with live, female hood ornaments (or so the posters lining my brother's high school bedroom had led me to believe).

My role in the festivities? That of accidental interloper. Having traveled to Puntacana on a totally unrelated assignment, I got a last-minute party invitation upon check-in.

No sooner had I entered the gala than my spectacle-savoring id was gorging deliriously: The hosts included Julio Iglesias (who would, before long, reveal his unique brand of cocktail chatter); the entertainment included Johnny Ventura (the most venerated *merenguero* in existence); and the little extras included New-Year's-Eve-meets-Fourth-of-July-scale fireworks.

But the true scene-stealers were the *Dominicanas* themselves—who bring us back to Benita, and her Pentagon of pre-party preening.

Though I couldn't tell you whether the room was actually five-sided (too many bodies obscured its angles), it was unquestionably the nerve center of a complex, high-level operation that demanded militaristic precision of all concerned. And I joined the fray at T-minus five hours.

Having spent the day diving, I sported the full complement of associated flourishes: a red, rectangular trough embossed impeccably across my face; knotted, salted hair; and eyes-gone-bloodshot during the brief incursion that the Caribbean Sea had made into my mask. And thus was I deemed an esthetical emergency.

"*¡Ay, mi madre!*" were the only words Benita could muster when I turned up on her doorstep. And solely because she was morally opposed to unleashing such a creature on the party did she agree to add me to her already-jammed docket.

But I would have to be patient. Endless numbers of brows, talons, and manes awaited, often requiring a deftly choreographed, three-on-one approach. The client in question would stretch out   locks tossed back and extremities flexed—while beautician A plucked; beautician B filed; and beautician C...well...beautician C's role was in a category unto itself.

By far the stoniest of the bunch, beautician C was the blow-out boss. And let me tell you: In matters of hair straightening,

Dominicans don't fuck around. Nobody wields a dryer more authoritatively—or to sleeker effect—than they do. Between their heroic displays of elbow grease and sheer force of will, no nanowave is left behind. Literally, every last strand—however obstinate—is plied into submission. Watching these women work, I felt I was in the presence of some ancient magicians' guild. And the fraying, patinaed diplomas on display did nothing to discourage that impression.

"Benita Carmona Rodriguez, *Primero Nivel de Corte y Estilo*," read the owner's own parchmented proclamation, translating to "First Level of Cutting and Styling"—and recalling (God help me) the Ordinary Wizarding Levels of Harry Potter fame. But despite her official credentials, alchemy was clearly her strong suit—as I learned during my mandatory pedicure. Failing to find quite the right shade of polish for me, she casually blended a thousand lacquers in about half a second to produce precisely the color I'd have chosen if left to my own devices (and in Benita's domain, no one was).

But I'm getting ahead of myself—and all the clients who were there before me. And skipping over them would be unconscionable, such astounding specimens of my gender were they.

I tried to avert my eyes, lest my stare go from simply rude to outright creepy. But nothing was sufficiently distracting. A brief survey of the available reading material revealed that every magazine in the salon dated mysteriously to 2001 (while the requisite accessories—*quinceañera* crowns, bridal headdresses, and all other manner of cranial pageantry—were of a significantly older vintage…circa 1983, if I had to guess). And though I did find something in the September 2001 *National Geographic Traveler* that would normally suck me in—a Croatia piece by travel-writing demigoddess Jan Morris—I couldn't have cared less at that moment about Draguc, Buzet, or even Hum.

Basically, I was in the middle of an estrogen lightning storm—and I was powerless to turn away.

The women in question were not only startlingly beautiful; they were—without exception—the most detail-oriented bunch of primpers I'd ever seen, to the extent that each brow shaping became a lengthy negotiation between owner and groomer.

"*Mas pa'arriba*," the former would instruct, indicating that she'd like a higher arch.

"*Imposible*," the latter would respond, drawing a line if not exactly in the sand, then certainly across the supraorbital ridge.

And so the parleying would begin, often requiring third-party mediation. But once an accord was reached on the exact altitude and angle of the brow, there was also the linearity of the nails to consider (straight edge or subtly rounded corners?); the volume of the hair to calibrate (on a scale of Demi to Beyonce, the most popular pouf quotient fell exactly in between); etc.

How different this scene was from the one I had witnessed months earlier, when my husband and I decided to walk the length of Broadway, from our home in Manhattan's Financial District to the last subway stop in the Bronx. About four hours into the trek, just past Columbia University, we hit Dominican territory, where every other storefront is a salon/barbershop. And unless we were there at a totally anomalous time, these bastions of beauty were also the epicenter of daily life. Every baseball game in progress on the face of the planet beamed out of their tiny, wall-slung TVs; dueling merengues blasted from countless, jury-rigged speakers; and people's perpetual comings and goings formed a sort of bodily

Brownian motion that went on for blocks. The mood was light; the conversation breezy; and the jokes decidedly dirty.

★

I'd heard many a story about the Dominican Republic, most of which involved sunburns and drunken spring break antics, and so I went, but under slightly different circumstances. While enrolled in a doula-training course, I met Annie Heath, a nurse-midwife and director of Proyecto Adames (www.proyectoadames.org), an organization aimed at lowering the rate of infant and maternal mortality and morbidity in the DR by offering a midwifery model of care. Annie brings volunteers to Hospital San Vicente de Paul, where they participate in the daily realities of the maternity ward. In the week I was there, I attended births that ranged from beautiful and smooth to truly scary. Never have I seen the stuff of life so rawly. Life and death and love, these things I discuss so abstractly in my college classes, were there before me in the most concrete of forms.

—Noelle O'Reilly,
"The Maternity Ward"

But beauty was no laughing matter at Puntacana Resort & Club, where the event at hand was high society and high stakes. Blowing away fellow celebrants was paramount, and no one would be caught dead looking anything short of impeccable.

Except, evidently, for me.

The last one to have her hair done, I had the misfortune of being dismissed just as a hurricane was dropping by. Of course, the stylists did everything in their collective power to protect my delicate do, whereupon I learned a new word: *tubis.* Previously known to me only as *Abu Agella* (a term I had picked up from Yemenite-Israeli friends), this coif configuration is familiar to every culture that believes freshly smoothed strands can triumph over adversity (read: humidity). Starting on one side of the head, you meticulously brush, wrap, and pin your way across the back—and eventually, over the forehead—until you've created a self-sustaining hair turban. The idea is to release the locks at the last possible moment, ideally in a hermetically sealed, moisture-free environment.

But even with the expertly wrought *tubis*, and the garbage bag the girls threw over it, my hair was no match for this storm system. By the time I got back to my room, all their hard work had been undone. And my only option was to proceed to the party sans damage-control, or risk missing Johnny Ventura. So off I went, looking almost as beastly as I had when Benita first laid eyes on me.

At least one person didn't seem to mind: resident man-about-town and the party's titular host, Julio Iglesias. Mere seconds after we were introduced, he inexplicably—and repeatedly—told me I'd need to return to the Dominican Republic soon...to get pregnant. He reprised the line so many times, in fact, that I finally asked if my baby-hungry parents had paid him for his services. Turns out he was simply infatuated with the idea of pregnancy at the time (his wife was expecting his eighth child), and thought pretty much every woman at the party should get knocked up. His parting words to me: "I make love only once a year, but when I do it, I do it big!"

This revelation, of course, shed a whole new light on the subject of all the girls he'd loved before. Had Willie Nelson acceded to a radically lopsided duet? But then I started doing the math: Even if my new friend wasn't exaggerating, and really had been on a once-yearly schedule for a while, the fact that the man was sixty-three translated to a respectably high head count (so to speak), give or take a few repeat customers.

However bizarre the exchange, it receded quickly in my mind as I made my way through the crowd. In fact, dwelling on any one thing was impossible under the sensory-over-loaded circumstances. Liberally applied fragrances mingled and hung midair, creating their own foggy microclimates. Teeny-tiny halters (some with internal hydraulic lifts, apparently) hoisted glistening breasts skyward. And diamonds the size of small continents threw off a constant, blinding glare. All the while, Johnny Ventura's music shook everything—hips, asses, tectonic plates—indiscriminately. The sum total? The perfect spectacle.

Then I realized: I wasn't the only observer. I spied a familiar, imposing figure on the sidelines—and it was none other than Benita. But she had softened considerably since last I saw her in the Preen Zone. In this new theater of operations, she seemed to shed the mantle of *generalissima* for that of proud parent. As she surveyed all that lay before her—those nails, that hair, those shimmer-misted décolletages—her broad smile and subtle nod bore an unmistakable message: "My work here is done."

A recovering beauty editor turned frequent travel writer, Abbie Kozolchyk divides her time between New York and wherever the assignment gods take her. She writes for National Geographic Traveler, Forbes Traveler, Allure, W, Martha Stewart's Body + Soul, Self, Redbook, *and others. For a random sampling of her work, visit her online at www.abbiekozolchyk.com.*

DULCE MARÍA GRAY

* * *

One Night on Moses Mountain

A holy place delivers.

I'D BEEN IN AND OUT OF CAIRO MOST OF JULY AND FELT safer walking there at night than I do in New York or San Francisco. During the day as I explored mosques, the labyrinthine Coptic district, or any other area, invariably children greeted me with "I love you" and "Welcome to Egypt." At first I was startled to hear the words in English, and even more startled to hear them in Spanish, Russian, French, Italian, German, Japanese, Mandarin, or Portuguese—even Danish and Icelandic. The phrases were uttered easily and often everywhere I strolled. After two weeks I began to wonder if President Hosni Mubarak's administration had held a massive public campaign to teach Egyptians to shout multilingual endearments to tourists; by August when I left Egypt I was convinced that kids, and oftentimes adults, simply express genuine wonderment and cordiality toward tourists, especially when their sentiments are acknowledged with a smile or a thank you.

That's not what my family had expected. They worried when I told them I'd be joining a group of professors who would be spending over a month exploring the country. They feared terrorist attacks, and justifiably, I supposed, since Egypt has a history of such events: On April 18, 1996 a gunman opened fire and killed 18 Greek and Australian tourists who were about to board a bus outside Cairo's Europa Hotel near the pyramids; on September 18, 1997 a gunman attacked a tourist bus outside the Egyptian Museum in Tahrir Square in Cairo killing 9 and wounding 35 tourists; on November 17 of that same year, 4 Egyptians and 71 tourists were massacred in Queen Hatshepsut's Temple in Luxor; after seven uneventful years, on October 7, 2004 attackers bombed the Taba Hilton in the Red Sea villages of Taba and Ras Shitan killing 34 and wounding more than 100; on April 7, 2005, just two months before my arrival in Egypt, a suicide bomber rode his motorcycle right into the historic shopping bazaar called Khan al-Khalili killing 2 tourists and wounding 18; then on the 30th of that same month 2 women opened fire on a tour bus wounding 2 passengers. On the 22nd of July I was awoken by the shocking news that earlier that day simultaneous bombs had gone off in the Ghazala Garden Hotel in Sharm El-Sheikh; our group had just been there. Over 80 people were killed; over 200 were wounded. But none of that worried me when I decided to go to Egypt, nor is it what I remember of having been there—perhaps because I firmly believe that traveling (and meeting a country's people) can spur profound growth, and that if I anesthetize myself, I diminish the experience.

I found Egypt to be mesmerizing, culturally rich beyond measure, and an enlightening location for pondering the contentious relationship between Muslims, Jews, and Christians. Moses Mountain, located 250 miles from Cairo in the middle of the Sinai Peninsula, like no other place in Egypt, epitomizes that connection. All three Abrahamic religions have venerated and fought for Moses Mountain. No one really knows which of the cluster of granite mountains the prophet Moses actually climbed millennia ago, but currently most agree that it was Mount Sinai, which the local people call Jebel Musa—Moses Mountain. For months, I had been looking forward to hiking it. A few of us in our traveling group decided that in order to avoid the scorching heat we would make the trek at night. Depending on which of the two routes taken, for most people it is merely a three-hour hike, but our Bedouin guide, Tawhid, timed our departure around midnight so that most of us could be sure to reach the summit by sunrise.

We met Tawhid early in the evening at the foot of Mount Sinai, where Saint Catherine monastery reigns as the oldest continuous place of Christian worship in the world. It's an impressive fortress built by the Roman Emperor Justinian in the first half of the sixth century; its forty-five-foot high by three-foot thick walls have consistently prevented invasion. Justinian picked the site because reportedly he identified the Burning Bush, as it's mentioned in the Book of Exodus, where God revealed Himself to Moses and then gave him the Ten Commandments. The descendant of the fabled bush sits inside behind a rock and cement wall and is watered from a well believed to be the same one where Moses met Zipporah, his wife. Since early in Christian history, hermetic monks have considered the monastery and surrounding area hallowed ground. Today, there are several monks in the monastery, including one from the United States, and only one hermit who lives in a cave-house he carved out of a nearby cliff and surrounded with olive and date trees.

Tawhid explained that Saint Catherine Protectorate is a busy place, especially since being declared a UNESCO World

Heritage site in 2002, and that the Bedouin of the Jebaliya tribe who live in the area have become integral in the thriving tourist business. No matter the time of year, there's a steady stream of visitors who trek to the summit at 7,496 feet (2,285 meters) above sea level. When one of my colleagues asked about him, Tawhid hesitantly talked about being from a long line of traditionally nomadic Bedouin who migrated in search of water and grazing for their livestock, mostly goats, and who now live in el-Arish. Distinctly different tribes have co-existed in the Sinai Peninsula since ancient times. Living in this demanding region has forged in them a resourceful and collaborative attitude. Today most are desperately impoverished and the men attempt to earn wages by trading animals and other goods in nearby villages, tending flocks, laboring in mining companies, picking olives, and working at menial jobs in tourism. I knew that there's 30 percent unemployment in North Sinai and its capital el-Arish, the major commercial center where most of the population of 219,000 is concentrated, and that the area is considered a hotbed for terrorist activity. Following the most recent attack numerous Bedouins had been arbitrarily arrested.

Tawhid came along for our privately arranged insider's tour of the monastery. Although the building is in need of much repair and updating, the monastery holds a precious Byzantine art collection, the second largest and important batch of illuminated manuscripts in the world (the first is in the Vatican), and part of the remnants of the 350 A.D. Codex Sinaiticus, one of the world's oldest copies of the Greek manuscript of the New Testament. (The other parts are in the British Museum.) Tawhid told us about the legend of Saint Catherine: She was a beautiful woman who lived in fourth century Alexandria and refused to renounce her Christian beliefs; thus she was persecuted and killed, but, as the mystical legend goes, angels took her and placed her on the highest mountain in the Sinai Peninsula, Saint Catherine Mountain. Seven centuries later, monks found her and enshrined her in a golden casket inside a marble chest. Supposedly, the fragrant smells that emit from her body have powerful healing powers, and today hoards await impatiently the occasional opening of her casket.

Tawhid showed us that from Saint Catherine monastery there are two routes leading up to Mount Moses: The faster and steeper one is called Stairway of Repentance; the easier but longer one is called Camel Path. We took the seven-kilometer long Camel Path and started the initial 4,000-step snaking ascent through a narrow trail packed with throngs of people, braying camels, and Bedouin men selling *shemaghs* (fringed scarves), camel rides, torches (flashlights), water, tea, blankets, food, and even souvenir mountain rocks. We wended our way in the dark, dodging sharp rocks and camel droppings, thankful to have brought water and worn layers of clothing and hiking shoes and amazed that some people actually intended to make it up wearing just flip-flops. All you could see were myriad stars and thousands of single-file flickering torches pointed downward. We meandered up and up, some of us huffing in the cold of the night.

When he noticed I was getting very tired, Tawhid walked with me for a distance. He lit a cigarette. "How often," I asked, "do you climb Mount Moses?" His green eyes darted, his body leaning toward me as he helped me to quickly recover from almost tripping. "Four times a week, maybe more depending on the tourists." No wonder he's so slim and agile, I thought immediately. "Why did you come to Egypt?" he asked as if wanting to deflect my questions. "I want to learn about your culture and history." He responded, "I want to learn more about America. I want to go there." I don't know if I actually spoke the word "why," but he explained: "I want

to go to school there, to university. Do you know how I can
be accepted in your university? I have been saving money for
five years to go." Tawhid volunteered the amount he'd saved
and I simply could not tell him that once converted it would
not cover the cost for one class at most colleges in the United
States. He was at least the fifth young man who had asked me
that same question. "I have an uncle who moved to Germany
and he has been trying to help me to go with him, but I want
to go to America." "Why not stay here in Egypt, Tawhid?" I
questioned a bit dishonestly since I pretty much knew what
the answer might be, but I wanted to know his opinion.
Calmly, surprisingly candid and very matter of fact, he said:
"No jobs. I'm twenty-five. I went to university. My brothers
and cousins did not. We cannot find jobs. I went to Cairo for
two years but no jobs. My brothers and cousins and some of
the women left here. My mother died. My father is here but
cannot work like before." I didn't want to make him uncomfortable by asking more personal questions and simply let him
lead the conversation toward a long description of the wonders of Egypt.

Three quarters of the way, after camels could no longer
climb and Bedouins stopped trying to sell their arm strength
to pull you up each stair, I could only hear the sound of my
breathing and pumping heart in rhythm with the crushing of
stones beneath my measured steps. Some time after five in the
morning, by then gripped with fatigue, I began to notice the
outline of massive mountains rippling like an endless open
ocean. Slowly, the luminescent horizon began to appear as we
almost reached the summit. I didn't stop to absorb the sight of
masses gathered in front of teashops and vendors, or the cam-
eras flashing like fireflies. I wanted desperately to greet the
morning sun from the highest peak. My second wind propelled me toward the additional 750 steps; I leaped through

the jagged ridge, stepping mindfully on an astounding staircase hewn by monks hundreds of years before any crane or electrical tool could help them. I sat at the very pinnacle, feeling the crisp wind on my face, and I waited for the sun to appear.

Bit by bit it made its majestic entrance warming my chilled body and permitting me to see for miles and miles. Awed, I allowed myself to cry.

I'd read that I would be able to see the southern tip of the Sinai Peninsula and the resort city of Sharm el Sheik, the Gulf of Suez, the Red Sea, Gulf of Aqaba, and on to the Arabian peninsula. But I focused on the ridged monotone red granite mountains of all heights; the speck of Saint Catherine in the barren jagged valley below; and right next to me the small Christian chapel and Muslim mosque, a few people nestled alone, like me, in crevices; a French group of nuns enjoying Mass; a charismatic English Christian family reading the Bible aloud; ten Hasidic Jews chanting; and

People who know nothing about these things will tell you that there is no addition of pleasure in having a landscape to yourself. But this is not true. It is a pleasure exclusive, unreasoning, and real: it has some of the quality and some of the intensity of love: it is a secret shared: a communion which an intruder desecrates: and to go to the lonely and majestic places of the world for poor motives, to turn them to cheap advertisement or flashy journalism, jars like a spiritual form of prostitution on your true lover of the hills The solitary rapture must be disinterested. And often it is stumbled upon unthinkingly by men whose business takes them along remoter ways: who suddenly find enchantment on their path and carry it afterwards through their lives with a secret sense of exile.

—Freya Stark, *The Valleys of the Assassins* (1934)

twenty Muslims kneeling in prayer. I suddenly realized that I was not alone; every inch of this steeple was occupied by a multitude of distinct groups. I welled with the naïve desire to see this communion enacted in every corner of the world, and with the deep awareness of that impossibility.

At about seven I walked down the 750 steps to a landing filled with snack stands, sunglass-wearing, cell-phone-toting, coffee-sipping tourists, pilgrims, and guides, and all manner of vendors offering to take your photo, renting blankets, and selling postcards and trinkets. I found some of the members of my group in one of the stands, ordered a hot mint tea and sat in a corner. When I peeked through the blanket covering what seemed to be a window, I froze with the recognition that the shop was teetering on a peak as if on the head of a pin. Way below in the stark desert, in between the massive boulders, I could see a few tiny goat herders. Tawhid offered us Bedouin breakfast: goat milk with bread, called *gourass*, made from salt water and baked under ashes then soaked in tea with goat milk. I drank the delicious *bonn* (coffee prepared from green coffee beans that are roasted in a small tin container and ground with ginger and cooked in a *gabana*, a round earthenware container with a long narrow neck).

Shortly after, we descended slowly through the precipitous Stairway of Repentance, Tawhid leading the way and telling us about the chapels built along the path throughout the centuries. All of us stopped to admire occasional bright yellow flowers pushing through crevices—struggling, I imagined, to bask in the early morning warmth of the sun. The images of those exquisite, hardy flowers flourishing in one of the world's most inhospitable conditions are still vivid in my mind; the experience continues to remind me of one of my favorite thinkers and the author of *Black Skin, White Masks*, Franz Fanon, who wrote in 1952: "In the world through which I travel, I am endlessly creating myself." Fanon learned that lesson the hard way—colonization having forced him to travel—since he was born on the island Martinique, was educated in France but worked and felt at home in North Africa. He journeyed and indeed allowed his diasporic wanderings to infuse in him an awareness of his place and responsibility in our world. Like Fanon, I know that traveling is the most palpable way to grow and be(come) who I am—especially when it's to places that are very different from what is familiar to me, and particularly when I can exchange ideas with the people I encounter.

Dulce María Gray is a professor of Cultural Studies, Composition, and World Literature at West Valley College in Northern California, and an avid traveler who passionately supports the inclusion of travel as an integral part of the curriculum. Right now she is working on a collection of essays about the relationship between traveling and the construction of self-identity. Her major publication is an ethnographic study called High Literacy and Ethnic Identity.

SYBIL BAKER

✦ ✦ ✦

The Kind of Traveler I Am

She had to travel alone to find out.

As an American woman living and teaching English in Seoul, South Korea, for the past seven years, I was no stranger to travel. During our semester breaks, my husband and I were often schlepping our backpacks around the world for months at a time. We'd drifted on a raft made of used tires down a secluded river in Sumatra just to glimpse the endangered orangutans hanging from the jungle trees on the river's edge. Once, in Siem Reap, Cambodia, we paid to have a "guard" accompany us and our guide in our jeep to protect us from roving bandits, who, a few months earlier, had shot an American woman for her camera. During that ride through the remote villages to see Bantai Seray, the "crown jewel" of Cambodia's Angkor Wat, I kept my eyes on the AK47 placed in between the front seats of our jeep. I was afraid to ask if the safety latch was on, or if there even was one.

We'd had many other adventures. We'd ridden in old Soviet jeeps through dust storms in the Gobi desert, eaten mutton until our pores sweated stale sheep, and listened to the infamous Mongolian throat singing. I'd sprained my ankle in Beijing, and shattered my elbow while bicycling down Milford Sound in New Zealand, and battled travelers' diarrhea in Vietnam. We'd camped next to Russia's Lake Baikal, walked around Australia's Uluru, and traversed Peru's Machu Picchu. And yet, despite a passport filled with stamps from more than twenty-five countries—many of them third world—I'd never traveled alone.

That changed when my marriage abruptly ended after I discovered my "perfect" husband had been engaging in a series of affairs for the last few years. Virtually overnight I went from someone South Koreans envied—a woman with a devoted husband, a job at a prestigious university, money, and time to travel—to (in my mind at least) someone they felt sorry for—an out-of-place American woman, adrift in Asia with no real career path, divorced, childless, and well past Korea's "old maid" status of thirty. And yet I knew that judgment in Koreans' eyes was really a mirror of my own. I felt over the hill, undesirable, and alone. I was a single woman on the other side of the world, away from family and friends, some of whom were urging me to move back to the States, where, they were certain, I wouldn't feel so isolated. Yet my job and my life in Korea were the only forms of stability I had. I didn't want to give those up, too.

While I wasn't ready to move back to the States, I did know that I needed to get out of Seoul for a while. I needed to forge a new identity as a "singleton," one built on self-confidence, self-respect, and self-knowledge. The best way for me to do that was to take my first trip alone.

"So what kind of traveler are you?" a friend had asked me once, meaning: do you like beaches or museums, the Hilton or hostels, planes or trains? This should have been an easy question for a person who had traveled so much. But it wasn't.

I *had* been the kind of traveler my husband was. Someone who didn't stay in one place too long, documented every event with hundreds of photos and notes, crammed in as many cultural wonders in as little time as possible, and, when there was time, sought out the non-tourist "authentic" spots. I don't begrudge that style of traveling—I did a lot and saw a lot. In fact, after a long day of sightseeing when my husband and I would return to our guesthouse, lunch skipped because we hadn't had the time, I would often encounter other backpackers who had not even left the hammock of the common room. Why, I wondered, had they traveled to Asia, if all they did was lounge at the guesthouse all day and party with their fellow Westerners at night?

I never thought that I minded my husband's way of travel. It suited us and our marriage. He enjoyed the planning and research phase, while I couldn't be bothered. After he planned our trip, he'd hand me the *Lonely Planet* guidebook transformed into a colored pinwheel of Post-it notes indicating the places he'd narrowed down for our itinerary. While my comments were welcome, I was content to skim over the marked sections and put in my one-cent's worth. Usually, I didn't feel strongly enough to suggest anything other than his course of action, and was happy to let someone else do the work.

Yet our jam-packed travel schedule left little time for sleeping in or slacking off. Sometimes the vacation felt like a forced march past a blur of famous temples and museums. Sure the sites were awe-inspiring, but even armies rest at fifty-minute intervals. Occasionally after a long day of sightseeing and another skipped lunch, I would suspend my judgment and instead cast an envious eye at those backpackers lolling about at the guesthouse, culturally deficient, yet infinitely more relaxed.

But if I wasn't entirely like my ex-husband, then what kind of traveler was I? I wasn't sure. I only knew that when our marriage ended, I wanted to go somewhere, but not to any of the places he—we—would have gone. I also knew that I would not research any places on the internet or thumb through travel books in a cramped corner of a bookstore. Instead, I summoned what remaining faith I had in God and the forces of life and decided I would wait for a voice to tell me.

It didn't take long. Even I was surprised at how quickly and assuredly that voice did come—only days after my husband left for Japan and our marriage was essentially over. This voice came from my subconscious, unexpectedly. But as soon as I heard it, my body tingled with excitement. I felt alive and hopeful about my life. I knew that this trip was vital to my recovery.

Prague, the voice said. *You must go to Prague.*

In my mind, Prague was a city of artists and romantics. The place had first interested me as a writer in the early 1990s, when the buzz was that Prague was the new Paris for expatriates. Ten years later, I read about a month-long summer seminar for writers sponsored by the University of New Orleans. I'd never even mentioned to my husband that I might be interested in such a program because it was not "our kind" of travel. Besides being tame and not so exotic by our third-world travel standards, my husband would not have wanted to stay in one place for such a long period of time, taking classes with a bunch of *Americans*.

Yet, I felt that a month surrounded by my own kind—Americans—was exactly what I did need. Even though I had gone back to the States every few years or so, the country, especially after 9/11, had become more inscrutable and incomprehensible to me than the villagers I'd met in Laos. More than that, I also felt that I would meet many creative older women who might be role models in my suddenly single life. I was curious about the college students, too. Although I taught at a university, college students in Korea were quite different: drugs (even pot) and casual sex were virtually nonexistent in their lives. Most of my students had never held even a part-time job. Many of their mothers still dressed, fed, and cleaned up for them. The students were sweet, innocent, and also widely naïve about many of the ways of the world. They often asked me about what life was like at universities in the States, and, except for a few generalizations and sweeping platitudes, I had little to say because I no longer knew.

Of course it wasn't just a connection with Americans I was looking for—I could have flown back to the States for that. Prague itself represented many things that spring—a return to my writing, a chance to live in a beautiful city full of art and artists, and, an opportunity to visit a place that I had wanted to go but I never would have, at least under those circumstances, when I was married. One month in one place. Exploring the city, absorbing its rhythms. A leisurely walk instead of a forced march.

I imagined strolling those streets of the "new Paris" with fellow writers, soaking up a bit of old Europe, a part of the world now more foreign to me than the rice paddies of Vietnam.

And so, at thirty-eight, I was taking my first trip alone.

My traveling experience did help with the arrangements. For one, I wasn't afraid of traveling to another continent. I knew where to get the best deals for tickets and how to pack everything I needed into one suitcase that I could wheel around easily. I'd become a veteran of the ten-hour plane flight and could pace myself with magazines, glasses of wine, and in-flight movies.

I arrived in Prague more excited than nervous. As the airport bus tumbled toward the ancient dorm that would be my home for the next month at Charles University, I was at first disappointed with the gray and desolate concrete buildings. It wasn't until we got into the "old town" that the Prague in front of my eyes matched the Prague that had stirred my imagination. The city was a soothing mix of architecture that encompassed Gothic, Art Nouveau, and baroque; cobblestone streets that led to imposing churches and castles and the bustling cafés nestled between them. Ah, Europe!

Inside the dorm at Charles University, the New World had taken over. Loud and boisterous Americans struggled with overstuffed trunks and double suitcases. They wandered about the cavernous halls in their shorts and flip-flops, making themselves at home, heartily embracing their new best friends. After checking in, I rode the elevator to the three-room suite and opened the door to my room. As I sat on one of the bunk beds, I heard shouts and giggles down the hall.

I felt it then, the fist in my stomach that was as tight as the emptiness in the room. I was alone. Just like back in junior high, on that first day of school, when everyone seemed to know someone except me.

That was the biggest change between traveling by myself and with someone. The delicious agony of being alone. I savored the pain because it reminded me that this was my life and that I could still feel something at least.

Over the next few weeks, I tested out my new life as a woman traveling alone. After the challenges of Asian backpacking, Prague in many ways was easy and ideal. I spent most of my time in the three-kilometer radius of the historical town center. I visited Kafka's grave, toured castles and churches, soaked in the museums, and "discovered" the Art Nouveau artist, Alfons Mucha. I joined in on the sponsored field trips out of the city and ventured to the parts of town where bleak concrete buildings and cracked sidewalks were the rule of the day.

Prague was a good city for someone who needed to recover from the betrayals of life. The streets were clean, the buildings scrubbed and renovated, the cafés quaintly European, beer cheap, and everyone, it seemed, spoke excellent English. The historical downtown felt almost like Euro-Disney, a place that held all the benefits and none of the hassles of foreign travel, though priced for the well-heeled tourist. The local citizens must have agreed, at least about the prices; most lived in old Soviet-style apartments and couldn't afford a beer in the downtown of their own city.

> ———— ✻ ————
>
> Most of us…cast longing eyes at the door marked with the magical word "Europe," and it has opened freely enough when the husband said the "Open, sesame;" it is only of late years that women have made the amazing discovery that they can say it themselves with like success, but it is well to keep the hinges well oiled, and the rubbish cleared away from the threshold. When my turn came, I felt as if I had been taken into a high mountain and been promised all the kingdoms of the earth, and had at once accepted the offer.
>
> —Ella W. Thompson,
> *Beaten Paths, or a Woman's Vacation* (1874)

I did, in no time, make a few friends. The students were mostly divided into two groups—undergraduate seniors and graduate students in their early and mid-twenties, and women over forty. I shared a suite with two women in the latter group. Generally the over forty group was single, by choice or not, established in their careers, and without the responsibility of younger children.

At first I admired these slightly older women, these glimpses into my not-so-distant future. Financially and emotionally independent, they seemed content with their lives. They also seemed at peace with their not so perfect Western bodies. After being surrounded by chopstick-thin, cellulite-free Korean women—genetic winners in God's body lottery as one man told me—I had begun feeling, well, frumpy, even though I was slim for my height by Western standards. After all, my husband had cheated on me with women younger and thinner than me, so that must mean I was old and fat, right? (Ask any woman who has been cheated on, and she will admit to similar self-defeating and wrong-headed recriminations). The visual potpourri of dozens of Western women's bodies reminded me that my hips were indeed normal. Many of those women were by Korean standards "fat," but in the context of the little America which made up our dorm, these Western bodies looked generous and accepting—of me and themselves.

These forty-something women were stable souls who spent their free time trying new restaurants or reading in their rooms. With their well-stocked fridges and early bedtimes they were like the mythical responsible older sister, maternal and welcoming. In many ways these older sisters showed me how I could be comfortable in my own skin, even if that skin was not to be caressed by someone else.

Those women showed me that I too was the architect of my life. They had traveled here alone as well, and were also writers, poets, and photographers. In homogenous Korea, I sometimes felt like a freak of nature. I saw now that I was one of many, a part of a sisterhood of independent women who were making their way in a world that had not been what they had thought it would be as young girls. I admired them.

Yet their confidence hid other things. Change and disruption of routine affected them more than my younger classmates.

They were often too tired and overwhelmed to leave the sanctuary of their rooms. Halfway through the month, one of my roommates, a D.C. lawyer, fell on one of the sidewalks and bruised her knee. She retreated to her room for three days, and confided she couldn't wait to get home. They had come here alone, but they traveled in groups, as they were often afraid to do anything by themselves.

They reminded me a bit of the backpackers in my other travels—people who'd taken the time and expense to travel to another country yet were content to recline in hammocks smoking a joint or recline in their beds reading a novel as the day hazed into nothingness. I didn't want to be like that, like them. I knew if I retreated from the pain—physical and emotional—that I would never move beyond the hurt and anger I felt toward my ex-husband. I would never move to a life of my own creation that I was, in the end, responsible for. Life was about taking risks, pushing myself out of my comfort zone. So, I usually respectfully declined my older sisters' invitations to the expensive lunches, and spent most of my time with the college students.

Things had changed since I'd been at college in the 1980s. At that time, we had worn baggy, thrift shop dresses belted with ropes or black t-shirts and formless pants and Doc Martens. We spiked our hair and listened to obscure bands played by our DJ friends on the college radio station. Now, the girls wore belly rings and cropped tops. Butterfly tattoos peeked out of their camisoles. Didn't they know their bra straps and thong underwear were showing? Later I realized that for them there was no shame in showing off their bras or underwear, but I never could quiet the "mom" voice in my head warning that a well-bred girl would never reveal her undergarments on purpose.

Even if these collegiate fashions had elicited a disturbingly prudish reaction on my part (forcing me to face for the first time a mini ohmygodi'mlikemymother crisis), the college students were fun. We danced at clubs three stories high, bar hopped, tried absinthe, and ate lunch together. I listened earnestly to gossip about who had slept with whom. For all their worldly airs, the girls were naïve in a way that my Korean students weren't, in that they seemed to so willingly confuse sex with love. My younger American sisters had their hearts broken many times over that one month because of that confusion.

The two classes I took, a fiction writing workshop and an American expatriate literature class, helped me feel like I was an artist in this city, and that I was also doing something for myself and my future. Our workshop leader was one of the few real ex-pat writers in Prague, and he inspired me to continue finding my own voice as an expatriate writer after that month. The American expatriate class also showed me the proud history of American writers living and traveling abroad, and I saw that I could be part of that continuum. Prague helped me see that my marriage had given me a gift. For without my marriage, I would have stayed in the States and missed out on my experiences abroad that now informed my writing, that gave me something say Traveling with someone had taken me to the place where I could now travel down my own road alone.

Then there were the literary ghosts of Prague: Kafka, Rilke, Kundera. The Czechs didn't want to have much to do with them. To be a Czech artist the requirements seemed to be quite strict—write in Czech and live in Czech. Rilke was barely mentioned, perhaps because he was only born and studied there, and wrote in German. Kafka, who also wrote in German, seemed to be trotted out more for the tourists than

the Czechs themselves. And Kundera was considered a traitor
because he didn't return to Prague from Paris after the Velvet
Revolution. Would my family and friends think me a traitor
when I told them I would be returning to Korea instead of
moving back to the States, now that I didn't have my marriage
as an excuse for living abroad?

For the many of the younger students, this was their first
time in another country. They loved Prague and schemed
wistfully of moving there, although this was more escapist fantasy than any concrete desire. Their enthusiasm reminded me
of my first trip abroad, at age thirty. That was my honeymoon
to Paris and Barcelona in 1994. The cities and people seemed
so much more sophisticated than life even in Washington,
D.C., where we lived. We fantasized about living in Barcelona,
this place that was not America, the place where art was happening, where people must have discussed only important
things like philosophy and politics. Where people didn't wear
shorts or sneakers and instead wore linen and Italian footwear
while drinking aperitifs in outdoor cafés.

Then out of chance more than design, we did move abroad.
Asia was not the U.S., but even more certainly it was not
Europe. After the initial "differentness" of Korea wore off, we
found we were living a life similar to anywhere else. We were
working and paying bills and going to the grocery store. We
soon discovered that, like Churchill's dictum about democracy,
the only thing worse than American television shows were all
the rest. Once we learned a bit of Korean, we were in for another disappointment. Instead of heatedly discussing Eastern
philosophy or ancient poetry, Koreans talked about the same
things Americans did, that is, money, sex, family, and TV.

And just as Korea lost its exotic glamour for me, so too did
the initial sheen of life in a beautifully romantic and artistic

city begin to wear thin for most after the third week. The young and the old were starting to miss things like their cars and friends and beds. Home. A solid image, easy for them to conjure. For me, though, home was an abstract line of tension that tethered me to the States and Seoul. My friends and family were scattered around the States, and I loved visiting them often. But Prague had confirmed that my life, my path, for the time being at least, was still as an expatriate, living and working in Seoul.

One of the last nights in Prague, I spied a group of Korean college students in the common area of the dorm building. They were drinking beer and keeping to themselves. I walked up to them, and using my passable Korean, I let them know that I lived in Korea and was a teacher there.

Two hours and many beers later, after many heartfelt cheers and reliving of the 2002 World Cup, which had been hosted in Korea the month before, the boys told me regrettably that they had to go to bed as they had to check out at 6:30 in the morning, four hours later, to catch their train out of Prague. I bid them goodnight and joined my classmates at another table.

Thirty minutes later the boys came back, sheepishly, with a new round of beers. They had felt bad leaving, they said, when the atmosphere had been so good. It was a very Korean thing to say and do, and in that moment, I was suddenly concretely homesick.

After a month in Prague, I discovered the kind of traveler I was. Sometimes, the fast track was O.K. But I had enjoyed unpacking my suitcase and settling into a place for a month. That month gave me the time to establish my regular haunts, like the place across from school where I had my coffee and chocolate croissant every morning before class. To learn a bit of the local language. To know my way around without having to pull out my map. To spend time in the old churches, to take in the museums, and afterward sit in a café with a coffee or beer, writing in my notebook. Like an artist. That summer, Prague taught me that I am the kind of traveler who likes to take her time in one place, so that when she writes about it, she'll say it in a voice that is her own.

Sybil Baker is a graduate of Vermont College's MFA program. Her essay, "Lost Generations: The American Expatriate Experience," was published in The Writer's Chronicle *in 2006. Her essay "Hope Streams Eternal" won the Seoul grand prize in 2005. Most recently her fiction has appeared in* Paper Street *and* The Bitter Oleander. *After living and teaching in Seoul, South Korea for twelve years, she now is Assistant Professor of Creative Writing at the University of Tennessee, Chattanooga.*

MARY TOLARO NOYES

✦ ✦ ✦

Leila's Gesture

The sins of governments are forgiven by the people.

"*BUONA SERA*, GOOD AFTERNOON, *SIGNORINA*," I SAID softly, as I approached a young woman sitting under the shelter near the train tracks. Snuggled up against the damp cold in her ample wool overcoat, she was studying my disheveled look, especially the muddy boots. She looked up at me and I noticed how young she was, how beautiful. Her dark eyes peered out from under a large, dove-gray headscarf, worn in the style of many Muslim women who live in Italy.

"Is it here we wait for the train to Bologna?" I asked, nervous about approaching a Muslim on that afternoon, March 20, 2003, the day the United States and her allies began dropping bombs on Iraq. I had scrambled down the steep side of the grassy hill from my friend's old stone farmhouse perched on top, and tramped across a field to the back of the tiny Marzabotto train station on the local Bologna-Porretta Terme line. The station offered few amenities at that late hour, certainly not a *capostazione* (station agent) to answer my question.

"*Sí, sí,*" she answered me with a smile. "I am waiting for the same train."

I thanked her and sat down close by. She wasted no time in beginning the litany of questions. First, she asked where I was from and I told her, hesitating slightly, "San Francisco, in California. I am American. Where are you from?"

"I am from Morocco," she responded, "but I have lived with my family in Bologna for three years now. My name is Leila. Did you know there is a splendid island called Leila off the coast of Morocco?"

"No, I didn't know about the island," I answered, "but the name is lovely and it suits you. My name is Maria. It's a pleasure to meet you."

"Oh, Maria," she said, "I like that name very much. You seem Italian too. I know many ladies here named Maria."

"Yes, I am also an Italian citizen," I admitted. "My grandmother's name was Maria Calogera. She was from Sicily."

"Oh," she exclaimed, pleased, "so your family's roots, like mine, come from the Mediterranean. We are cousins then!"

She went on to tell me about herself: twenty years old, the only daughter in a family of three children. She liked living in Bologna because life offered more possibilities. She was on the way home from her job at a nearby shoe factory. Her fiancé still lived in Morocco and she wasn't sure she wanted to marry him because he was very old-fashioned and would never consider moving to Bologna. "But my father is a wise man, and I am not too worried that he will insist I marry him," she said. As an afterthought she added, "My brothers are impossible though. They are like my fiancé." When I asked about her mother she had little to say. "She stays home and would prefer that I follow her path, which I don't want to do."

"Well, then," I responded, "tell me about the life you wish for."

"No, first you must tell me about yourself, *signora*. Perhaps I have been talking too much."

"No, you are not talking too much, Leila," I assured her. "I am a writer and I learn so much when I meet people like you."

The train rumbled slowly into the station and we walked together, climbing on board and into an almost empty railway wagon. We sat down opposite each other, next to the window.

I explained my reason for being in Bologna since early autumn, with only a brief trip home for the Christmas holiday: the editor of my book on Bologna lived there in Marzabotto, and we were collaborating as I revised and updated the material.

She had plenty of questions and relished our chance encounter. I described my family and our lives in California and asked, "Would you like to study at Bologna's famous university, Leila?"

"No," she replied, "studying doesn't interest

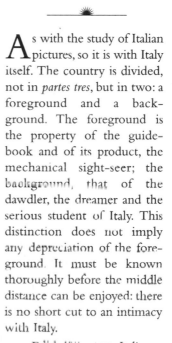

As with the study of Italian pictures, so it is with Italy itself. The country is divided, not in *partes tres*, but in two: a foreground and a background. The foreground is the property of the guidebook and of its product, the mechanical sight-seer; the background, that of the dawdler, the dreamer and the serious student of Italy. This distinction does not imply any depreciation of the foreground. It must be known thoroughly before the middle distance can be enjoyed: there is no short cut to an intimacy with Italy.

—Edith Wharton, *Italian Backgrounds* (1905)

me. I want to earn money so that I can be independent, too, like your sons. I want a future in Bologna, so perhaps you can tell me about her history."

"Where do you live?" I asked. "I could describe your neighborhood's past."

"We are just inside Porta Lame," she said, "and it doesn't seem very interesting to me!"

Then I described how she would have found it in the Middle Ages and Renaissance. "Just imagine the canal that once flowed where Via Riva di Reno is now, and the silk factories humming, turning out cloth, making the Bolognesi rich and famous. Bombs destroyed the neighborhood during World War II." I grew pensive and said, "What you see has been rebuilt since then. We have lost so much..."

The perfect opening...

Without missing a beat, her large expressive eyes, fringed with thick, black lashes, locked with mine, and I understood where our conversation was headed. My heart leaped up to my throat.

"*Signora* Maria," she said, her husky voice quiet, yet strong, "do you know what happened this morning?"

I know we must have blinked, but when I think back to that moment, it seems like even the miniscule flick of an eyelid would have severed the connection. "*Sí*, Leila. Yes...I know what happened this morning. Yes...yes...and I'm so sorry."

As I said it, my hands flew up and covered my eyes and the sobs, which had been caged deep inside me for weeks, exploded into the space between us. For the first time in my life I was ashamed to be an American. I had protested in the streets, signed petitions, voted, realizing finally that bombs were inevitable and the American people seemingly powerless against our government, which marched the world toward war.

She listened quietly. I could feel her eyes watching me as I sat there that afternoon, March 20, 2003. "I'm so sorry...so ashamed of my country...so sorry...*vergogna*...shame..."

In the silence, Leila looked up again, reached across the space between us and took my hands in hers. "Don't worry, *Signora* Maria," she whispered, "I understand. I understand that we must separate the actions of governments from the individuals that we meet. I can do that. Please don't be so sad. We have to understand each other and talk to each other. I understand." While she spoke, her eyes stayed focused on our joined hands and then she looked up at me watching her.

"*Grazie* Leila," I said. "Thank you for understanding...and...I hope together we can help to change..."

And she suddenly asked me, "*Signora*, do you know that the date of my birth is May 11? When is your birthday?"

Astonished, I answered, "My birthday is also May 11, Leila."

So, we sat together on the little train chugging toward Bologna, our hands still clasped, and my lovely companion met my gaze boldly and announced, without the slightest hesitation, "Our souls were meant to meet today, *Signora* Maria, don't you think?"

Mary Tolaro Noyes was raised in Bellows Falls, Vermont, where her Sicilian grandparents settled in the early twentieth century. She now lives in San Francisco, California with her husband of thirty-seven years, Tom. After years dedicated to teaching and to raising two sons, she has finally come to the writing she always meant to do. Her favorite tales involve chance encounters with people who help her understand their world—and herself. Inspired by rediscovering her grandparents' family in Sicily in 1989, she first visited Bologna in 1994 as a student of Italian. After frequent extended stays there, she has come to regard the Città Rossa as her second home and is still taken by the city's medieval magic and modern charm.

* ✱ *

Joy on Kilimanjaro

Africa's highest mountain is a gift to her spirit.

IN THE PINK-STREAKED AFRICAN SKY—THAT ALWAYS seems bigger than any sky on Earth—the sun rose over the great smoky plains of Tanzania, the horizon endless miles in the distance.

Alone at dawn in Africa.

Alone on the deck of the large A-frame dining hut at Mandara, first camp on the five-day tourist trek to Uhuru, the summit of Mt. Kilimanjaro.

Alone at 9,000 feet, looking down on the misty rainforest, unable to see the town of Marangu 3,000 feet below, where I began the trek the day before...

Ten thousand feet above me, a crown of ice gleamed—Hemingway's *Snows*. You can't beat his title for glamorous mystique, but he was wrong about the altitude. The summit, Uhuru, is 19,340 feet, not 19,710 as he wrote.

Joy's story was better than his. She told it while rowing a raft on the Green River in Utah, "testing my strength," she said, after months of treatment for invasive cancer.

Joy was a river guide all over the world for twenty years, since she was eighteen. When she and Butch Carber, also a guide, decided to get married, they got together a bunch of friends, climbed the highest mountain in Africa, and got married on top. What could be more fun?

"Our judge pulled out his robes on the summit," Joy said with delight, "and another friend surprised me with a bouquet of plastic flowers. Can you imagine carrying that extra stuff just for the ceremony? We were so exhausted we could hardly walk the last hundred feet."

A big smile and bright eyes illuminated her small face framed in short dark hair. In spite of the recent treatment her little body was muscled and strong. She looked twenty-two. Then she answered the unspoken questions. "That was a year ago," she said, "I was diagnosed a month after our marriage, during a routine post-trip exam."

Her vitality took me aback. Her name, Joy, how could she live up to it now?

She rowed and talked against the backdrop of broad river, red cliffs, and verdant banks, a fitting scene for her bottomless bag of adventures——the first exploratory river expeditions on the Zambezi in Africa and the Indus in Pakistan; the first descent of the Luangua in Zambia; the first female river guide on the Bio Bio in Chile; the Coruh in Turkey; the Watut in Papua New Guinea; the Tatshenshini and Copper rivers in Alaska; numerous trips on the Colorado River through the Grand Canyon and the rivers and canyons of her home state, Utah.

"I would love to go to Africa," I burst out, "but I haven't found a way to do it."

"I'll take you," Joy said at once, with the optimism and confidence that characterized her life. Joy and I shared a birthday, twenty years apart. If I had been born when she was.... Go to Africa with Joy? In a minute!

Two years later she was dead of cancer, in her prime, September 1992.

Years later it came to me I had said Alaska, not Africa. Grief altered my memory.

Hundreds of friends and family gathered atop a magnificent plateau in Canyonlands, Utah, to celebrate her life. Unknown to most, except for Joy's best friend whom I also met on the Green River trip, I silently added my paper prayer to the urn of ashes, although I longed to speak of my love and loss. Joy's husband would drop these ashes into rivers, above mountains, and into canyons worldwide.

In my long life I have been a hero to others—to many of my high school classmates in Woonsocket, Rhode Island, where I grew up; to Barnard College classmates who admired my independence in the conformist '50s; to work friends who thought me fearless, if eccentric, even mad; to strangers who longed to leave the city as I did to live in beauty as I do. Joy was my only hero

---

I reached the top of Parnassus: for half an hour I saw the whole of Greece below me, a vision of incredible beauty, all its rusty headlands and misty seas and Olympus (which they call Olybus because mp = b) in the far north and *everything* in fact somewhere in sight: and crocus and scylla, incredibly blue ones, on the edge of the snow. When we came off the top, my guide wrapped me in a blanket and I fell asleep and woke after an hour with an icy wind and have been suffering from a miserable cough ever since: but one must be prepared to sacrifice something for trespassing on the Gods.

—Freya Stark, Letter, 18 June 1939, in *The Coasts of Incense*

among the many lives I admired for many reasons. Joy's was the only life I would have liked for my own.

At the start of our river journey she chastised me for a small but significant lapse. I had not kept to the trail. At the end of the trip she praised me for being "river savvy and a great help." I beamed with pride. Praise from Joy was praise indeed. And now this girl, my spiritual child, my hero, a woman I had been with for only a few days, was dead. I was devastated.

I was in Tanzania to climb Mt. Kilimanjaro in honor of Joy Ungricht Carber. At least it was a gesture on the scale of her life.

Of the five climbers in my group one was a giant of a fellow, age twenty, three were fit young women about thirty, and me, thirty years older than the oldest. All of us were on a Guerba overland expedition in East Africa. At our pre-climb briefing at the Hotel Marangu, the outfitter told us, "Whatever you need, don't be afraid to ask your guide. His only goal is to help you get to the top." What I heard was: His only goal *in life* is to help you get to the top.

No doubt he meant food, water, help carrying day gear— the farthest things from my mind. My first goal was to create an understanding with my personal guide, George Kimaro. Even though I had more experience than the others combined, I insisted on hiring an extra guide to stay with me, in addition to the three guides and six porters assigned to us. If Joy and her friends struggled to get to the summit, I needed all the help I could get.

On the first day we walked as a unit, strolling on the dusty road that wound upward through the rainforest, exceptionally dry in early March.

On this day, the second, I intended to walk alone with George.

When we were well out of sight of Mandara and the many other groups of hikers, I held back, placing my hand on George's arm. "Wait," I said, "I have to do something."

Throwing myself to my knees in the grass, I bowed to the shining peak. George looked alarmed. I laughed. "What's your word for God?" I asked.

"*Hongo*" is what I think I heard.

"I'm praying to *Hongo*," I said, "for strong legs."

George laughed, a full-bodied sound with a huge smile that transformed his intense expression into easy camaraderie.

Why did I pray in that way? Because in 1984, I ran down a long steep mountain path through the rhododendron forest in Nepal, bounding from boulder to boulder, following barefoot Nepalese porters carrying six-foot wooden beams. At the bottom one porter pulled tufts of grass from both sides of the trail, bent slightly and rubbed the grass on his knees. "What's he doing?" I asked Kisan, the local porter I had hired that morning. "Praying," Kisan said, "strong knees."

For the next three weeks, all the way to Everest, at the top of every Up, at the bottom of every Down, on the far side of every rickety swaying bridge, we prayed and offered our thanks. *Namaste, namaste,* bowing, our hands in prayer before our lips. It comes easily in nature.

And so it came easily that morning in Africa.

George wasn't much taller than I. Compact, all lungs and muscle. He liked to wear two hats, a knit one and a faded red cap, an eccentricity that amused me. I was a cliché—the little old lady in hiking boots and a floppy safari hat.

George's languages were Swahili and Wachagga, the dominant local tribe. He was fluent in German and understood English better than he spoke it.

"I'm slow," I told him, in plodding exaggeration.

"I have only one good eye," I said, covering my left eye.

"I don't always know where the ground is." I shuffled, feeling the way.

"I wobble." I showed him, shifting my weight unevenly.

His eyes memorized my gait and breathing, my attitude.

I watched him, too, on the sly. The outfitter said the guides know when they first look at you who will make it, who won't.

"It's frightening," he added.

What was George thinking about me?

"When we climb to the top," I asked, "will you take my hand, like a child?"

George hesitated. "Do you understand? Like this," I said, taking his hand in mine.

He nodded. I felt better.

The final climb to the top was two nights away. I had heard the stories firsthand: sleeping poorly, if at all, at Kibo, the last camp at 15,500 feet; getting up in the freezing cold sometime between midnight and 2 A.M.; four to six hours to reach Gillman's Point at 18,640 feet by sunrise, a punishing 3,000-foot gain at altitude. That's where it's over for most trekkers, too exhausted to go another two hours, another 700 foot gain to reach Uhuru, at 19,340 feet.

"Gillman's Point is *not* the summit," the outfitter said at the end of our briefing. "You must make every effort to reach Uhuru. That is the true summit."

He told us the climb was 70 percent mental and "older people seem to do better because they discipline themselves to go slow."

Good news for me, the original tortoise.

Before leaving, each hiker had to sign the official register of Mt. Kilimanjaro National Park—name, country, passport number, age. While the various groups were still waiting around awkwardly, one of the South African men dashed up to me. "Are you Rona?" he asked.

"Yes."

"Darn it," he said, punching the air, "I wanted to be the oldest person on the mountain!"

"How old are you?" I asked.

"Fifty-three."

"Just a kid," I said.

The trail from Mandara was a fairly narrow, well-trodden path through a sparse forest that gradually declined to smaller trees and large shrubs, some flowering in the early spring. Without haste, slow and steady, George and I walked peacefully.

Like guides everywhere, George began his own ritual of connection.

"How many children do you have?" George was asking the introductory question in societies where the number of children signifies wealth, virility, worth as a woman, love of family, and so on.

"None," I answered. In India I adopted the habit of white lies when asked, to avoid culture shock, confusion, and unwanted conversation. With George, I had to tell the truth.

An involuntary look of surprise crossed his face. I quickly went on with the standard response. "How many do you have?" I asked.

"Seven," he answered. I concealed my thought—so many, how can he care for them?

"How old are you?" I asked, another polite question.

"Forty-five," he replied, older than I guessed. "How old are you?" he asked.

With some pride I answered. "In one week I'll be sixty-four."

We considered our partnership in silence.

I followed his footsteps exactly, incorporating his rhythm, a trick I discovered to compensate for being Mrs. Slow. It had worked many times—in the Grand Canyon, the Sinai Mountains, recently in the Okavanga Delta when we chased a lion. I first used it when I followed Fred Astaire down Madison Avenue in Manhattan. He was walking arm in arm with a woman, oblivious to the passers-by in that necessary way celebrities develop to create a barrier.

I followed two or three steps behind. It was like dancing with him!

With each step George lifted his heel noticeably, pushing his weight up and forward, a technique that later propelled both of us through deep, soft scree on a 45-degree slope through the last excruciating hours to the summit.

"How long does it take to become a guide?" I asked.

"Many years."

"How many?"

"Twenty."

"Twenty!"

I fell silent. Eighteen-year-old Joy beginning her career in wild freedom, worlds apart from the porters on this mountain, beginning with thirty-pound loads on their heads. How many years as a porter, then an assistant, learning the mountain in bitter cold, blizzards, rain so thick you could drown standing up, in mud, heat, and dust?

The exquisite weather of the past few days was remarkable. Even though March was the start of the rainy season, not a cloud, not one, obscured the mountaintop.

A few weeks earlier, on the Kenya side, someone on the overland truck shouted, "There's Kili!"

"Where, where?" I asked, hanging out the window, seeing only towering stacks of clouds.

"Look up, Rona, you're looking straight ahead." The young

man next to me tilted my head higher. "See it? At that break in the clouds, see the peak?"

Sometimes your jaw does drop. Miles away, across the flat Kenyan plain, the full height of the mountain was revealed, its full beauty and magnificence not visible in Tanzania.

What made me think I could do this? It was not the first time I had questioned my sanity. When I flew from India to Nepal twelve years earlier, my head was down as I filled out the entry card. Something made me look out the window. Another moment of astonishment.

The Himalayas below, so close I could easily see sharp peaks and deep valleys, precipitous trails, little villages, rivers, terraced farms on mountainsides. What made me think I could trek there? Well, I did. And now I would do this. "The heart has its reasons, that reason takes no account of." Pascal, *Pensees.*

The temperature was mild. We ambled through heath and flowers, then moorland of giant lobelia and giant senecio, a groundsel with the look of a strange cactus, clusters of flower-like leaves at the end of its arms.

It was time to tell my story.

"I had a young beautiful friend," I began quietly, "smaller than me and very strong." Immediately George's expression was anticipatory. This was Africa, where storytelling has been a way of life for thousands of years. In the previous two months, time and again in the intense heat of the afternoon, I had seen circles of young people talking together in the shade of a broad-leaved spreading tree. The scene was ancient, and poignant. Poor, sick, beautiful Africa.

"My friend's name was Joy," I went on. "She was a guide in America, Africa, Alaska, Asia, all over the world."

George's face lit up. Yes, a guide.

"She got married on top of Kilimanjaro," I said, pointing upward.

George looked skeptical.

"Yes, up there," I repeated, "on top of the mountain."

Now George nodded, believing me. I think he was impressed.

"The man she married was a guide, too, and many of their friends who..."

Here I choked. In broken sounds and tears, I went on, "...who climbed with them to celebrate the wedding."

George frowned, not understanding my tears.

"One month later," I cried, "she was operated on for cancer. Cancer," I said, looking up into his face, "you know?"

"Yes, yes, I know," he said.

"She promised to take me here, to Africa." My voice became shrill. "She thought she was O.K. She wasn't. She died."

My face was distorted, hot in my hands. No one could see or hear my sobs but George.

"Don't cry," he said, with great kindness.

I uncovered my face and implored him. "That's why I must try to get to the top, to Uhuru, to honor her spirit." My hands rose in the air. "Her spirit, George, do you understand?"

"Yes, yes," he said, taking my hand. "Come, rest." He led me off the path and sat me on the grass. My back sagged against a boulder.

"I do have children, George, many," I said, sighing and sniffling. "My young friends who lead me to beautiful places. This girl was like a special child."

Grief never expressed had found its voice. The injustice of Joy's death when miserable people thrive. Her tight little body that crammed life into it, minute by minute, in her span. Her fierce spirit that burned to the end. Her failing body, eviscerated, burdened with bags, living by will on her final river trip through the Grand Canyon.

A writer on that trip, on assignment for *Outside* magazine, intended to write about his own adventure. Instead he wrote about Joy, a dying woman:

> "Aren't you sad it's all over?" I asked Joy. She raises her chin proudly, smiling, and tells me, "No, not at all. One trip has to end so another can begin."

Only at the very end, she cried to her best friend, "I want more."

Her life, so rich and full. I could not understand her passion for more.

George wiped my tears. "Don't cry," he said again. He looked away, into space. His words came from deep within, a pledge. "You will make it," he said.

Horumbo, the second and largest camp on the Marangu route, was a crisscross of trekkers departing early in the bright clear morning. Some were headed up, hopeful, to the final camp at Kibo. Others were on their way down, elated or glum, depending on whether they had reached the summit the day before.

George and I greet each other with warm smiles. We have a bond.

I bow gaily to the peak. Its beauty makes me happy. Or maybe the thin air makes me high. At 12,000 feet I have no signs of altitude sickness. No headache, no diarrhea or nausea, no lack of appetite, no shortness of breath. No difficulty sleeping except for getting up three or four times to pee, proof that I am drinking my obligatory four cups of tea in the evening. I feel wonderful. After weeks of drinking heavily treated water with things floating in it, I am drinking pure cold glacial water drawn directly from the stream.

I am drinking the mountain.

By early afternoon we reach the Saddle, a moonscape. Before us stretches a high desert plain that sweeps from Mawenzi, a volcanic cone almost 17,000 feet, across to Kibo, the highest cone of Kilimanjaro. Nothing grows but tiny plants and lichens. The flat-topped massif stands alone, revealed, capped north and south by glaciers. We can see the trail to the top, a whitish scar on a long gray body against a pale gray sky. The wind picks up. Time for another layer.

In three hours we reach a gray wooden sign outside a long cinder-block building that looks like a prison: KIBO, 15,500 FEET. Inside the air is stone cold. Trekkers bundled in down give off no body heat. Each group finds its bunks. Ours is a small room off the main corridor. The porters bring tea, then soup, cold rice, cold pasta, bread, and biscuits —cold comfort, literally, especially after the steaming plates of delicious meals urged on us in the lower camps. Every night I ate my share and as much as I could of the others', who neither ate nor drank enough. Too late now. No fancy cooking at Kibo, where every drop of water is carried in on porters' backs and heads.

At this altitude I force down a full bowl of soup and rice and the essential four cups of tea. The others play with their soup, nibble at biscuits, ignoring the warnings of the outfitter. "Urine must be copious and clear," he said, more than once.

By 7 P.M., submerged in my rented sleeping bag in all my layers except my long down jacket, I lie awake and restless, waiting for the wakeup call at midnight.

Four times in the next four hours I get up to pee. I will myself out of my sleeping bag, fumble in the dark and cold for my boots, hunch into my down jacket, clomp down the frigid hall into the freezing air and behold!, the amazing glory of a full moon floodlighting bare slopes above, thick layers of clouds floating below.

Sky, moon, clouds, and mountain. Mountain, moon, clouds, and sky.

Glory, glory!

The outhouse is freezing, but clean. Maybe nobody gets up to use it. The shelf is so high I have to climb up to squat over the hole. I move my bowels, also amazing. Many trekkers are constipated or have diarrhea, two of the many reasons they don't make it. Less than one-third will get as high as Gillman's Point, even fewer to the true summit, Uhuru.

Lying in my sleeping bag, my brain protects me from facts. It allows only the necessity to get up and get going when the call comes.

A sharp knock at the door startles me. The call! I dress quickly, drink my tea, secure my water bottle inside my jacket so it won't freeze and leave the others huddled over the table as I step into the hall. There is George already waiting for me, his smile excited, bright as moonlight in his dark face. He greets me with two words—"We go?"

Outside I grab George's arm. "Where is it? Where is the top?"

He points to the summit, invisible at this angle. I bow. We laugh together. We go.

Two hats for George are not enough. He also wears a balaclava and the hood of his heavy jacket. Insulated pants cover his sweats, padded mittens cover his gloves.

From the skin out I wear silk long underwear, a long-sleeved cotton t-shirt, a rented, worn track jacket and pretty good sweat pants, my own insulated pants, a bright purple tubular scarf I can pull up over my nose and chin, less than adequate rented gloves and my excellent knee-length down jacket with its more than cozy hood, like a puffy pumpkin head. Tucked inside, hanging from my neck, is my floppy safari hat.

We walk in beauty. The moon is elsewhere. The night sky is close, the stars closer, the starlight intimate. We climb in silence, arm in arm, all but alone at that early hour.

A line of Germans pass silently, like macabre pilgrims, hooded and shrouded in parkas, ski poles moving in unison, a methodical rhythmic machine. Not too long after, they stop above us to rest. We pass them. I am pleased. Even the Germans have to rest.

My outside person tells me, "You got up early, you were ready, you didn't hesitate." My inside person smiles at this and murmurs, "You have a chance."

Sooner than I expect, sooner than I like, I start to pant. Bad form. Increases dehydration. I count off steps, one to one hundred, out loud. We pause every one hundred steps. Every fifty steps. I cheat. Bad form. Too many rests, too early. My rented walking stick is chest height. I stop, lean my chin on it the way the outfitter showed us, and close my eyes. George nudges me. I sit on a rock and nod off. George wakes me. "No sleep," he says.

I'm sweating and unzip, unsnap, and take off my inner jacket. George stuffs it in his pack. My fingers are freezing from the brief exposure. George whips off his mittens and gloves and rubs my hands vigorously, shelters them in the warmth of his underarms, the way my grandmother used to. I feel foolish. Doing O.K. but no great shakes. Not good enough, maybe.

I have an idea. "Sing to me, George, sing the Kilimanjaro song."

The night before we left the Hotel Marangu, boisterous singing and clapping came across the garden to my room. What was going on? Were these people going to keep me up all night? I had booked a room so I could have a comfortable bed, peace and quiet, not my tent. I didn't have a sleeping bag, no room in my backpack for that and my down jacket. I had been cold, sleepless, and miserable many nights in the past two months. Earlier I had been in a panic. I couldn't remember where I packed my Kili gear, or what I brought. I got lost on the grounds looking for the building where the briefing was scheduled. I needed a good night, desperately.

Like a thief, I watched from the edge of the dark.

Around a roaring fire a rowdy bunch of climbers sat in a circle with their porters and guides. They all looked six feet tall and 180 pounds, beer bottles raised. Their noise was the joy of success, a traditional celebration on the return, a way to say goodbye, to thank the porters and guides for their hard work and dedication.

The laughter died down. The guides and porters looked at each other, then began a stirring song, the Kilimanjaro song. Their big voices filled the night. They clapped their hands and moved their shoulders from side to side. It ended in cheers and applause.

I wanted that.

George sings, but even George has trouble singing, breathing, climbing, and leading me by the hand, all at once. What stupid, selfish thing had I asked of him?

By now many people have passed us. Around 17,000 feet, we come to a shallow cave, large enough to hold a dozen or more climbers, resting, resting. It might be 3 A.M. I am allowed to sleep.

George shakes me several times before I awake. "We go now," he says, gently this time.

＊

Not long after, a giant fist belts me in the gut. I double over with shouts of pain. For the next three hours it hits me every few feet, knocking the breath out of me, draining the strength from my legs. Sobbing from step to step, moaning between spasms, I entrust myself to George. I gulp air, too hard, too fast. Dangerous. I could pass out. The rests are closer, more urgent. At times I brace my foot against his to keep from sliding down the slope, or lean my whole body against his side, to stay upright, no longer thinking about the top, or even getting to it, only willing to try, step by step.

I cling to George when we stop, lay my head to his heartbeat, steady and strong, pulsing through layers of clothing, breathe with him, trying to come down to stillness.

Closer than if we were naked, suspended in dark space, timeless in this mortal world of mountain, moonlight, and silence.... George presses my body to his, one hand on my back, one at my waist. He bends me backward in a beautiful curve. I feel the warmth and swelling of his body. A bottom breath rises from a mysterious depth inside me, filling my lungs with life. It hesitates, then slowly, slowly eases from my lips into the night. Two human beings joined to the mountain.

It is beautiful to look into his face. He kisses me on the mouth, his lips warm and gentle. I smile. My eyes tell him, we go.

Every rest is touch and emotion, rhythm and movement. Again and again, we go.

The mountain is unforgiving, impersonal. The pain, relentless. Words erupt. "This...is not...a mountain...you climb.... This...is a mountain...YOU SACRIFICE YOURSELF TO!"

Its beauty is unbearable in grief. The moon, the stars, the

black night. I wail the litany of rage. "Why did she have to die? So young, so beautiful, so good, so strong..."

George turns to me again in great kindness. "Don't cry." I cry anyway, but more quietly, until I stop.

The path narrows, ever tighter, steeper. If I look up I'll tumble backward. But I must look up. The full moon rests on the ridge, in arm's reach. The stars are in my face.

George walks a step ahead. He holds his arm stiff behind him, grasping my hand, first one, then the other, as we zig and zag. He never, never lets go. I close my eyes, walk blind, stagger, stumble, sink in deep, soft scree, no longer a matter of trying. I must be worthy of Joy. "I *must* go to the top," I shout into my legs, "I must *go* to the top, I must go to the TOP!"

George turns to face me. "Yes, you must," he says solemnly.

More people pass, even though they started an hour or more later. "I'm too slow," I hiss, on the edge.

George soothes me, murmuring, "*Poli, poli,*" Swahili for "slowly, slowly." "It's good," he repeats.

The pain becomes a fact.

I see images of Olympic runners, swimmers. Is this what they endure to become who they are? I see a note scribbled on a cereal boxtop, left in my tent in Amboseli Park, Kenya. "I wish you success," it said. He was the leader of an Israeli group that reached the summit in December. The words fuel my mind and body.

Most of all, I see a photo of mountaineer Dougal Haston on the summit of Mt. Everest in 1975—hood pushed back, head tilted up, a wide white smile on his browned face, white snow reflected in his sunglasses. Something in the lift of his head, the attitude of his body, the beauty of the scene, expressed ultimate joy.

I wanted that for years, long before Joy, to stand on the summit of somewhere that demanded as much of me as these climbers had given to Everest. I didn't know it was the kind of joy you have to work for, beyond anything you could imagine.

Somewhere in the pain I start to climb for myself. In my soul it feels this is what Joy's spirit intends—to produce a person I hoped was inside me but had never been sure existed—to turn myself inside out from a place I feared and desired with no idea how to get to it.

Enlightenment comes, a sense of peace and confidence in my being, without answers.

Dawn is breaking. The ridge is visible. The trail has vanished into a tumble of rocks and boulders. Climbers are crawling upward, everywhere. For the first time George urges me forward. "Hurry," he says, "sunrise is at 6:30."

Only a few more feet. Legs like diver's weights. Organs, a dense mass. With each gain, the mass contracts in extreme spasms, cutting off my air. Breath to breath, hands gripping the rocks, pulling, pulling my body higher, a little higher. From the corner of my eye, I can see George a few feet parallel, keeping an eye on me. I am on my own, but George is there.

I lunge over the top, stagger and throw myself over a huge boulder dead ahead, arms splayed, legs dangling like the Straw Man, eyes huge at the spectacle before me—a startling white ice field—the glacier—the roof of Africa!

Waves of grief and exaltation break into uncontrollable sobs. I collapse face down on the boulder, my head hidden in my arms.

A gentle hand pats me on the shoulder, a man's voice speaks in my ear.

"Well done," says the voice. "You are one tough lady."

In a daze I raise my eyes to blinding sunshine. The man is one of the South Africans, so much fun the past three days, clowning in camp, tossing off jokes along the route. I bow my head, uncomfortable with his compliment.

"I was highly motivated," I answer, without my usual smile of self-congratulation.

"Obviously," he returns.

The respect in his strong young face undoes me. Tears fill my eyes again. Humility is a new emotion.

Gillman's Point, 18,640 feet. All around on the narrow ridge other climbers rest here and there among the rocks. I find a spot and lean back against a boulder. My emotions are spent, my heart quiet. Joy kept her promise. She brought me here. George knows. Where is George? There he is, resting against a boulder, twirling one of his hats in his hand. Light-headed, I float to him.

"Are you ready to go to the top?" he asks.

The top? What top? It takes a moment to register—Uhuru. "The top," I snap, "are you mad?" George stares dumbfounded at the madwoman in front of him. In another moment I come to my senses. Uhuru, the true summit, where Joy and Butch were married. I squint at the long gentle ridgeline. It doesn't look too bad. Another two hours, another 700 feet. It even looks easy after the ordeal of the last six hours.

The outfitter's words are imprinted in my brain. "Gillman's Point is not the top of the mountain. You must make every effort to reach Uhuru. That is the true summit." If George thinks I can make it, I can. I must, for Joy. My smile is an apology. "We go," I say.

The sun is shining like a day at the beach. This feels like fun. It's cold. I have on all my jackets and my floppy safari hat. I tie my broken sunglasses to my hat with a shoelace. George laughs at me. "A new style," I say with dignity.

In minutes pain shocks me. Again? Still? What's wrong with me? George presses on, always a little ahead, beckoning. We meet groups of two or three or four returning from Uhuru. "We're late," I gasp, "they're coming back already."

"It's O.K.," George assures me, "plenty of time." He lies, I'm sure. It's much farther than it looks. It's hard, it hurts. It never occurs to me that I'm above 19,000 feet, I've been climbing for eight hours with little sleep, no food.

Every few feet I crumple and cling to George, gulping air, feeling his heartbeat till my breath measures his. At a point, the mood of our embrace shifts subtly. George breathes stronger, deeper. His hands move down my back, pressing me to him. Our breath unites. My head floats. We breathe out together, separate slightly and look into each other's eyes. I see deep wonder in his face. Perhaps. I am amazed and at peace, again.

A noise. A man and a woman step through a cleft in the rock. They stare in silence, unintentional intruders. We stare back in silence. They pass. We go.

We climb higher and higher. What I see comes through a glass wall of fatigue—magnificent views of the ice fields, blurred by pain and exhaustion.

We top a little rise. The summit!

Before me is a rock-strewn elevation, its edge round, like the pictures of Earth from space. It feels like the top, like balancing on a beach ball. Puffy white clouds hang in the distance, far away and below. Flanking one side, separated by a narrow chasm, is the face of the glacier, a shimmering blue-green ice cliff, a table mountain, dazzling white in the pure light, lost in clouds on the horizon.

The famous crude sign hangs lopsided. It proclaims in large yellow letters:

YOU ARE NOW AT THE UHURU PEAK

THE HIGHEST POINT IN AFRICA

ALTITUDE: 5895 METRES A.S.L.

I feel happy as I walk around, taking in the scene, strangely at home, fulfilled. Nothing is an effort. But when I look down into the famous crater, my eyes feel the bare ground like bare skin. Like me, naked, exposed, bare to the soul. I turn back to the ice. Its beauty and mass comfort me.

Nearby the South Africans are taking pictures, asking me to be in their video. Their guide talks with George, guide talk.

I take out my little pocket camera, a disposable panorama. I have to call George to come stand beside me. George and I behind the sign, George and I in front of the glacier.

This mountain took me completely, more than any person, thing, or event in all the days of my life. There was nothing to do now but leave.

The deep fine scree that was so hard to ascend was like a ski run going down. Whoosh, whoosh, zig, zag—until my boots filled with sand, and the slope jammed my toes into the front of my boots.

I sat on a rock to adjust my boots, and lingered. George interrupted me abruptly, ordering me, if you will, to hurry up. What for, I wondered dimly, it wasn't that far to Kibo.

We were the last to return, twelve hours up and back. Bodies sprawled everywhere—hikers, guides, porters, all prone, soaking up energy in the noon sunshine.

Many of them grinned at us, showed thumbs up. It felt like a big party. It was, a party for me. The word was out. Mama made Uhuru. Mama, the Swahili form of address for every mother and all women who are not young, a mark of respect and affection.

George instructed me to rest in my bunk for a little while before we had to leave for Horumbo. What? Leave? Yes, we had to make room for the next hikers who would begin to arrive soon. Yes, we had to return to Horumbo to sleep, didn't I know that? Another three or five hours of hiking.

Did I know that? The outfitter surely told us. Either I didn't hear or comprehend something too remote to my purpose. My mind was on UP.

I lay quietly in my bunk, the only one of our group who made it to the top. The others were sleeping. Two of the young women made it to Gillman's Point, one, Marie, by sunrise, the other, long after. The third turned back after an hour, too sick to continue. The young giant, crippled by massive blisters, never left the hut.

Mama made Uhuru. What a lovely sound.

The lead guide, a man of sixty or more, poked his head in the door. He saw me awake and came in grinning, arm outstretched. Pumping my hand as if I were the greatest person in the universe, he chortled, "Congratulations, Mama," over and over.

Outside again, George brought me a little fruit before the march to Horumbo. I did march, full of energy, mostly by myself. George was needed to help the others.

I have little memory of that night. The dining room was abuzz with excitement. I ate very well. The young man with blisters was resigned, very much an English good sport of the old school. The young woman who turned back was depressed. Marie, who made it to Gillman's Point by sunrise, glowed with happiness, even though all her toenails turned black.

The next morning, fully refreshed, I felt thirty years younger.

"C'mon, George, let's run," I said, as we started out. Once again he looked at me as though I were crazy. I was thinking about that day in Nepal, bounding fearlessly down the rocky trail. "C'mon, take my hand." He did, and we flew down the mountain.

Uhuru means freedom.

At last, I understood Joy. I want more.

I get more.

In the early afternoon, as I walked into the lovely gardens of the Marangu Hotel, I came upon some of our overlanders who elected not to make the climb. Ulla, from Berlin, shined with joy, for me. Penny, from Canada, came to me beaming, arms outstretched. "Chuck and I are so glad it was you," she said, meaning the one who made Uhuru.

Allan, from Wales, in his fifties, had made the climb on a previous trip. "Well done," he said shaking my hand vigorously. Connie, American, a fragile-looking sylph, had lived alone in a hut in a Congolese village ten years earlier, as a Peace Corps volunteer. If anything, her smile was bigger than mine.

When I went to the office to pay my bill, the beautiful office women seemed to levitate from their chairs and float toward me, white teeth shining in dark faces, arms extended. They embraced me in turn, softly kissing me on the lips.

"Congratulations, Mama," they said, one after the other.

"Well done," said the hotel manager/outfitter. When I praised George for his kindness and skill, the manager remarked, "Yes, it's uncanny how they know what you need." Then he waived the extra fee I should have paid for hiring a personal guide.

The hikers were to meet in the garden for our celebration. George reappeared with my certificate, No. 1566/96, March 6, 1996, Uhuru, 10 A.M., Age 64 minus 4 days, the paper of heavy stock bordered in gold. The Gillman's border was green. I always was a gold star kid.

Nothing, nothing, nothing would restrain my happiness, not even sympathy for the two who failed—but what was happening to Marie? Her face was bright red, stained with big fat tears. I rushed to her. "Marie, Marie, what's wrong?"

"Nothing," she sobbed, "I want to be just like you when I grow up! You're my inspiration!" Indeed, she went on to climb wonderful mountains in the next ten years, never failing to send me long letters and excellent postcards.

It was good to sit down with a bottle of cold beer. We toasted each other many times. The tip envelope was generous. I gave George my purple scarf and a sharp new Adidas cap. Then it was time for the song. We joined in, clapping and swaying from side to side. Oh please, one more time, I begged, forgetting how tired they were. Again they sang.

Goodbye. Thank you. Goodbye, goodbye.

The guides and porters rest for a week before their next climb.

Around midday the next day we stopped at a village for a break. Inside a shop I couldn't hold back, I had to say it again, *I climbed Mount Kilimanjaro.*

The young African clerk I spoke to stopped trying to sell me a piece of fabric at his price, not mine. The fabric sagged on his chest, forgotten. His eyes went deep. "How far can you see from the top?" he asked.

I hesitated. To a place deep inside me. He was looking for an answer I couldn't give, words to reflect his own sense of mystery, awe, wonder, desire.

"It's very beautiful," I said quietly, with respect. He nodded, it was enough.

I bought the fabric, a wild print of stalking yellow cheetahs, jaws open, teeth bared, on a red background with blue vines supporting narrow yellow blossoms. It wasn't pretty, or fashionable. What it had was energy. Originality. What it had was Africa.

In the summer of 1996, writing most of the above, I looked out the window and announced to myself, I don't want to be a gardener anymore, I want to be an adventurer. I want to see as many of the beautiful places on this Earth as I can, before they or I vanish, as long as my body and bank account hold out.

For the next ten years that is what I did. My body and bank account failed about the same time, but I am working on recovering both. In the meantime, desperate for water in the awful heat last summer, I booked a last-minute river trip through the Grand Canyon.

I was so happy I decided to go downriver every summer for the rest of my life. Marble Canyon is a tough place to live, but one big advantage is this—it's only ten minutes to the put-in for the Grand Canyon!

Someone will ask, as someone always does, how did you wind up in Marble Canyon from New York City?

I'll answer as I often do: in 1976 I took a river trip and lost my mind, which I was greatly in need of losing.

But that's another story.

Rona Levein has been a word lover since the age of four when she first realized she could read. She has been devoted to traveling and telling her stories, and hopes to write a book before she dies. She attributes her lust for life and writing to her many teachers and mentors who have put her on the path to become "a writer worth reading." She lives in Arizona.

STEPHANIE ELIZONDO GRIEST

* * *

Abandoned in Uzbekistan

Sisters come through again.

I WOULDN'T HAVE ADMITTED IT, BUT I WAS LONELY.

I had just put Lareina, my confidante of the past year, in a taxi and watched her disappear into the deserted streets of Tashkent. This had become a ritual over the past few days: waving from the curb and trying not to cry as yet another member of my tight-knit group departed for their next adventure. Lareina was bound for Hong Kong, where a new apartment, high-powered job, and boyfriend awaited.

Not for me. My year-in-China Luce Scholarship had just ended and I had no clue what to do now. Join a potential love interest in Colombia? Hustle for rent in New York City? Return to my family in South Texas and get a "real job"? Or continue traveling, *sola*? I had opted to stall for time in Moscow where couch-surfing opportunities abounded, but had just learned that my best friend there had been denied permission to send me a visa. I could be stranded in Uzbekistan for days—even weeks—while the Russian embassy scrutinized my papers.

65

After Lareina's cab pulled away all I felt like doing was sulking in my motel room, but I knew that indecision would drive me crazy if I did. Absolute freedom can be as paralyzing as confinement when you don't know what you want. So I took to the street instead, hoping for a distraction.

Strolling through the old neighborhoods of Tashkent is like thumbing through the pages of Scheherazade's *One Thousand and One Nights.* The high wooden doors of mud-plastered compounds lead to inner courtyards that serve as dining nooks, with low-to-the-ground tables set atop Persian-style rugs and brocade pillows used as seats. I peered inside one and saw a family of five breakfasting on unleavened discs of *lepeshka* and fresh honeydew, sipping their tea out of bowls. Within these medieval corridors, you can almost feel the presence of Tamerlane, the fourteenth-century conqueror who left so many majolica-tiled mosques and terra cotta minarets in his wake.

Continuing on to the farmer's market, I arrived in time to see the vendors unloading crates of meats and cheeses and burlap bags of grain from their trucks. Old ladies in kerchiefs were selling bottles of homemade yogurt; butchers in blood-soaked aprons hacked at carcasses. Eggplants, squashes, cherry tomatoes, and yellow melons glistened in the sun. I considered buying a tiny gourd filled with cloves for the day I actually owned a cabinet—and, moreover, a kitchen—but panicked when I realized what that symbolized. Stability. Responsibility. A job with benefits. A husband and 1.5 kids. I tossed the gourd back in the bin and hurried out of the market.

A neon sign soon caught my eye: Mir Burger [translation: World Burger]. My heart pounded. Would they sell french fries there? I usually avoid food I can buy at home but my body had ingested little but yaks and sheep the past month. Slipping inside the burger joint, I ordered a jumbo pack of fries and a vanilla shake and slid into a yellow booth. Mir Burger was no misnomer: Mongolians, Iranians, Turks, Russians, Koreans, and turbaned Sikhs ate side-by-side while Celine Dion belted out the theme song to *Titanic*. I watched a pair of sixteen-year-old Uzbeks smoke cigarettes with one hand and dip fries into ketchup with the other. Their generation had grown up in the Communist era and was now coming of age with the dawn of capitalism. They looked so hip in their stretch pants, halter tops, and hoop earrings, it was hard to believe they were only a generation or two removed from the skull-capped, bearded vendors preparing kebobs and vats of *plov* over an open coal fire outside the storefront window.

The french fries left me feeling nostalgic and even more lonely, like I should be rushing off somewhere fun with friends. How was I going to travel *sola* if I couldn't handle being alone?

Needing some company, I decided to return to the Indian restaurant where our group had held our final meal together. The co-owner—a bubbly Uzbek named Sveta—had urged us back. Hoping she'd remember me, I descended into the dimly lit tavern that emanated cumin and cardamom.

"Where have you been? I have been waiting all week! Sit down, you must be starving," Sveta sang out in Russian, pointing at a table for two. She disappeared behind a tapestry featuring Ganesh that was pinned over a doorway, resurfacing a few moments later. She had changed into a silky blouse with spaghetti straps, a side-slit black skirt and five-inch heels, her bleached-blonde hair streaming down her shoulders. After shouting out to someone in the kitchen, she joined me at the table and fired off questions about every member of my group, whom she had met only briefly but recalled with remarkable detail.

A teenager in a black miniskirt and frilly white apron soon emerged from the kitchen carrying a tray full of food. To my amazement, she plunked down everything I had ordered on my first visit: basmati rice, vegetable curry, and a hot cup of chai. Sveta introduced her as Albina, an architecture student at the local university.

"Is that what people wear in America?" Albina asked, staring down at my mud-caked hiking boots.

"It's what we wear when we leave it," I offered.

"And those?" she pointed at my well-worn corduroys.

"When we want to be comfortable," I replied.

"I thought Americans wore Calvin Klein and Polo," she pouted.

I could relate to Albina's disappointment: my own discovery that communists didn't wear star-crested berets had been equally disillusioning. Since we were on the topic of fashion, I inquired about the women I'd seen in the countryside who connected their eyebrows with charcoal pencils and had mouths full of gold teeth. Did their head scarves indicate they were Muslim?

"*Nyet*," Sveta laughed. "They just do that to keep their hair out of their faces, like *babushki,* old women. Muslims don't have to wear scarves here. We can dress any way that we like."

They can thank the Soviets for that. In 1927, the Soviet Union launched a *hujum* against customs it deemed oppressive to women, including dowries, child brides, and veiling. Unfortunately, these measures were insensitively implemented with tragic results in many cases. Rather than educate Central Asian men about the emancipation of women, the Soviets simply mandated that veils be burned at public ceremonies. Women received no protection against the wrath of their families for following these orders and thousands were reportedly killed or maimed by husbands, fathers, and brothers.

Women throughout Central Asia started veiling again after the collapse of the Soviet Union but the Uzbek government took a firm stand against it, passing a "Law on Religion" in 1998 that forbids religious dress in public. At that time, men could wear skullcaps but any woman caught veiled in public was subject to arrest. When I asked Sveta and Albina if they knew any women who wore the veil, Albina tossed her auburn-dyed hair and scoffed, "*Nyet,* this is Tashkent. We're very cosmopolitan here."

"You're Muslim?" I asked, eyeing her mini-skirt.

"Of course," she said, pulling out a necklace tucked inside her cleavage and holding it up for me to see. The tiny gold charm said "Allah" in Arabic script.

Post-Soviet Muslims! I'd never met any before. I eagerly started quizzing them. Did they pray five times a day? (*Nyet.*) Eat pork? (*Nyet*—too fattening.) Attend services at the mosque? (*Nyet*—women were forbidden there.) Make a pilgrimage to Mecca? (A what? To where?) Read the Koran? (*Nyet*—they couldn't read Arabic. Nor Uzbek, for that matter.)

Now I was disappointed. "And you're still Muslim?"

"*Da,*" they replied, sounding bored.

Sveta changed the subject: "Let's go shopping!" Albina clasped her hands in excitement. "I'll go change!" she exclaimed, bounding toward the kitchen. She returned seconds later in an off-the-shoulder silk dress and matching silver shoes.

I was feeling rather butch in my hiking boots and corduroys as I hoisted my backpack onto my shoulders and watched Sveta and Albina touch up their makeup and grab their dainty handbags. As we headed into the street, they reached for my hands in the innocent, school-girl fashion of Slavic women. We skipped over to the nearest shopping mall and beelined to the cosmetics department, where the sales attendants had the same snooty smugness as their American counterparts (only instead of Chanel and Estée Lauder, they sold Ivory soap and Vaseline). Sveta sampled every brand of hand lotion before settling on a bottle of Yves Rocher.

Our next stop was a black-and-white checkered ice cream parlor. Having downed two meals already, I insisted I wasn't hungry, but they ordered me an enormous hot fudge sundae (and two glasses of water for themselves) anyway. While I force-fed myself the whole milk ice cream, Sveta and Albina filled me in on the restaurant's scandalous clientele. One gentleman had been bringing in his wife and mistress on alternating evenings for years. His wife had recently caught on, however, and retaliated with an affair of her own with one of the cooks. The night before, the mistress and the husband had dined on lamb chops in the front of the restaurant while the wife and the cook shared dessert in the back.

Albina had to return to her shift at the restaurant, but Sveta had an appointment at the sauna and invited me to join her. We hailed a cab that took us to an upscale part of town and dropped us off beneath a sign portraying a seductive woman winking from beneath a broad-brimmed hat. The front door opened into a café where half a dozen, well-to-do women nibbled on caviar. They all turned to stare at my hiking boots and corduroys as we walked through the doorway. A receptionist handed Sveta a key and she led me down the hall.

Having frequented the Russian version of a sauna in Moscow, I had an idea of what the afternoon would entail—

namely, stripping down to nothing and roasting on a communal set of bleachers with a dozen other women—but Sveta's key opened to a faux marble room with its own whirlpool Jacuzzi and connecting private sauna. Plastic conch shells and starfish lined the pea-green-tiled Jacuzzi; two lounge chairs were propped up against the vanity. Russian pop music blasted through hidden speakers. Sveta kicked off her heels, slipped off her clothing and hopped into the Jacuzzi before I had even removed my boots. "*Tak khorosho!*" she sighed, her cheeks flushed from the heat. "Aren't you coming in?"

Having also disrobed in front of Russian women before, I knew what was coming. I peeled off my clothing quickly, hoping to hide under the suds before Sveta could notice—and inevitably comment upon—my body's imperfections.

"Your breasts are too small!" Sveta chirped as I removed my bra. "And you've got pimples on your back. Don't you get enough sex?"

Dear God—did it show? I peered down at my neglected body.

"My gynecologist says you should have sex with your husband or boyfriend at least twice a week and a lover once a week to clean out your system and keep everything balanced and in order," Sveta said as I slid into the warm water.

I tried to imagine my seventh grade sex education teacher breaking this news to us. "Now your dermatologists may recommend Oxy pads, girls, but there's only one way to *really* get a good complexion...."

"What's so funny?" Sveta demanded. "You don't see any pimples on *my* back, do you?" She turned around to show off her flawless skin, then briskly changed the subject. "Time for the sauna!"

I climbed out of the pool and followed Sveta through a

narrow doorway into a tiny, smoldering chamber. As the woody heat penetrated my pores, sweat trickled out like a saltwater spring. I eased myself onto the scorching wooden platform and started to sizzle. In Russia, trips to the *banya* generally conclude in a tribal dance where women beat each other with birch leaves to "bring the blood to the surface." Yet here, there was nothing but a sack of salt. When I asked about it, Sveta scooped out a handful, grabbed my arm and started scrubbing.

"It helps you sweat out your oils," she explained.

This seemed logical: I had been doing the same to eggplant for years. So I closed my eyes and tried to relax as Sveta worked her way from fingertip to fingertip. Then she lowered me flat on the platform, scrubbed a path from my ankles to my neck and flipped me over to tackle my back and butt. Satisfied, she handed me the gunny sack, stretched out onto the platform and motioned for me to begin. Trying to imagine Sveta as a giant purple vegetable, I set about scrubbing.

"*Tak khorosho,*" she grinned like a cat in the sun.

Coated with salt and slick with oil, we returned to the first room and hopped into the Jacuzzi to rinse off. As I dried myself off with a terry cloth towel, I felt the loneliness of the past twenty-four hours seep clean out of my pores.

To my considerable surprise, the Russian embassy approved my request for an emergency visa the following day. I booked the next day's flight to Moscow.

I rose with the sun my last morning in Uzbekistan. My bags were already packed; I sat beside them for a long while as uncertainty churned in my belly. This was it: I was about to begin life post-college and post-fellowship. From here on out, there was no prescribed path—a prospect that both exhilarated and terrified me. I wanted someone to mark this moment with me—to chase my taxi halfway down the street blowing kisses, as I had done for every other member of my group. But I had only my yak-smelling backpack for company.

I walked along the creaky floor boards toward the front desk, handed in my key and headed out the door. To my astonishment, Albina and Sveta were huddled together on the front steps. I'd only told them that I would be leaving "early" in the morning. There was no telling how long they'd been waiting. They slipped their hands into mine and led me down the steps to the curb, where a taxi waited. As the driver loaded my pot-bellied backpack into the trunk, I hugged them fiercely.

"You have your passport, *da*? And your ticket, Stesha! Do you have your ticket?" Sveta asked anxiously.

"When you get to the airport, don't forget to check in!" Albina instructed. "And keep your backpack with you! *Bozha mou*, don't leave it on the plane!"

As my taxi rolled away from the curb, Sveta and Albina began to trot alongside, waving and blowing kisses. I blew kisses and waved back until they blended in with the mosaics on the misty horizon.

Stephanie Elizondo Griest has mingled with the Russian Mafiya, polished Chinese propaganda, and belly danced with Cuban rumba queens. These adventures are the subject of her award-winning first book, Around the Bloc: My Life in Moscow, Beijing, and Havana *and inspired her guidebook,* 100 Places Every Woman Should Go. *Her memoirs from Mexico are scheduled for publication in 2008. She has also written for* The New York Times, Washington Post, Latina Magazine, *and numerous Travelers' Tales anthologies. Stephanie once spent a year driving 45,000 miles across the United States, documenting its history for a web site for kids called The Odyssey, in an '81 Honda hatchback. Visit her web site at www.aroundthebloc.com.*

AUDREY FERBER

* * *

April in Paris

Listening is an essential ingredient for romance.

I WOKE UP ONE DAY, I WAS FIFTY-FOUR, AND I'D NEVER been to Paris. My husband, sixteen years my senior, had gone once with college friends in 1957. Would he want to go again? I hummed "April in Paris" while I folded the laundry. I bought brioche instead of bagels. I rolled my black skirt above my knees and struck so insouciant a pose, Brassaï's lovers leapt from their pages and ravished me with kisses.

Paris the beautiful, Paris the romantic, Paris the bohemian. Was it too late for me? My husband slept beside me, his snores punctuated by full apnea halts. Was it too late for us to find romance in the capital of love?

On the suggestion of friends, we rented an apartment in the Sixth Arrondisment. I raced ahead of him as he fought our suitcases through the cigarette fog hovering over the last winding flights of stairs. I threw open our door and headed straight for the bank of windows with rooftop views. Yesterday, I was one of the uninitiated. Now I had my very own garret with rooftop views.

That night, we sat in a restaurant next to another couple from Northern California. The wife showed me a photo of their new baby. I discreetly checked the guidebook on my lap. "An inviting *boîte* adored by Parisians…" Where were all the French people? McDonald's?

"When I was here in '57…" My husband began the story of his post-collegiate grand tour.

I cleared my throat. Why did he have to sound so old?

Later, while he snored next to me, I listened to the noise from the café below. The outdoor tables were jammed with fresh-faced, *louche*-faced young people. I should have come when I was in my twenties. I'd kept ending up in Mexico buying the same embroidered blouses. I'd lain slathered in oil on more beaches than I cared to remember conspiring with the sun to age my skin.

Someone laughed below. The music got louder. I wrapped my arms around my husband's back. A first night in Paris demanded making love. He shifted toward me in his sleep, his skin as warm as a *daube*. Then my sleeping pill kicked in.

In the morning, after croissants and *caffé pressé* in the patisserie outside our door, we explored our neighborhood. Two women in slim suits stood talking on our corner. Their nude hosiery and the scarves looped through the handles of their handbags looked formal and iconically French. At home, my jeans and clogs identified me as a cultural creative out to buy a free-range chicken but here my thick juvenile clothing felt all wrong. I left my husband practicing his French on a fruit vendor and entered a shop with one rack of perfect clothes.

"*Figure*," the *vendeuse* announced, belting me into a twelve hundred dollar black trench coat.

The silhouette may have been right but the armholes were so tiny, my arms sprang out from my sides.

It started to rain. Hard pelting drops. "April in Paris." I felt
foolish for planning our trip around the lyrics of a song. My
husband and I put on our matching all-weather hats and
walked down to the Seine. I didn't expect to feel much. But
as soon as I saw the river and the bridges, an affirmative chord
of "yes" resounded inside me. My steps quickened. I was the
heroine of every movie set in Paris. I was inside all the novels
and songs. The rain stopped and a disc of sun appeared. A
surge of joy crescendoed through me. Paris *was* magnanimous.
I'd arrived so late but still she took me in.

"Wait. My hip hurts," my husband said as we started across
the bridge. He rested against the railing. I tried not to sound
snappish when I offered ibuprofen but we'd just started out. I
turned away from the Walkman cord tangled in his eyeglasses
and studied a man at the other end of the bridge. A vision of
Parisian elegance in a chestnut suede jacket and flannel pants.
He was perfection. The man I'd have an affair with if I was
single. But as he got closer, I saw that he wore an inky black
toupee tipped off-center and that his wet microfiber jacket
was more orange than brown.

"Are you O.K.?" I turned and hooked arms with my husband. "Should we go back?"

"Are you kidding?" he said. "*Allons.*"

Saint Chappelle stirred me. The deep red columns and navy
blue ceiling made me reconsider my entire white-walled life.
In the Marais, we marveled at the kosher restaurants. Our
Jewish identity always ignited abroad. We photographed each
other in the sexy curves of the Picasso Museum. That night,
we ate at a brasserie so atmospheric I expected Piaf's nylons
to be soaking in the sink. We sat inches from a sylph-like
woman in her seventies and her male companion.

"When I was here in '57," my husband began.

"We have been travel partners for thirty-five years," the sylph said before draining a glass of ox-blood-colored wine. Her cascading white hair trembled on her back. "When my benefactress suggested Paris, we jumped at the chance," she continued.

"Partners." "Benefactress." Her language cast a rosy glow. Maybe all my marriage needed was a vocabulary adjustment. The sylph's partner mentioned Rome.

"My daughter and I toured Italy in eighty-one," my husband said.

"Bread?" I rattled the basket at his mouth, close enough to nick his teeth. The daughter from his first marriage. His ancient travel itineraries. You didn't hear me going on and on about my other lives. What kept him so focused on the past?

We loved the Musee d'Orsay, the flea market at Clignancourt, and a shop where they made silk umbrellas by hand. Then, too quickly, our week in Paris reached an end. On our last night, we taxied to an outlying neighborhood to try a Basque restaurant too au courant for the guidebooks. We ran through a lashing rain from the cab towards the light pouring from its broad windows. A small blond woman huddled inside the door holding a wet umbrella across her hips. Raindrops quivered on my husband's silver beard as he admitted to the maitre d' that we had not reserved. The man lowered his chin and raised one eyebrow as if he were insane. Then, he started to lead us to a table.

"Excuse me," the blond woman quavered. Her hair was plastered to her scalp and her wire-framed glasses sat crooked on her nose. "I was here first."

The host spoke rapidly to one of the waiters in a language that wasn't French.

"Oh, never mind." The woman's voice broke, crying, as she slammed out the door.

"What just happened?" I imagined that she'd fought with her husband or cracked under the pressure of visiting Paris on her own.

"They don't want to seat her because she's alone," my husband said. "They think we'll spend more. We should leave too."

"Why?" My stomach growled as I tried to decide between the braised rabbit with prunes and the piperade.

"To support her," he said.

I looked into his eyes. He wasn't kidding. I didn't think he knew the word "support." Warmth flooded through me. I thought of his patience, his generosity, the loving way he helped my father tend his bonsai trees. Then he turned to the couple at the next table.

"When I was here in '57," he began.

"Why did you come?" I exploded as we walked to a main boulevard. "If you've been everywhere in '57 or '81, why the *hell* are you here?"

He flinched. "I've never been here with a wife. A lover."

The word "lover" quivered on his lips. He still touched me when he spoke from his heart. The rain stopped. A gypsy woman in smeared eye makeup tried to sell him a rose. He bought the whole bunch. Concertina music from a distant café floated in the air. I held out my arms. We waltzed on the cobblestones.

Audrey Ferber ate cuy *in the Ecuadorian jungle, blistered in Israel, and searched Costa Rica for the elusive quetzal before she found Paris. She teaches writing at the University of California Extension in San Francisco and is at work on a novel about the Shakers.*

BRITTA SCHROEDER

* * *

The Bug

*It creates a state of mind that is hard
to get rid of once infected.*

I'm a cliché, I thought to myself as I made another
kick step in the knee-deep snow, only a few feet from the top
of the mountain. Just another lonely, brokenhearted individual
trying to drown her sorrows in some enlightening pilgrimage.
I stopped staring down at the blinding snow and ice, and
looked up to the top of the mountain, where tattered
Buddhist prayer flags fluttered in the wind, sending prayers up
into the pure blue sky. At roughly 18,000 feet, I was the only
living being within sight. The sun reflected off the snow,
burning my nostrils and the roof of my open, panting mouth.

"Trust me," my boyfriend said. I didn't want to do it. He
sweet-talked me into it, claiming we would understand each
other on a deeper level and that he wanted to prove his love
to me. We would become more intimate, he insisted, and I finally caved to his desires. Afterward I felt dirty. Indeed I was
so, returning to the tin-roofed shack at the end of each day
covered in a layer of mud. Under his pressure, I had consented

to take my first trip abroad, accompanying him on a research trip to the depths of a South American rainforest.

I can honestly say that the thought of traveling had never crossed my mind before. Travel agency brochures of bikini-clad women, drinks in hand on a white sandy beach, never held any appeal for me. But my boyfriend's minimalist type of traveling opened a new world to me, a world where I could be myself in all my unwashed, unshaven, unemployed glory. Indubitably, he was correct in his prediction, for traveling does bring people closer when they share a bathroom and intestinal parasites.

Yet, after the various intimate connections on our first trip, I brought home more than just stomach bugs. I had contracted a disease from him: the highly contagious, incurable Travel Bug, known to speakers of Latin as *Travelus addictus*. It hides discreetly in the traveler's system, waiting until the hallucinations of the last malarial medication have barely worn off and then BAM! It hits hard and fast, usually when the person is least suspecting, so that one quiet Sunday afternoon, the victim suddenly feels the pressing urge to shave all their bodily hair and weave the belly button lint of some remote tribal members in Burkina Faso. Other symptoms of The Bug include the desire of travelers to show painfully long slide shows of past trips and reminisce about flesh-eating viruses in a vaguely boastful tone. And now, all thanks to the efforts of my beguiling boyfriend, I too was infected with the disease.

Unfortunately, when the closeness we achieved on our various travels proved in fact to be too close for his comfort, I found myself looking through yet another guidebook, this time as a single traveler. "Traveling alone will help clear your head," my friends said. I didn't have to go to another country to speak a different language. What my friends really meant was, "We don't know why he broke up with you and wish you would leave the country so you would stop asking us." My friends were correct though, no matter how they said it. I needed to appreciate my newfound freedom, and hopefully discover a way to fill the hole my previous traveling partner had left at my side. I was in search of a revelation, a life-altering epiphany, of the sort people find while wading through the jungles of Papua New Guinea or while looking out to the ends of the Earth at Tierra del Fuego. A solo adventure sounded like the perfect way to find such an epiphany, and, as a self-proclaimed mountain junkie, I believed my epiphany was waiting for me somewhere within sight of the tallest obstacle in my world, Mount Everest. Therefore, I once again succumbed to the nagging voice of the Bug, which is how I found myself knee-deep in snow completely alone in the upper limits of the troposphere.

My destination was not

————— ✳ —————

We go into the wilderness with our whole selves. It asks no less of us. It asks the utmost of our bodies. It asks that we perceive it with accuracy. The price can be high if we do not.

If we look intently we find a great deal more than we knew we would find. Scientists have accumulated a vast hoard of facts and know that they still may not have more than pricked the mother lode of knowledge. But if facts are all they perceive, they have not yet learned wisdom.

In the wilderness wisdom comes on the wind and in the stillness; it shows us ourselves, our deepest, archaic, forgotten and truest selves. We recognize that we are of the Earth and of the Universe—a part of the structure, and it is within us and of us—inseparable.

—Margaret P. Stark,
How Deep the High Journey

Everest Base Camp, where the lower flanks of Everest obscure the view of the mountain, but Kala Pattar, the mountain across from Everest, which allows for the best view of the monolith. As I stood catching my breath a few feet from the summit, I remembered the second day of my trek. Resting on a rock along the switchbacks to Namche Bazaar, two teenage girls from Japan had conversed between themselves before turning to speak to me in broken English.

"You are…lonely?" one had asked me.

"Yes, a little bit," was my reply. Lonely or alone, either word meant the same thing to me at the time. Her question was not only well formed for my present situation, but also well founded. A single Western female, without a guide, a porter, or even a hiking partner still seemed to be a strange sight for many of my fellow trekkers to see. Beyond traveling without any form of companionship in the tourist off-season, the previous week's snowstorm had left me even more isolated than I had expected. For the first time in five months, rain clouds covered the Kathmandu valley the day before my trek, and what had been rain at a lower elevation was snow higher up. Most trekkers had turned around at 12,000 feet when faced with knee-deep snow, but I couldn't turn back. I had yet to find my epiphany, and, as a native of the state of Colorado, I knew that epiphanies could rarely be found below 14,000 feet. Besides, to a young woman with a broken heart, frostbitten extremities are the least of her problems.

For three days after the storm I saw only a handful of defeated *bideshi*, or foreigners, coming down the trail and the occasional Sherpani leading her yaks to lower winter pastures. More often than not, though, the trail ahead of me was a sea of white and when I rested, I could see only my tracks behind me. Just like winters at home, I was reluctant to break the spell of the perfectly formed crystal mounds glittering in the sunlight. The sky had returned to the deepest blue, birch trees dripped with icicles to create a fairyland archway, and the frozen icefalls cascaded down the moraine boulders, with no one else to see it but me. While hundreds of lone trekkers had come before me and many more were sure to come behind, very few would have the solitude I took for granted.

I took a few more kick-steps up the last of the slope, and squinted at the glaciers surrounding me. After ten days in the snow, and nothing but cyclic thoughts in my head, I had arrived at the top of Kala Pattar, utterly alone. A glance down the side of Pumo Ri revealed the beginnings of a base camp, but I had the entire mountain to myself. As I crouched on the slippery ice, using the rock cairns as a windbreak, I gazed at Mount Everest and let my accomplishment slowly sink in. I had made it! I had made it through knee-deep snow, uphill the entire way, completely alone to 18,192 feet. As I so cleverly punned to myself, I was completely "solo in the Solu Khumbu."

I sat on Kala Pattar for a while, looking behind the rock cairns and prayer flags for the life-altering epiphany I knew awaited me. Surely it was hiding somewhere around the windswept summit. Visions of myself suddenly realizing that I was better off without a traveling companion and basking smugly in my solo success danced through my head. Unfortunately, as always, the epiphany is an elusive creature and after many minutes of exposure to the wind, I gave up my search. I was completely alone on a mountaintop, epiphanyless, all because of my transmitted disease. In short, all because of my now MIA travel partner. On top of everything, I could feel a case of giardiasis coming on. My elation with my accomplishment slowly faded, for in my blind striving and subsequent failure to find my epiphany, I was faced with yet another reminder of my absolute isolation: who would take my picture?

Descending the trail the next day, I turned a corner and came face to face with the Everest Base Camp setup crew. A continuous line of over a hundred yaks threaded down the valley and disappeared behind the hill. Utter chaos prevailed, and I sat on a rock watching the circus continue upward, since it was no use to fight the onslaught of yaks. Two days before, the virgin snow had been evidence that I was totally alone. Now yaks snorted, porters struggled under their burdens and trekkers chattered away in every imaginable language. I watched the train subside, not the least bit envious of the fifty-some trekkers and mountaineers whose memories of their trip included the view of a yak's backside. Passing the last of the stragglers slowly hiking up the now dung-covered trail, I resumed my descent, feeling a force gripping my insides. I hurried down the mountain, hoping the strange feeling in my stomach was not giardiasis, but a different kind of bug. The kind of bug that is the only mesmerizing companion a traveler needs.

Britta Schroeder is a resident of Colorado but works for the Forest Service in Alaska during the summer to subsidize her winter travels. She volunteered in Nepal for four months before trekking and avoids men who have an aversion to matching socks. If she grows up, she wants to be an environmental lawyer.

TARA KOLDEN

* * *

The Etiquette of Apple Tea

Don't be afraid to dance with
the carpet salesman.

I DON'T REMEMBER WHERE I PICKED HIM UP; MOST
likely it was on a corner near my hotel. Istanbul was just
shrugging off the last snowfall of early spring, and there wasn't
much foot traffic on the slushy sidewalks, even though the
neighborhood was blocks from the Hagia Sophia and the Blue
Mosque and would likely be overrun with tourists in a matter of weeks. There weren't many lodgers at the budget hotels
that lined the street, so the few foreigners who came and went
were subject to immediate scrutiny from the locals living and
working nearby. It took me barely a day to learn that a woman
traveling alone was sized up the same way from doorway to
doorway—she must be in need of a drink.

"Lady, you come and drink tea with me?" This from the
proprietor of the hotel next door to mine, purportedly a
cousin of my landlord. He lounged in the entranceway of his
own establishment. "Hot tea. Nice on a cold day."

I smiled at him, but begged off. And I declined a similar invitation from the front desk clerk at the hostel down the
street. From the shop on the corner came another appeal.

"Apple tea," cried the shop owner, "or coffee—you like coffee? Come and drink with us."

I shook my head again and walked faster. It was my first time in Turkey, but hardly the first time I'd met a friendly proposition on my travels. Before Istanbul I'd been in Athens, where the come-ons had been fast and frequent. There were the uniformed guards at the gates of the National Gardens— they were supposed to stand silent watch, but they clicked their tongues when women walked by. Or the middle-aged man who'd attached himself to me in Syntagma Square and, before we'd walked two blocks, suggested a weekend tryst at his country home (in his favor, he'd quoted Homer). This unwanted attention was something I had expected as a solo traveler, but if over-familiarity was an occasional nuisance in Athens, in Istanbul it was as constant as my shadow.

I had rounded the corner on my way to Topkapi Palace before I realized that someone had quietly fallen in step beside me. A young Turkish man was matching my pace, stride for stride. Our eyes met and he smiled at me—it was only left for him to offer me tea. Instead, he asked if I was looking for a carpet.

The question caught me off guard—surely nothing in my demeanor suggested an urgent need for a floor covering. I was grubby and hollow-eyed after a week of trekking through the Mediterranean and living off cheap foodstuffs, and the beat up daypack slung over my shoulder did nothing for my mien. I probably could have passed for homeless. I did not need a rug.

I told him so, but he wasn't easily dissuaded. "My shop is just here. Please, you will come and look?" He gestured to a shop across the street. Against the gray of the icy pavement and surrounding buildings, the shop windows stood out like jewels. They offered a glimpse of several hundred Turkish carpets, some rolled and stacked against the walls, others laid out on the floor, the better to show off their intricate patterns. They were beautiful, and the price of just one was probably more than I had budgeted for my entire trip.

"Thank you, but no," I told him. I enunciated the words, but he understood perfectly.

"No pressure to buy," he assured me. "You can only look."

I couldn't walk any faster than I already was. Beside me, he wasn't winded. "Really, I can't."

Abruptly he changed tack. "You are going to the Hagia Sophia?"

I nodded.

"You would like a guide?"

I shook my head. "Thank you, no."

Still I couldn't lose him. We turned another corner and were faced with the magnificence of the Blue Mosque. I didn't want to rush past the minarets without pausing to appreciate the view, but neither did I want to stop with this strange man.

"No, thank you," I repeated, but he was impervious.

"You are here for how long?"

I sighed. "Just a few days."

He took stock of this and nodded. "You will visit the Hagia Sophia, Sultan Ahmet...perhaps Topkapi?"

"Yes," I admitted. In the distance, I could see the fortification wall of the palace.

He eyed me carefully. "You need a guide, you will come to my shop? I promise you, I can show you many things. Many interesting things. You will come to me?"

"Sure," I said, relieved that our meeting appeared to be at an end.

"You know where to find the shop?" He was insistent on this.

"Yes," I said. Anything to be left in peace. At last he slowed his pace, and I made my own way to the esplanade and the main gate of the palace.

Topkapi was a labyrinth of imposing gray walls and room after room of treasure. I devoted the afternoon to an exploration of its many displays: porcelain and silver, spoils and relics, imperial costumes. Most beautiful of all was the harem, with its many tiled and gilded rooms and shimmering divans. I wondered at first whether the sultan's concubines were unhappy in their captivity. Did they get enough attention? Did the sultan remember all their names? But as I passed through the final rooms of the harem and returned to the inner courtyard of the palace, I wondered if it was instead the sultan who felt imprisoned. Where the harem was delicate and inviting— both in architecture and in decoration—the rest of the palace seemed more a utilitarian outpost than a royal residence. Who, then, had the upper hand: the sultan or his women?

It began to drizzle in the late afternoon, and the wind off the Bosphorus left me chilled. The palace was unheated, and eventually not even the lure of more treasure could keep my mind off the cold. Near closing time, I made my retreat. The esplanade in front of the castle was busy with vendors, and from one of them I bought a wool scarf to supplement my inadequate outerwear, which mostly consisted of a faded jacket meant for spring in other latitudes.

The view from the palace was magnificent. The Hagia Sophia's immense outline coupled with the Blue Mosque's lofty minarets to form a silhouette that reminded me of my childhood copy of *The Arabian Nights*. But if the buildings seemed familiar to me, so did a face in the crowd.

The carpet seller was waiting across the street. Waiting for me? Or another female tourist? I wasn't sure, but when he spotted me threading my way through the tea vendors and the postcard hawkers, he detached himself from his corner roost and glided to my side. I couldn't help but acknowledge him.

"You enjoyed your visit to the palace?" he asked.

I was still wary of him, but I was also tired, and so very cold. I saw no reason not to let down my guard a little and answer him honestly. "Yes, I did. The rooms were beautiful. And the sultan's costumes. I bought a scarf." I showed him my purchase, and he nodded his approval. I let him walk with me down the esplanade and back toward my hotel.

"It is colder here than you expected?"

I hardly needed to answer. I was hugging myself in my thin jacket, and burrowing my chin deep within the folds of my new scarf.

The carpet seller gave me a sympathetic smile. "Won't you come inside and drink some tea? No pressure to buy, just have some tea. It won't take long. And your hotel is just there, yes?" He pointed down the block toward a group of hotels, one of which was indeed mine.

I allowed myself to be led into his carpet shop, where two clerks were busy unrolling a series of rugs for an American couple who were deliberating between carpets in shades of green and beige. My host sat me in a chair beside the couple and went off to fetch the tea, and while I waited for him I looked around at the rugs. Here were colors as opulent as the tiles I'd seen in the Topkapi harem—vivid blues and greens and golds. One of the clerks explained to the Americans the provenance of the carpet they were considering, and I tried to imagine the look of the loom that had produced such a treasure.

Soon my host returned with the tea set. He poured my tea into a delicate tulip-shaped glass, and offered it to me with a saucer and a tiny spoon for stirring. It tasted like hot apple cider, and was just the restorative I needed after my hours in the frigid palace.

We sat in silence for a time, drinking our tea. I couldn't bring myself to ask how much the carpets before us cost. The Americans had still not made up their minds.

"You like this?" the carpet seller asked, pointing to a rich maroon rug the clerks had just unfurled.

"It's beautiful," I admitted.

"You could buy one from me. A very good price. Take it home with you."

I explained to him the nature of my trip; such a carpet would never fit in my backpack, and that was the only luggage I had.

"You know," he said, "we ship worldwide."

The next day dawned just as cold, and with no fewer invitations to drink tea. And as before, the carpet seller was beside me before I had reached the first corner outside my hotel.

"What will you visit today?"

I paused and thumbed through the dog-eared guidebook that had served me throughout my trip. "I've heard there are ancient cisterns beneath the city. I'd like to see them."

He beamed with enthusiasm. "Yes, I know them. Please, allow me to be your guide."

I hesitated. "I have no money for a guide. Really, I must save for the rest of my trip."

He waved his hands in the air. "No cost. None at all. I would just like to show you my city."

I weighed his offer. What was he after? And how much trouble could I get into if I accompanied him to the cisterns?

We each bought our own tickets at the entrance to the cisterns, and descended with the other tourists to the dark, subterranean caverns beneath the city. We did a delicate dance on the wooden catwalks—I would stray ahead and he would catch up; I would linger beside a particular column and he would find me—never too familiar, but not exactly strange. He told me a little of the cisterns' history, and pointed out the giant stone heads—remnants of pagan statuary—that had been incorporated into many of the cisterns' supporting columns.

As we left the cisterns, he stopped me. "What will you do for dinner tonight?"

In truth, I didn't know. I made mention of my guidebook.

"Have dinner with me," he said. "There will be many people there. You will enjoy it."

I told him I'd think about it, and he didn't press the issue. He also left me free to wander by myself in the afternoon, and I spent a quiet hour in the Hagia Sophia.

Evening found me returning to my hotel, and the carpet seller was there on the corner to greet me. Dinner was soon, he explained. The taxi was on its way. Indeed, as he mentioned it, the car pulled up outside his shop. I was aware then how dangerously close I could be to catastrophe. Wasn't this how modern tragedies began, with women getting into cars with men they didn't know? Still, I climbed into the back seat.

The taxi took us through parts of the city I hadn't seen—crowded, busy areas brightly lit with advertisements and flashing neon. It was a cold night, but that had not deterred the local citizenry from hitting clubs and bars that looked a lot like those I'd visited at home. After a day of ancient history, I had emerged into a modern Turkish night.

But dinner, my host assured me, would be traditional. The taxi dropped us at a small *lokanta* where a long table was already waiting. The people seated there greeted the carpet seller warmly and made room for us at one end. Most of our companions were Turkish, but there were a few foreigners like me. A South African woman sat across from me and offered up a few pleasantries. As I sampled the rabbit stew and had my first taste of *raki*, I wondered about my fellow diners, all of whom seemed connected to my host. Who were they? Were they family? Old established friends? Or had he scoured the city, building a collection acquaintances, and summoned us here…for what? I'd been trained to equate skepticism with self-preservation, but I could find no evidence for an ulterior motive at this table. Did the carpet seller sit a little too close? Refill my glass of *raki* once or twice too often? Did it matter?

There was live music in the restaurant, and after the meal the men got up to dance. They formed a line that snaked its way around the tables, but their efforts were clumsy, prompting both laughter and applause from those of us still seated. By the end of the festivities I was red-faced from laughter and exhilaration.

Late that night I climbed into the back of another taxi for the return trip to the hotel, joining some of the same people I had sat with at dinner. There was much multilingual bantering as we crossed the bridge back to the European side of the city, and we dropped a few passengers here and there in neighborhoods I could barely make out in the darkness. I didn't recognize my own stop when it came, but the carpet seller nudged me helpfully toward the curb.

"I must pay you," I told him. "For dinner, and the taxis." I held out what cash I had, and he accepted a wad of lira. It was a lot, more than I had budgeted for the day, but this evening had been far from typical.

"Sleep well," he told me, just before shutting the door. "Tomorrow you will come and drink tea with me."

And that I would have, if I had not left Istanbul the next morning to continue with my travels. But even now I sometimes raise a glass to my Turkish carpet seller, although I never learned his name.

Tara Kolden lives and writes worldwide, but most often calls Seattle home. Her travel essays, fiction, and poetry have been published in journals such as Student Traveler *and* Paris Eiffel Tower News, *and in anthologies from Lonely Planet and Seal Press.*

CATHERINE WATSON

*　*　*

A Place Prepared

One might call it the very heart
of North America.

THE ANCIENT PUEBLO OF ACOMA, NEW MEXICO, IS
perfectly nicknamed: Called the Sky City, it commands the
most exotic location of any inhabited place in the United
States—the top of a 376-foot-high mesa, a natural citadel of
golden rock, an island in the sky.

It's also amazingly well-disguised.

I'd driven there from Albuquerque in late afternoon, turning south off Interstate 40 at the Acoma tribe's booming
casino complex and picking up a small, scenic road. At first, it
ran past scattered homesteads—old stone houses, trailers, a few
brand new ranches—but for most of its nearly twenty miles, it
took me through a gorgeously empty landscape of red and
gold mesas, polka-dotted with plump, dark cedar shrubs.

Finally the road curved, and the vista I was waiting for
opened out below—a wide valley, studded with mesas and
giant rock towers, like sentinels along a sacred way. I pulled
over where the road starts down, got out of the car and, as
usual, stared in awe. The Sky City was right there in front of

me, three-and-a-half miles away, but its camouflage is so perfect, I couldn't see it, even though I knew where to look.

I drove a mile closer, down onto the valley floor, and still saw nothing but banded mesas and golden rock. I had to drive another full mile before I could finally distinguish the twin bell towers of San Esteban del Rey, Acoma's 1629 Spanish mission church, rising above the fringe of little flat-roofed houses along the mesa rim.

This place is North America's Machu Picchu, and in some ways it's more impressive: It's older than the world-famous mountaintop ruin in Peru—and it's still alive. Acoma people have lived up there for more than a thousand years.

The Sky City mesa is a tribal emblem now, and the Sky City nickname functions like a brand. But its real name—Haak'u—means something hauntingly different. It means "a place prepared"—a reference to a cosmic promise made to the tribe when it first emerged into this world.

"It was already foretold at the time of Emergence that there was 'a place prepared'—in all senses of the word—for our eternal occupancy," Brian Vallo, director of Acoma's new cultural center, explained while the center was being finished. "It is the traditional homeland of the Acoma people," he said. "A very sacred place."

Twenty pueblos—the Spanish word can mean village, tribe or individuals—still survive in the Southwest. One tribe, the Hopi, lives in northeastern Arizona. The other nineteen pueblos are in New Mexico, arrayed on the map like a backwards L, with Albuquerque at the hinge.

The pueblos are different nations, speaking different languages—Keresan at Acoma and Laguna, Zuni at Zuni, Hopi at Hopi, Tewa and its variants along the Rio Grande.

They look different, too. Taos is famous for its ancient pair of multi-story apartment buildings. Tiny Picuris is set high in lush hills. Jemez, beside a mountain river, has narrow, tight-knit lanes and the feel of a Greek village. Nambe's homeland is a miniature Monument Valley bounded by modern suburban homes. And Acoma—well, Acoma is like nothing else in this country.

But those are superficial differences. All the pueblos share something more important—a powerful belief system so encompassing and so interwoven with every aspect of daily life that even to call it "tradition" or "religion" is to limit its scope. It is deeply rooted in the land, and the pueblos have managed to hang onto it for 400 years, ever since the Spanish conquest.

Whenever I visit, I try to imagine what it is like to inhabit the Pueblo world, a world where everything is sacred, where everything has meaning, where everything—and everyone—is connected to everything else. "The connections to place and people—that's HOME," said Brian Vallo. "And that's a LOT."

For me, imagining a world so complete is like trying to picture a color

> The sun had been set for some time, when, being within a quarter of a mile of the ferryman's hut, our path having led us close to the shore of the calm lake, we met two neatly dressed women, without hats, who had probably been taking their Sunday evenings' walk. One of them said to us, in a friendly and soft tone of voice, "What! You are stepping westward?" I cannot describe how affecting this simple expression was in that remote place, with the western sky in front, yet glowing with the departed sun.
>
> —Dorothy Wordsworth,
> *Journal* (1803)

that isn't in the spectrum, and it turns every trip to this part of the Southwest into a spiritual journey.

It was a long way, in more than miles, from the sacred Sky City back to Acoma's Sky City Casino-Hotel and Travel Center on I-40—so far a distance, in fact, that at first I had trouble picturing them in the same universe, let alone the same landscape.

But the casino complex and its huge, adjacent truck stop are the economic engine fueling Acoma's future, and that future includes the preservation of its past. Gaming revenues, for example, paid for most of the tribe's $17 million cultural center at the foot of Haak'u mesa.

The handsome center is intended to be many things, Vallo said, but they all involve the precious concept of home—a home where visitors can feel welcome; a home for repatriated Acoma artifacts; a home where the Acoma themselves can study their language and heritage.

Even the architecture tells a story about home. It includes elements of every dwelling style in Acoma history—from ancient stonework like that found at Mesa Verde and Chaco Canyon, right on up to HUD housing built by the U.S. government.

From my room in the casino hotel, I could look across the swimming pool and see the force that is driving Acoma's economy now: the raised roadbed of Interstate 40. It took the place of old Route 66, and it's still the Mother Road across New Mexico.

Rivers of semi trucks glittered in both directions, and steady streams of them were pulling off at the Acoma exit to tank up and let their drivers fire down. More than 120 semis were parked at the tribe's truck stop my first night there—I drove along the rows, counting—and more were arriving by the minute.

Inside the casino hotel, there were the familiar clangs, whoops, and jingles from the gaming hall off the lobby. But the complex does not serve alcohol, and the hotel was surprisingly tasteful and quiet, even with the Fourth of July coming up. Families jammed the casino restaurant, and Sky City staff was setting up folding chairs out back for a casino-sponsored fireworks show. It felt more like a community social center than a subset of Las Vegas.

Haak'u, by contrast, draws a different crowd to the ancient mesa top, but it too draws large numbers: In summer, hundreds of tourists a day descend on a village of fewer than a dozen families.

To protect it, the tribe has been tracking tourism to the Sky City for more than a century. It began guided tours as early as the 1930s, and tours are now the only way you can visit the mesa. Small buses shuttle visitors up there from the new cultural center at its base, on a road built in 1950 for a John Wayne movie.

The rules are strict: No photography without a permit, no wandering off or hanging back, and you need to get the name right. "It's pronounced AAAAH-coma," my group's tour guide said firmly, as we began our tour of the old city. "We aren't in a *COMA!*"

What looks enchanted from a distance is stark up close, and that always startles me. The houses of the Sky City are plain and box-like, one or two stories, made of stone or adobe plastered with mud.

Gusts of wind whip through the narrow streets, flinging sand against skin and into eyes. There is only one small tree—"the Acoma National Forest," my tour guide joked—

and the blistering New Mexico sun always feels as if it's right overhead.

The mesa-top tours take about an hour under that sun. The guides move fast, and they cover a lot. Pause, and you're guaranteed to miss something—an ancient window made of mica, for example, or the hole in the cemetery wall that allowed lost spirits to come home, or an explanation of the tribe's matrilineal system—how the youngest daughter inherits from the youngest daughter, down through time.

But visitors do pause—caught by stunning views at the end of every lane, by the tables of distinctive black-on-white pottery set out in front of artists' homes, and by the food—apple turnovers, straight from the oven, and fry bread so fresh that the grease burns your tongue. A lot of these tourist pauses, I suspect, are really just ways of extending the experience, of getting to talk with people who actually live in this strange and sacred place. At least they are for me.

At the end of the tour, the guides always offer a choice of how to get back: Ride the bus back down the mesa or take the hidden foot trail that the Acoma people used for centuries before the road was cut.

I always choose the trail.

Almost vertical in places, it follows a steep, narrow slot in the cliff face. Getting down safely requires trusting the ancient builders, who knew what they were doing when they carved the footholds and handholds. It's also a good idea to follow the guides' advice and climb down backwards.

I turned around to face the yellow rock and then descended as if I were on a ladder, reaching my toes down step by step, sliding my fingers into ancient niches placed exactly where I needed to find them.

Of all the good experiences on this trip, that descent was the best. I liked feeling that I fitted into something that went so far back in time, with so many connections to other people—even if they could never be my own. The scale of the steps was human, and the warm, golden stone felt good and secure against my hands. It felt, in fact, like comfort.

Catherine Watson took her first trip at the age of five, by train, from Minneapolis, Minnesota, to Grand Forks, North Dakota, in a blue suit her mother had sewn and a new white straw hat. She has been fascinated ever since by the relationship between "home" and "away." She was the award-winning travel editor of the Minneapolis Star Tribune *from 1978 to 2004 and is the author of* Roads Less Traveled: Dispatches from the Ends of the Earth *and* Home on the Road: Further Dispatches from the Ends of the Earth.

BETH E. MARTINSON

* * *

How to Strangle a Pigeon

Money won't buy wisdom or joy.

MY ROOMMATE IN PARIS KNOWS I'M BROKE. SHE COMMENTS that Hemingway was always hungry when he lived in Paris. She's reading *A Moveable Feast*. If it were my book, I would put some ketchup on it. Bon appétit!

Hem would understand. It was rumored that Papa used to strangle pigeons in the Luxembourg Gardens. So far I have been unsuccessful with the pigeon hunting, but it's only my second week in Paris. After a week of living on a pauper's budget, I've come to the realization that being a starving artist isn't so glamorous.

I signed up for a writing program at the Paris American Academy for the month of July. It was supposed to be a chic rite of passage like my forefathers of writing. I didn't realize that in order for me to afford the program I would spend every dime I had and forfeit all Parisian luxuries once I got to the city of light. Being an MFA student has had its broke panic attacks, but a month on a hundred euros has been the biggest challenge of my life.

Paris is so expensive that it's easier to drink than eat. I didn't expect to become an alcoholic here, but the wine goes down smooth and it's the cheapest nourishment in France.

Every night I thank my lucky Parisian twilight that the apartment came included in the cost. Hunger and homelessness often go hand in hand, but in this particular circumstance, I have a roof but no protein.

I spend the majority of the day searching for cheap nourishment or classmates that are eating. But Paris is the "bling bling" capital and the only items I can afford are, incidentally, fashionably French. I eat baguettes and cheese for most meals. I drink bottles of wine for three euros that taste like red clown shoes. On my modest budget I could hardly afford to attend a wine and cheese tasting party in the states, but in France, it's cheaper than a box of Cheez-its.

In class I watch my peers eat. They think I'm weird. I try to explain it's the hunger, not me, but it usually comes out as drool. My roommates hide food in strange places. I found a baguette in the cabinet with the broom. I ate it while I swept.

My professor hands out stacks of papers for us to read. All I can think about is what food group paper might fall into. I've considered trying to sauté the handouts with some brie or perhaps put it in a baguette. One night our professor invited us all over for a party with the instructions, "Bring some wine and food." I bought the usual red clown shoes wine and a baguette for seventy cents. I ate half the bread on the way.

My best friend here is poor, too. Every day we decide who will pay for what. We don't argue, as that takes too much energy. When you are hungry, you waste little energy. We buy cheap foods and lots of red clown shoes. We walk around aimlessly after the bottles are empty and we're still hungry. Most of the time we sit on public fountains and laugh at the lengths we would go for food. When you're hungry, you get delirious and always feel drunk especially when you only drink red clown shoes for dinner.

We get creative in our meal preparation. Everything tastes delicious. The other night we made fried eggs and added mayonnaise. It was awesome when I washed it down with red clown shoes.

Little things get pushed aside in favor of food and wine. We forego necessities. Laundry is taking a shower with our clothes on. Personal hygiene products are overrated. We smell most of the time and usually shy away from normal people. Our classmates think we're strange. Our professors think we're on drugs. The Parisians leave us alone. The bums are our friends. We have names for all the pigeons and work as a team to get food. But they're all still an option for meals.

We walk around the Luxembourg Gardens as ghosts. We are invisible to most of the tourists. All we talk about is food. We play a game in the park instead of writing. I say, what would you do if you had one hundred euros right now? He says, what would you eat if you could have any meal? Those details can go on for hours.

We talk about childhood memories of eating. Holidays are full of lovely meals. Birthdays are brimming with tasty treats. We have hunger fantasies of going berserk. I entertain the thought of toasting a large quantity of Japanese tourists on a hibachi the size of Notre Dame. He prefers a horde of Germans on a George Foreman grill the size of the Eiffel tower. Now that's fat-reducing!

I pass flowers and think if they would taste sweet. I wonder if the grass would be a good vegetable alternative. And of course, I laugh about what Hemingway may have done with the pigeons, and examine which method of strangulation he may have used. I watch French women with their petite poodles and think about how lucky those bitches are and what their meat might be flavored with. I look for bigger dogs with fuller thighs. I wait for absent-minded pet owners.

We sit by the fountain outside the Paris American Academy and count pigeons, cars, and tourists. Counting games make it easier to stifle the hunger. It's almost as if we're children waiting for someone to feed us. Where is my mother? Where is the lunch lady? Damn them both for not giving me a peanut butter and jelly sandwich.

Thank god for red clown shoes! Without it, we wouldn't sleep at night. We would toss and turn with hunger. I would sleepwalk into the kitchen and eat all my roommates' food.

This is the most perfect dreamless sleep. If I couldn't drink, my mother would be following me around all night saying, "I told you not to go to France with no money." She would be cooking chicken a la king, spaghetti and meatballs, steak tips, apple pie. Holy God I am hungry.

The other day I fell asleep in the garden outside my school. I fantasized about what Paris could be if I had money. Visions of champagne and crepes under the Eiffel Tower, fine Burgundy with an aromatic aftertaste, three-ply toilet paper, clean socks, laundry detergent, 300 thread-count sheets, etc. I drool over it, asleep in the garden in the middle of the afternoon. Hungry people need to sleep a lot. We're not lazy, just hungry.

My best friend and I became friends through writing, hunger, and an affinity for alcohol of all kinds. On good days we can buy beer. We get the strongest/cheapest combination—usually it's Amsterdam beer from the grocer across the street from my apartment on Rue Bertholette. The family who runs the grocery store thinks we are alcoholics because we giggle at the sight of wine and beer and also because we hold food as if it's our firstborn child.

We buy strange things. We count change. We try our credit cards every other day just to make sure they don't work. Together we make fun of the situation. We never complain or get depressed. Friendship forged during famine lasts forever. I think I will make that a bumper sticker.

The other night we went to another random fountain, each with our own bottle of red clown shoes. There we took turns balancing on the fountain, at times slipping in and laughing until we snarfed red. While I was enchanted with the way water looks like macaroni and cheese, he climbed to the top of the fountain and screamed, "I am the king!"

Funny how a three-euro bottle of wine makes you monarchy. A cheap bottle of tequila deems you at least a jester in the court. A simple bottle of champagne makes you a Dame.

Beer, of course, makes you some sort of sports star. At least that's what usually happens after drinking too much of it. We think phone poles are linebackers. Gates become feeble defenders. We sing "We Are the Champions" and "Eye of the Tiger" as we walk in circles trying to find a familiar landmark.

Like occupational drunks, we sometimes pass out wherever the bottle takes us. We walk the streets at all hours of the night like ghosts searching for where their lives left them. One night we went to the Pantheon and marveled at its haunting presence. I rubbed the stone to see if it would hurt if I bit it. I was really hungry that night. I considered losing teeth for a chunk of marble.

Hunger is the third person in our friendship. We collaborate on meals, on wine, on taste. Before eating we decide how best to use the food, how efficiently we can make a meal.

Hunger is an evil bitch. We argue with her constantly. She is stubborn and never flexible. When we want to go out, she wants to stay home. When we are drunk, she is sober. We always do what she wants to do and I'm getting quite sick of her. I try not to invite her over, but she comes uninvited and stays way past her welcome.

You have to get creative when you're poor. Today we ate mustard and goat cheese—the two last holdouts in the fridge. It tasted good to me with a bottle of red clown shoes. If I am hungry later I will go to sleep. I play games with my hunger—what can beat hunger in a sort of *rock, paper, scissors* game. I know that sleep beats hunger. Drunk beats hunger. Love beats hunger. Passion beats hunger. Sex beats hunger. Anger beats hunger. Laughter always beats hunger. As I sip this glass of wine I ponder what doesn't beat hunger…those things I don't need.

One evening I thought I had some more money. My mother mentioned she may put some cash in my bank account. Excited and giddy at the thought of having a warm meal, I invited all of my classmates over for a dinner party. It was the least I could do after having mooched off of them all the time. Most of my classmates avoid my friend and I because we invite ourselves to their apartments in search of meals. The dinner party at my apartment was to be a peace offering for all our rude discrepancies.

At 8:45 P.M. my best friend and I had no money. The guests were due at 9 P.M. My mother forgot. My ATM card was empty—just about as empty as my fridge and cabinets. We had fifteen minutes to create a party. When you are poor and desperate, your mind is nimble. You have to be manipulative and crafty, not because you want to, but because goddamn it, you have no choice!

We invited many people that night. I called each one and let them know which particular item they could bring. Sarah and Dorothy came with dessert. Jeremy brought pasta and sauce. Kelly made a salad. Everyone else brought wine and cheese and bread. It was perfect! I had nothing to offer but the party itself. Everyone saluted me while eating their food and drinking their wine, both of which my best friend and I consumed ravenously. I hid the leftovers from my roommates. There are four baguettes under my bed for real emergencies.

I know that when I leave here and get back to a life of money—a life of the ordinary everyday mundane—nothing will be the same. Taste will be less powerful. I won't savor the flavor of every bite knowing that it may be the last. I won't create strange concoctions with condiments and laugh at their absurdity. When I leave Paris, being broke will be about bills. Here it is about being an artist, a writer, someone who wants to be touched by raw emotion. Here my hunger is stifled by beauty and friendship, at home, my hunger is stifled by efficiency.

Living on wine and friendship is a beautiful experience. When I get home I will look back at this time as a model against which all else will be compared. I'll meet new people and wonder if I could survive on their friendship without food. Pigeons will never look the same again. I will apologize to my own dogs for considering their French relatives as a meal. I'm sure I will never find a bottle of wine that tastes like red clown shoes.

Eventually I will look back on these days and not remember the hunger pangs or the laughter or the taste of red clown shoes, but I will never forget that I've lived the richest days in the poorest times.

When Beth E. Martinson isn't finding herself in funny situations, she's helping her students learn, grow, and change the world. She writes both nonfiction and poetry and recently completed her Master of Fine Art in Creative Writing at Chatham College in Pittsburgh, Pennsylvania. She has studied writing in Italy, France, and India but is now back in the Boston area where she is a teacher, counselor, writer, and purveyor of the arts.

* * *

Pilgrimages to the Edge

Home is in the heart, and everywhere
the heart holds dear.

IF I HADN'T BEEN SPOOKED BY A NEWSPAPER HEADLINE, I wouldn't have found myself in an ambulance on Achill Island, off the coast of Ireland. Of course I wouldn't have met Pat either, and that would be my great misfortune. The bold headline, glimpsed over the shoulder of a fellow passenger on a Galway-bound bus from Shannon International, read as follows: TEN DEAD IN ROAD ACCIDENTS IN ONE WEEKEND. Hardly encouraging news the day before I was to collect a rental car and begin working my way up Ireland's jagged west coast.

Being in Ireland is one of my greatest pleasures; *driving* there is not. And this time I was on my own, which meant I'd have to both drive and navigate the narrow roads, all the while dodging unforgiving stone walls on one side and oncoming traffic on the other. The one side and the other were, of course, the opposite of what I was used to at home.

My destination was Ballycastle, a seaside village in north County Mayo, where my parents were spending six weeks.

With a rented cottage as their home base, my mother happily painted in a nearby studio while my father made the most of a sojourn in the county where his parents were born and where many of his cousins still live. When my parents had stayed there the first time two years earlier, I'd traveled to Ballycastle with my sister and her family, taking the direct inland route, a three-hour drive from Galway. This time, I wanted to explore a few more pockets of western Ireland, so I'd set a slower course along the coast, allowing myself three days to reach Ballycastle from Galway.

I'd planned my moves carefully, breaking the drive into short segments and rewarding myself with cozy hotel rooms in mostly pedestrian-friendly towns where I could park once, then do my exploring on foot. One of my planned stops was Achill Island, which had been on my Irish to-do list for some time. But would I dare to drive around the beautiful, roller-coaster terrain of Achill on my own? Even before I spotted the off-putting headline, I had my doubts. I'd booked a room at *Ostan Oilean Acla* (Achill Island Hotel), just steps from where the bridge from the mainland makes landfall, thereby hedging my bets. I'd be on Achill for less than twenty-four hours; if there was even a whiff of rain or fog, I could skip the sightseeing and write postcards.

Why was I going to Achill anyway? What was I trying to prove, and to whom, by driving myself around steep cliffs on a remote island where I didn't know a soul? In half a dozen visits to Ireland, I had developed this habit of island-hopping—leaving the mainland to explore obscure specks of land that fringe the coast. On every trip, I found myself seeking out new islands, flirting with the western edges of Ireland and, therefore, of Europe. Where had this urge come from? Literature, I'd always assumed.

Long before I first set foot on Irish soil in my mid-thirties, I yearned to visit the Aran Islands, off the coast near Galway. I'd developed a romantic attachment to these stony scraps when, as a college student, I read J. M. Synge's plays, set in rural western Ireland, and his memoir, *The Aran Islands*, which is part ethnographic study, part valentine to the hardy inhabitants of Inishmore, Inishmaan, and Inisheer. My grandparents all had emigrated from Ireland as young people, and Synge painted a picture of rural Irish life as I imagined it had been for them. He also captured the odd blend of optimism, fatalism, and humor that made them who they were—sons and daughters of Ireland, but also survivors, adventurers, who left everything they knew and ferried their dreams across the Atlantic, where they'd taken root in Philadelphia's burgeoning Irish community.

As a child I learned that the words "home" and "back home," when used by my grandparents, always referred to Ireland. But not one of my grandparents had ever gone back home. I never asked why, or even if they had wanted to. By the time these questions had fully formed themselves in my mind, it was too late to ask. I grew up with the impression that when you left Ireland, you said goodbye for good. For my grandparents' generation, there were few exceptions to this rule. One of my father's aunts did go back—twice, in fact—voyages I learned about long after the fact; I imagine those trips as bittersweet, for in the end she'd had to leave again. When I was eight, two of my mother's aunts came from Ireland and stayed with us for several weeks—the only time in my grandfather's life he was reunited with these two sisters, nearly forty years after he'd left home. We called them "the flying aunts": no one we knew had ever crossed the ocean in an airplane before.

In those days I never dreamed I'd visit Ireland; the world was a bigger place then, and people didn't move about it so freely. I could not have imagined I would be reunited with one of the flying aunts near the end of her life and would meet four generations of cousins scattered clear across Ireland. A well-fingered book of Irish fairy tales was the only passport I carried as a child. I memorized Irish emigrant and rebel songs, leafed through yellowed songbooks, played Irish record albums over and over. Ireland was the bravest, most magical place I knew, but as unreachable for me as Shangri-La.

When the world shrunk and eventually I did get there, I was struck by the way my Irish cousins—in Mayo, Sligo, and Derry—all used the word "home" in relation to their American visitors. They talked about *us* coming *home* to Ireland—my parents, me, my aunts and uncles, my siblings. They said "home" without even thinking about it—"that time when James was home" or "now that you're home."

Each time I hear "home" in that context, the word falls on my ears as equal parts welcome and something else, too; the faintest of accusations, perhaps? It's almost as if *we're* the ones who left Ireland—not the aunts and uncles they never met, but the cousins they never played with as children, the daughters and sons of those cousins. We're prodigals returned to the fold, welcomed with open arms. This doesn't erase the sense of loss that was felt —on both sides of the ocean—for all the decades in between. But each journey from here to there is a kind of homecoming, a way of going back on behalf of my grandparents and the great aunts and uncles who comprised the transplanted Ireland of my childhood.

Among my Irish and Irish-American relatives, I alone seem to find it necessary to touch the edges of the Irish world every time I visit. My Irish cousins smile at my island-hopping, but don't understand the appeal of these hard-to-reach, not-much-to-do places. I've never gone to Ireland without venturing off the coast at least once; I can't help myself, or so it seems.

On my first visit, my parents humored me by agreeing to an overnight excursion to Inishmore, the largest of the Aran Islands. The adventure began with a ferry ride on which we all three got sunburned, then continued with a wittily narrated, but bruising, five-mile donkey-cart trip to our thoroughly isolated B&B; I was in love with the island long before we climbed the rocky hill behind the house to view the ruins of the ancient fortress known as Dun Aengus, atop a crumbling cliff perched 200 feet above the sea.

I've gone back to Inishmore—usually for a night or two, sometimes as a mere day-tripper—half a dozen times. So far I've only floated by the middle island, Inishmaan, owing to the vagaries of the ferry schedule. I've spent three delightful

> How can I describe the joy that filled my heart when the shores of my own country first greeted my eyes through the gray atmosphere of the sea, or what emotions took possession of me while sailing up the stream. I saw the grand Statue of Liberty, the great city, and thousands of flags waving in the fresh morning's breeze. No one who has not wandered away from home and friends can understand the pleasure of being once more among their own. I simply drank deep breaths of calm, sweet gladness, and gazed about me so eagerly that my "seeing machinery" was out of order and needed a rest. I was trying to see everything at once, and was in danger of having a curvature of vision, and a chance of never having a good, straight stare again.
>
> —Mrs. William Beckman,
> *Backsheesh* (1900)

afternoons on Inisheer, the tiniest Aran Island. Once I boarded a motorboat, then made a mid-water transfer, owing to the vagaries of the tides, to a slightly under-inflated orange raft steered by a slightly inept pre-teen to reach the famously "evacuated" Great Blasket Island off the Dingle Peninsula in County Kerry. Already on this trip I had visited one new island—tiny Clare, in Clew Bay near Westport. I'd spent five hours strolling Clare's quiet, gentle hills in the sunshine, wearing only shorts and a t-shirt on a remarkably warm September day.

Until now my Irish island adventures all had begun with boat rides, then mostly proceeded on foot; on Inishmore, I once crossed the island by bicycle and once in the aforementioned donkey cart. No doubt the walking is one of the reasons I visit these remote, nearly traffic-free islands. Feeling a place beneath my feet somehow makes a travel experience more authentic, leaving me with a deeper sense of having been there. But Achill would be different from my other Irish islands: I'd reach it by car, driving from the Curraun Peninsula across the Michael Davitt Bridge and right onto the island. Walking routes abounded, but I'd have to drive inland to reach a jumping-off point for any of them. To appreciate the views from the island's majestic sea cliffs, I'd have to tackle the most challenging roads.

After my sunny day on Clare Island, I stopped into the tourist office in Westport in search of a detailed map of Achill. A friendly, dark-haired, twenty-something woman in the bright green uniform of Ireland's tourism staff raised her eyebrows slightly when I said I might drive around the island, then encouraged me (or meant to) by saying, "You'll probably be fine." She was unaware, she was sorry to say, of any guided tours. I thanked her, then purchased a combination map/guide to Achill Island along with a stack of postcards, just in case.

Back in my room I unfurled the Achill document, compiled in 1988 by Mr. Bob Kingston. The annotated map was as big as the interior of my car, so it would not be terribly useful for driving. Still, it offered a wealth of information under headings such as The Name, most probably from the Gaelic *acaill,* derived from the Latin *aquila,* for "Eagle" Island. Other topics included Physical Features, Settlement, People, Tides, Wildlife, and Walks. I read through Things to See—a list of eighty-three sights strewn across Achill's roughly fifty square miles. Some sounded mundane (#33, Old Coastguard Station), some exotic (#4, Carrick Kildavnet Castle, outpost of Ireland's sixteenth-century pirate queen, Grace O'Malley). Numbers 24 and 66 were too sad to contemplate—children's graveyards, or *killeens,* straddling the middle of the island, where un-baptized babies once had been buried to prevent their "unclean" souls from tainting consecrated burial grounds.

By far my favorite section of the guide—for its sheer Irishness—was one called Tragedies. Only in Ireland, I mused, would a place promote itself to visitors by listing a series of accidents that had befallen its residents: group drownings, mostly; a fire in Scotland which claimed the lives of ten migrant potato workers; a plane crash; and, most recently, the loss of three farmers while "attempting to rescue sheep from cliffs." The tragedies listed accounted for a grand total of seventy deaths between 1894 and 1983, on an island whose current population is roughly 2,900.

In 1841, before the Irish famine, the island's population was recorded as 4,901. Yet there was no mention under Tragedies of the Great Hunger, which took a significant toll on Achill through starvation and emigration. Mr. Kingston did allude to the famine under Settlement and in a section titled The Achill Mission, about the Church of Ireland's nineteenth century efforts to convert local Catholics to Protestantism, using soup and grain as inducements to the starving populace.

In the same way that only an Irish travel guide would include a section on Tragedies, the third and final paragraph of this section veered unexpectedly toward the positive: "Despite the harsh environment, the island people are a hardy, good-humoured lot," Mr. Kingston wrote, "and man's indominatability was well marked in September 1987 when Don Allum stepped ashore in a severe gale at Dooagh, having rowed the Atlantic in both directions in a twenty-foot boat, and received a welcome that lasted for more than a week!" Very Irish, I thought, to deftly switch the subject like that from tragedy to triumph.

As I collapsed the sheet back into neat squares, I noticed a listing for Tours. The heading proved misleading, however, as the text described "three spectacular drives which should not be missed," but then made it clear the tours were meant to be self-propelled. "All of these drives are best done on clear days and in mechanically sound vehicles," Mr. Kingston cautioned. Again, the recent newspaper headline loomed large in my mind.

Would I or wouldn't I? I still hadn't decided as I turned into the small car park in front of *Ostan Oilean Acla* late the next morning. The friendly receptionist confirmed that, unfortunately, no tours of Achill were offered. She readily (too readily?) understood my hesitation to attempt the scenic drives alone. She thought for a moment, then suggested that a local gentleman who "sometimes drives people around the island" might be willing to give me a tour. She phoned him and, as it turned out, his afternoon was free. He'd meet me at the front desk after lunch.

The gentleman was Pat, a wiry septuagenarian with a full head of gray hair brushed straight back from his forehead. He wore black slacks, sturdy shoes and a white shirt open at the collar and topped with a navy blue v-neck sweater. The sleeves of the sweater were pushed above his elbows. His leathery face attested to a windswept island life, and his blue eyes gave off just a hint of mischief, although he wasn't smiling. He greeted me wordlessly with a firm handshake and motioned for me to climb into the front seat.

The maroon van was large, a little clunky-looking, but perfectly neat inside. No name or phone number appeared on the side panels, nothing to suggest it was a commercial vehicle. There were three rows of seats. A large mobile phone perched on the dashboard. Before turning onto the road, Pat offered a caveat: "I should tell you I'm the driver of the island's only medical transport vehicle, so our trip will have to be cut short if anyone needs a ride to the hospital." I nodded my understanding. Clearly, sightseeing was secondary to medical emergencies.

Pat bought himself time by indicating that the first noteworthy point was a few miles off. Several minutes passed in utter silence. Pat was friendly to other drivers, lifting his right index finger in the standard Irish road greeting as we passed, waving them on if we came to a tight spot. I was glad to see he was a careful driver. But I was troubled by the awkward lack of communication and wondered what I'd gotten myself into. I supposed he was sizing me up, guessing at what I might know about Achill, what I might expect to see.

After about a mile Pat broke the silence, picking up where he'd left off: Despite the existence of a perfectly good, fully equipped ambulance, no one on the island was certified to drive it. That's why he—and the very van we were in—comprised the island's *de facto* medical transport system. When summoned, his role was to pick people up and deliver them to the hospital, about twenty-five miles inland. He had no medical training and did not tend to his passenger-patients. "Over the years," he said, "I've driven some people who were in a bad way, with open fractures and the like. A few of them never made it home. One lady just barely made it to the hospital alive, although I never did find out what was wrong with her."

I looked around. Not so much as a first-aid kit. To keep our fledgling conversation aloft, I told Pat that a few years earlier I had fallen and broken my ankle. Alone and unable to reach anyone I knew, but not so desperate that I needed an ambulance, I called a taxi to take me to the hospital. I told Pat how the driver kindly lent me his shoulder as I hopped into the emergency room on my good leg. Under the circumstances, it seemed the perfect story to tell. But from the look on Pat's face—and the silence that once again filled the space between us—he clearly thought I was daft. I thought to myself, but didn't dare say, how funny it was that when I needed an ambulance, I'd called a taxi, and when I needed a taxi, I unwittingly had called an ambulance.

When we reached the turnoff for The Atlantic Drive, some minutes after our last verbal exchange, the "official" tour began. Pat doled out tidbits of geography and history, if somewhat perfunctorily. I felt the need to make a fresh start, to establish myself as a visitor worthy of his time, someone genuinely interested in his island—just too wimpy to drive herself around it. I wove threads of my story into the conversation between his comments, which remained sparse. Pat was not impressed with my 100 percent Irish ancestry, although he glanced over briefly when I mentioned I'd been to each of my grandparents' childhood homes. As if to test me, he asked where they were from. I recited the litany: "My father's parents came from Bohola and Knock in Mayo, my mother's parents came from Draperstown and Magherafelt in Derry." He perked up slightly at the mention of Knock, but it would be another two hours before I knew why.

It apparently helped my case that I'd been to the Aran Islands and Great Blasket. Like my Irish relatives, Pat had been to neither. I scored points by casually mentioning the elementary Gaelic classes I'd taken. It didn't matter that I could barely string two Irish words together—he confessed he had long since "lost" most of his Irish after too many years away working in England; it seemed enough that I'd made the effort. Nearly half an hour into the trip, I felt I had redeemed myself. My status had been upgraded from mad American woman on holiday who wishes to be chauffeured around Achill, even though she has a perfectly good car sitting in the hotel car park, to Irish-American visitor who might actually be interested in this island.

The scenery was increasingly spectacular. Achill's sea cliffs are among the highest in Europe, and as we climbed steep roads that skirted the island, the sun sparkled on blue-green waters far below. Sandy beaches, including the two-and-a-half-mile-long strand at Keel, explained why there were as many holiday cottages as sheep dotting the landscape. On this warm September day, every beach was packed with bathers, many up to their shoulders in the water—a sight I'd never seen in Ireland before.

Pat navigated the roads masterfully. Occasionally he pulled over so I could get a better view and take pictures. At one scenic overlook he offered to take my picture so I would have a record of myself at Achill; this became our routine. His narration swung into higher gear. As he coaxed the van up one particularly nasty corkscrew, he recalled the first time he brought his mother up this road "in a motor car." She had vowed to find another way down. I understood why: A sheer drop began mere inches from the van's flank. "I'm glad you're driving," I told him, catching my breath.

When we reached the top, Pat let the scenery speak for itself and switched to local gossip and lore. A cove far below evoked the memory of a BBC television crew who, intent on capturing a shot from the water's edge, had failed to notice the approach of a sizable wave and had been flattened by it, to the utter delight of the locals. We passed a crumbling house with a tenuous link to Pat's family. There was a slight chance he might someday lay claim to this land and its top-of-the-world view, but the legal dispute had been simmering for years, apparently without his involvement, and he was not counting his chickens.

As we descended toward the coast, Pat glanced at his watch. We'd been on the road for an hour, and he asked if I'd like to keep going. I sensed he'd reached the end of what he thought would qualify as a respectable tour of Achill, if such a tour existed. I said I'd love to see more if he had time. So we set off on the second leg of our journey, with Pat describing other passengers he'd shuttled around between hospital runs: young people who spent weekend nights at two local discos, then called for safe rides home, often near dawn; a girls' football team, which included one feisty lass who dazzled Pat by teaching her teammates (in the moving van) a stealthy maneuver to knock the wind out of an opponent without being seen by referees; and last, but hardly least, the ladies of Achill, who enjoyed free rides in the van to the island's scattered shops every Friday. Pat rolled his eyes for effect when he mentioned the latter group.

The golf links, where sheep hungrily mowed the course as we passed, contrasted with remnants of older ways of life, like "booley" villages, stone huts set high in the hills near summer pastures. We stopped at the deserted village in Slievemore, which burrowed into the south-facing slopes of Achill's highest mountain. Before the famine this had been the island's largest settlement. Pat and I didn't speak as we climbed out of the van, but the silence between us was different now, a shared silence, as if we had entered a church. We walked toward the village, the roofless buildings and their mountain backdrop all awash in grays and browns; then we turned and saw what the residents of Slievemore would have seen on any clear summer day—the glimmering teal waters of Lough Keel sprawling toward the sea in an ocean of green, green grass.

Just after Slievemore, we passed a woman walking along an otherwise empty road. She and Pat waved to each other, then she stopped in her tracks and watched until the van disappeared. Pat's eyes danced with glee. His shopping rounds with the ladies tomorrow were going to be great fun: "They'll be dying to know the identity of the lady who was spotted with me in the van on Thursday afternoon." I could tell he would keep them guessing. I liked being in on the joke.

As we drove through one of the island's twenty-two villages, Pat pointed out his home—a tidy, whitewashed, one-story house near the road. Around the next bend, he pulled into a low-walled area beside a narrow inlet, where we inspected a fleet of upended Achill *curraughs*, traditional wood and canvas fishing boats. Pat snapped my picture, then let me persuade him to pose for one. He recounted a stormy fishing misadventure that had nearly required a coast guard rescue. His point was not the danger he and his companions had faced, but the embarrassment they'd been spared when they managed to reach the shore safely, on their own: "If we'd called for help, it would have been heard on every radio on the island, and we'd still be living it down."

A short time later as we passed a stony mountain, Pat pointed out a footpath that wriggled up the steep rise. He explained that in the old days it had been customary for funeral processions to go up and over the mountain to the church in Kildavnet. Everyone walked, the men taking turns as pallbearers. Boulders had been strategically placed to provide resting places for the coffin, thereby minimizing the risk of an undignified slip down the slope for the dearly departed. "Those were hard times," Pat recalled. "Following a funeral, the women climbed back over the mountain, out of respect for the deceased," he noted solemnly. "The men," he added with a wink, "went from the cemetery to the pub, where they offered their own respects. Some hours later, the men went home around the mountain, not over it." Pat grinned. It crossed my mind that free Friday shuttles for the current generation of Achill Island ladies might represent a form of communal atonement for the old funeral custom.

We had circled the mountain and were nearing Kildavnet, which hovers just above Achill Sound. Pat pulled in beside the church and cemetery and recited the details of Achill's two great tragedies—the thirty-two young people who drowned on their way to Scotland in 1894, and the ten who perished there in the 1937 fire. The remains of the victims were buried here, beneath commemorative markers. It was clear from Pat's tone that the people of Achill did indeed still carry these sad events close to their hearts, even generations later. Why the emphasis on these two stories, I wondered. Both my Achill tour guides—Mr. Kingston and Pat— seemed determined to impress upon me their significance.

It occurred to me while we sat there, comfortably quiet with each other now, that what made these events so tragic for the island community may not have been the deaths themselves.

Drownings had long been a fact of life in this part of the world. Certainly other islanders had perished tragically in a rural community with such a modest emergency-response system that even today it lacked proper ambulance service. Surely the "hardy, good-humoured lot" Mr. Kingston described ought to have absorbed these old twin sorrows by now. The deeper tragedy, I thought, may have been that those lost souls found it necessary to leave Ireland in the first place, to seek work in strange lands and, saddest of all, that they came home only to be buried. Ireland's great shame—her inability to provide work, or land, or education, or hope for so many generations of her young people—may have been the real tragedy on Achill Island, as elsewhere. The many who left, never to return; that old refrain again.

Pat, who had left as a young man but later found his way home, had been shuttling me around his island for two hours now. I sensed Kildavnet would be our last stop, and I felt my once-reluctant tour guide had done well to save it for last. It offered both a dramatic view toward the mainland and a poignant reminder of the island's links to the vast Irish Diaspora.

But Pat had one more stop planned for me. As we pulled away from Kildavnet he asked, a bit eagerly, "Did you say you've been to Knock?" "I have," I replied. "My grandfather was baptized in the old church," I continued. "My father has cousins nearby, some still live on the farm where my grandfather was born. I've been to see them, and I've been to the shrine." "Well then," Pat continued slyly, "If you've been to Knock, I'm surprised you haven't asked to see the House of Prayer. Most Americans who come to Achill are keen to see it, especially the women." He was being sarcastic now, although I didn't catch on right away. "I'm afraid I haven't heard of it," I said. Pat beamed. I had cleared the final hurdle, passed the ultimate test. He'd been waiting all afternoon for me to ask about the House of Prayer. Once I let him know I'd never heard of the place, and he let me know he wholeheartedly disapproved of it, he insisted on taking me there. "It's almost beside your hotel," he coaxed, when I tried to resist.

The House of Prayer required a lengthier preamble than any of our previous stops. We'd crisscrossed the island so often I'd lost my bearings, and I'd left Mr. Kingston back in my room. But I'm nearly certain Pat went the long way around to allow himself time to properly set up the House of Prayer as a sort of punch line. His approach was to compare and contrast the House of Prayer—"a bogus shrine," in his words—with one of the holiest places in Ireland, the shrine at Knock, roughly thirty miles away. Like virtually everyone from County Mayo, Pat had made countless pilgrimages to Knock: on holy days; before he sailed for England; and just after his brother's sudden death, when he'd gone there with a friend to have masses said. He offered a dizzying account of the latter trip, although his recollections admittedly were a bit blurred: "Everyone we met insisted on buying me a drink, for my troubles like, you know."

As Pat drove, I remembered stepping into the small parish church in Knock on my first trip to Ireland. I wasn't really there for the shrine. My father wisely had steered me away from the busy main street and led me first to the old church, where I'd felt a genuine connection to my grandfather and to the past. I was in a place where he had been a century earlier. I imagined him being baptized, receiving first communion, muttering his prayers; I couldn't recall ever thinking of him before as being young—he was nearly eighty when I was born.

Knock Parish Church is known throughout the world as a Marian shrine, a site where Mary once appeared, like Lourdes in France or Fatima in Portugal. On August 21, 1879—just a few weeks after my grandfather was born in nearby

Ballyhaunis—fifteen people witnessed the apparition, which lasted two hours. After lengthy enquiries by the Vatican, Knock was designated as an official shrine. Pilgrims immediately began trickling in, and they haven't stopped since: Today Knock welcomes 1.5 million visitors a year from around the globe.

The tiny wood-frame church is dwarfed by a towering glass-and-stone basilica, surrounded by a vast car park, a long row of shops and restaurants, an ever-expanding ring of hotels and B&Bs, a caravan park and one of Ireland's few international airports. Bumper stickers abound, along with souvenir medals, statues, rosaries, and various-sized plastic bottles for holy water. The web site for the shrine proclaims, "Knock is a crash course in the Christian life," as if that were a good thing. The bustling scene bears a vague resemblance to the boardwalk in Atlantic City, minus the slot machines and massage parlors. I say this not to disparage Knock or its visitors, merely to observe that the humble origins of the site where Mary appeared are now buried beneath layers of infrastructure that have evolved to support the weight of so many pilgrims.

As I reminisced, Pat described how the House of Prayer had grown beyond its own humble origins. His facts were sketchy and his editorializing seemed a bit harsh, although the information he relayed jibed with other accounts I would discover later. The House of Prayer was established as a retreat center by Mrs. Christine Gallagher in 1993, and its first few years were unremarkable. Then vague claims of minor miracles began to circulate, including possible stigmata (marks resembling crucifixion wounds) on Mrs. Gallagher and messages delivered directly to her by Our Lady of Peace. The rumors began to attract significant numbers of self-styled pilgrims— as many as 10,000 a year—lifting both the Achill Island economy and the eyebrows of Ireland's bishops.

An official enquiry revealed "no evidence of supernatural intervention" at the House of Prayer. Church officials did, however, go out of their way to emphasize Mrs. Gallagher's sincerity and good intentions. Her supporters refer to her as an "Irish mystic" or "visionary"; detractors use terms like "alleged stigmatic." Her own web site proclaims, "Christine Gallagher delivers heaven's messages to the world," which sounds pretty confident. The site cautions believers to be wary of imitation "Matrix medals" available from less-than-scrupulous sources, citing only a handful of legitimate distributors; the web site further notes that "Our Lady has said that She desires the proceeds from Her Matrix medal to provide upkeep for Her House."

Despite Church-imposed restrictions against masses and confessions there and a brief stretch in 1998 when the facility temporarily closed, the retreat center remains quite active. Visitors from around the world proudly publish online "miraculous photographs" and testimonials in support of Mrs. Gallagher and her prophesies. Some B&Bs boast of their proximity to the House of Prayer, although Achill's official tourism materials are mum on the subject. The one island resident I spoke with clearly did not feel blessed to live so close to such holy controversy.

From what I could gather, Pat's greatest objection to the House of Prayer—aside from its inability to hold a candle to Knock (so to speak) as an authentic shrine—was its over-the-top commercialization. "She's got a gift shop there now and everything, wait until you see." Having seen Knock in all its modern-day splendor, I braced for the worst. I was surprised when Pat pulled into a parking lot beside a modest two-story house roughly the same size as my own, except for a one-story chapel off to the right side, where I have only a small screened-in porch.

Pat had to be sure I knew what kind of an operation this was so, despite my protests, he insisted I step inside the House of Prayer so I could see for myself what a sham it was. I reluctantly approached the entrance. I balked when we reached the foyer and heard voices reciting the Hail Mary, but Pat wouldn't let me turn back. He blocked the exit and gently nudged me into the back of the chapel. A pleasant middle-aged woman— "That's herself," Pat hissed—was leading a small group in reciting the rosary. When she spotted us, she stopped praying for a moment and graciously invited us to join in. Pat yielded then, and I mumbled an apology as we both backed away. He tried to persuade me to have a look at the gift shop, but I won that round.

My formerly reticent host had morphed into an evangelist. There was an urgency about our stop at the House of Prayer, a significance I was meant to grasp. He'd had time to think about this and apparently had decided Knock was the place where our personal histories—mine and his—most closely intersected, or at least raised a finger in greeting as they passed each other on the road. If I understand the gesture—a grand one considering how we'd begun—Pat showed me the House of Prayer to underscore the holiness of Knock, to emphasize the difference between this place and an authentic shrine; he gave me credit for being able to see the difference, at a glance, which I recognized as a compliment. Pat did not offer compliments lightly.

Nearly three hours after leaving *Ostan Oilean Acla*, we finally turned back. Only after the van pulled into the hotel car park did we discuss, for the first time, financial terms of the tour. Pat suggested what I thought was a fair price, and I gave him a little extra. I would have hugged him if it had seemed even remotely appropriate, but I didn't dare risk a breach of our hard-earned entente. So we ended as we had begun, with a handshake, although this time he did smile.

That evening as I thought about my ride with Pat, I found an answer to an old question, a reason for my Irish island-hopping. I had halfway figured it out as we sat beside the cemetery in Kildavnet and I'd thought about all those young people leaving Ireland, never to return. But in a roundabout (and therefore Irish) way, it had taken the House of Prayer— bogus or not, who am I to say?—to complete the thought. Pat's discourse on the retreat-house-gone-bad and his reflections on Knock made me wonder what draws people to these places, what they find that resonates within, what they seek that leads them on to the next shrine, the next pilgrimage. Our meandering tour of Achill brought into relief my own small pilgrimages to Ireland's edge; it made me see I had come here for more than breathtaking views from the island's cliffs.

My island-hopping is a mock form of leaving Ireland, a way of multiplying the number of returns I can make for my grandparents. On ferry rides, I've tried to imagine how it felt for each of them to sail away, to look back at Ireland, to watch her disappear for what they probably knew would be the last time. Whenever I venture off Ireland's left coast, I push myself out to that edge—and then, of course, I scurry back. Like the House of Prayer, my pilgrimages may not be the real thing, but they nevertheless are sincere. I never will know how it felt to leave, for good; I do, however, know how it feels to come back, again and again.

After just a brief visit, I knew Achill Island was a place I'd return to. Having had the benefit of such a thorough orientation, I wouldn't hesitate to drive myself around next time. I would, however, be sure to find Pat and catch up on the latest gossip. Mr. Kingston's map shows some small islands near

Achill's coast. Maybe I could persuade Pat to leave the ambulance behind and take me on a boat ride so I could add a few
more islands to my collection. We'd be spotted, of course; and
what a tasty morsel that would make for the long-suffering
ladies of Achill Island.

Next morning a steady rain fell as I loaded my bags into the
car. The string of perfect days had ended, and so had my island hopping, for now. I pulled across the road and turned
right toward the mainland and my next stop, Ballycastle.
Somewhere on the Michael Davitt Bridge, I glanced back at
Achill in the rearview mirror and realized I was, once again,
going home to Ireland.

*Eileen Cunniffe is a recovering corporate communications manager
who lives and writes in Havertown, Pennsylvania—a Philadelphia
suburb with so many Irish transplants and descendants it is sometimes referred to as "Ireland's 33rd county." Her writing also has
appeared in* 400 Words *and* Wild River Review.

JANN HUIZENGA

* * *

Feeling Fizzy

*Mix two parts flirtation and
one part temptation...*

"Now I must go move my cows," says Fabio in Italian. "Do you want to see my farm?" The invitation seems innocent enough, and I readily agree. *Certo!* In my desultory Sicilian life, there's nothing I *don't* want to see, no frontier to my curiosity.

We fold ourselves into his little yellow bee of a Fiat, briefly trail a truck brimming with oranges out of Ragusa, then buzz down the arrow-straight road toward Marina di Ragusa, windows at half-mast, my hair whipping around. The landscape is dotted with sheep and white rocks, one indistinguishable from the other. We veer right onto a narrow coastal road toward Santa Croce, the Ionian Sea shimmering moiré-like off to our left. Spring has burst out all over. Everything hums and glows. Sprays of Spanish broom—my all-time favorite—explode like sparklers along the sandy roadside while tender blooms of pink bougainvillea and vermilion geraniums clamber impatiently over the perfectly-stacked drystone walls, stretching their new necks toward the warm breath of the sun.

Then we're heading back inland, bouncing along on a ser-
pentine lane past dusty blue agaves and groves of whorled
olive trees straight out of a Van Gogh. I get a whiff of Fabio's
spicy cologne—Sicilian men perfume themselves lavishly—
and study, in a dispassionate sort of way, the muscular hand
gripping the gearshift. *I bet he gets those big bear paws from
squeezing cow teats all day long.*

Around another bend, meadowlands undulate as far as the
eye can see—a smiling ocean of yellow blooms—interrupted
here and there by a massive carob tree. Not a soul or edifice
in sight. *Should I worry? Don't be paranoid. Where in hell are we
going? Just relax.* Fabio's busy rhapsodizing about the fifty-six
types of grasses, clovers, and herbs that grow in these pastures,
modestly attributing the international success of his artisan
cheeses to the flora that enfold us.

I point at the masses of oxeye daisies bordering the lane. "*Le
mucche mangeano anche queste?*" Do the cows eat these, too?

"Oh, no, the daisies are only for playing she-loves-me, she
loves-me-not." He shoots me a *look.*

I'd met Fabio the week before, when my friend Mary, her
husband Enzo, and my sister Linda had gone to eat fresh ricotta at a *masseria*, dairy farm, owned by Fabio's cousin. They'd
cooked up a huge copper cauldron of steaming ricotta for us,
and grilled coils of fat sausages. Then we'd all broken bread together around a long table draped in gummy oilcloth, dunk-
ing the crusts deep into the floaty-as-chiffon ricotta—Sicily's
ultimate comfort food—which turns surprisingly stone-heavy
in the belly.

Enzo had arranged the outing with Fabio—a casual ac-
quaintance of his—in his usual bighearted way, because I'd
posed a simple question: *How do you make ricotta?* The answer
turns out to not be so simple. For two long hours, I'd
scratched notes as Fabio poured and mixed liquids and stoked

the fire, pontificating all the while in Italian—but when I got home the notes made no sense. My photos are clearer: a ruddy Fabio stirring the hot pot of foamy whey over roaring flames; an agile Fabio straining to get the cauldron off the fire once the liquid had clotted; a jovial Fabio bringing up ladlefuls of diaphanous curds for our red clay bowls; a languid Fabio basking, after all the hoo-ha was over, out on a stoop in the sun.

"*Allora*," he'd said then, squinting up at me. "*Sei scritore?* You're a writer? I can help you with your research. You will write about our *cacciocavallo ragusano*. Next week, I will show you how we make it. It's famous, you know."

I was dimly aware that day that this *contadino*, farmer—a decade my junior—was gorgeous, registering the fact in the same detached way I admire the Doric pillars at Agrigento. "We should be Hollywood talent scouts," my L.A. sister kept raving during her visit, "and bring these heartthrobs back to Hollywood!" Fabio's a doppelgänger for Vince Vaughn, though a bit blonder and buffer. I attribute his caramel coloring to recessive Norman genes dating from the Norman occupation a thousand years ago, which still pop out in the Sicilian population like toys in Cracker Jack boxes.

We've just toured a high-tech research lab on the outskirts of Ragusa dedicated to preserving traditional cheese-making techniques, where Fabio periodically delivers vials of milk for testing. Scientists in white coats huddled around computer screens and shouted into cell phones in funny English. A few told me they'd recently returned from a cheese conference in Vermont. Others were eagerly talking about the upcoming Slow Food conference in Torino, which Fabio also plans to attend.

In the car, he asks if my sister has left Sicily. For the first time, I notice his boot-shaped sideburns. *Is that the Italian peninsula on his cheeks?*

"Yes, and my husband's arriving soon."

"Oh, how long have you been married?"

"Over twenty years."

His eyes go round, and his sugar tone turns to vinegar. "*Vent' anni?*"

He says he's doing *lo scapolo*, leading the bachelor life. Hasn't found the right woman. Likes a quiet life alone in the country.

We pull into his bone-jiggling cobbled courtyard, where a pack of dogs rush pell-mell at us. I reach down to pet one, a slip-up that fuels the frenzy of the others. They launch themselves at me like rockets on a rampage. We escape into Fabio's cottage as he points to the two-story villa next door, where his mother lives.

Aha! One of Sicily's quintessential mammoni, *mama's boys.*

His thick-stoned cottage, dark and homey as a bunker—*why do so many Sicilians live like moles?*—is a typical, no-frills man-space with a raw, cheesy smell. The dining table sags under a veritable hummock of dirty dishes. He's in the middle of a renovation, hoping to turn the house into an *agriturismo*, a farm version of a bed-and-breakfast.

The kitchen, Cheese Central, is a new addition. Tiled wall to wall and floor to ceiling in white—European Union regulations for sanitation, Fabio explains—the kitchen feels like a public restroom at Penn Station. White globs ooze in mesh baskets on countertops, presumably becoming cheese. Whether or not the whole operation would be deemed hygienic by EU standards, I'm not qualified to judge, but some innate Martha Stewart-ish compulsion makes me want to tie back my hair, roll up my sleeves, and scrub those tiles till my hands bleed.

"Ragusano used to be made in wheels," Fabio says, indicating the block-shaped cheese baskets, "but the wheels didn't fit into the suitcases of the emigrants leaving for America. So cheese makers began producing it in blocks." The Great Migration, a heart-wrenching exodus of 5 million dreadfully poor southern Italians from their ancestral villages a century ago, never fails to move me. But still, I laugh. Italians are so chauvinistic about food.

Fabio seems to want to linger in the house, but I edge us out the door into the light. The day has unfolded bright as a white sail. The garden makes up for what the house lacks. There are fragrant mulberry, lemon, fig, and citron trees. Dwarf palms and huge prickly pear plants with dangerous, leathery leaves. Almond trees wave in glorious bloom.

We walk out to the barn, where a half-dozen cows eye us in their docile, long-lashed way, flicking at flies with their tails.

"*Sono incinte*," he says. They're pregnant.

The animals have ivory-tawny spots, pink nostrils, and names like Hope and Happy. They carry their babies for nine months, Fabio informs me, just like humans. The calves will come soon. He forks hay into their mangers as I photograph. *Ah, pastoral life!* It seems exotic to me.

"You should play them classical music. I've read that cows like Vivaldi."

"Yes. I have to remain very calm when milking them. They can feel any human stress. Since milking is already stressful for them, they must be made to feel very calm and happy."

He tells me that farmhands from India are pouring into the area to help out on Ragusan dairy farms, and that Hindu cow worship makes these immigrants ideally suited for the job. "But the Indian I've hired," he says, "shows too much reverence. I lose patience with him."

We go out to the pasture to bring in the cows. One side of his property is edged by groves of carob and olive, another by an arroyo that runs to the sea. Fabio bounds through the sweet,

knee-high grasses toward his cud-chewing cows and does a series of demented jumping jacks to shoo his charges back to the
barn. He's in his element. *Click click.* I snap away. He picks
handfuls of herbs and grasses, grinds them between his palms,
extracts the kernels, and funnels them into my cupped hand. I
look and let them fall to the ground. He pours more.

*Why does he keep doing this? He's got a monstrous fixation on
seeds.*

The cows back in the barn, Fabio asks if I want to see the
bonsai carob tree he's discovered growing in a rock out beyond the orchard.

By now I should be braying, "I'm on to you, buddy!" I don't.

He whisks me off
through the glossy-leafed
carob orchard, then blazes a
trail through a thicket to
the wild place. We hear
birdsong and the babbling
of an underground spring
and emerge into an ab-
sinthe-green lotus land
smelling of chlorophyll.
Here is Sicily at her sweet-
est—green and ripe and
soft.

"My secret spot," he
says. "I've never shown this
to anyone."

Travel is always that way:
you go in search of one
thing and find something altogether different. I wanted
krill, the prey crucial to life
on earth today, but instead
found an ancient predator,
from a time when Antarctica
was warm.

—Lucy Jane Bledsoe,
"How to Find a Dinosaur,"
Antarctica: Life on the Ice

And there, as in a fairy tale, growing from a large, round
rock—a Lilliputian carob tree. My heart leaps.

"Molto romantico," he says. *"No?"*

Ah. His lair.

"*Dipende.*" It depends. Gulp.

"*Di che cosa?*" he asks. On what?

I have the scary sensation of being a teenager again, enduring some kind of creepy courtship ritual—and try, furiously, to ignore him. *Dum-do-be-do.* Spout some silly-ass rubbish about the tiny old tree.

His lips curl into a laugh. "You can't call a tree *anciano*, old! You can only say a person is *anciano*. A tree, and everything else, is *vecchio*, old."

"Your language is an *incubo*, nightmare."

Then we're in a field of clover, climbing toward the olive groves. The air is warm and I catch a whiff of the sea. It comes into sudden view on the horizon, no more than a kilometer away.

Fabio keeps climbing, scrambling over a waist-high wall.

"*Dami la mano,*" he says. Give me your hand.

I give him my elbow before jumping down, holding my camera tight. Then, just like that, he's looming over me, face tilted downward. He's got the gentle brown eyes of his bovines.

"*Sei bella.* You're beautiful."

I keep walking with studied nonchalance—smack dab into an olive bough. Tomorrow I'll have a scratch across my forehead, a trophy of the moment.

"Hasn't anyone in Sicily told you that?"

Nuh-uh, unless you count the homeless man who roosts in a cardboard box out in front of Oviesse department store. My otherwise oh-so-loving husband, let's be frank, has grown a little miserly with compliments—like so many men, I suppose, in easy, long-term relationships. Is that why these two little words bewitch me so? I can hardly keep my limbs from twirling around the orchard. *I feel pret-ty, oh so pret-ty!*

Get a grip, for crying out loud.

It's alarming how charming I feel!

Helios, at its zenith, bursts in the cerulean sky. *I feel dizzy, I feel sunny, I feel fizzy and funny and fine!*

Married men of America, are you listening?

I glance Fabio's way, half-expecting to see him prancing about on furry haunches and hooves.

"*Devo andare a Ragusa,*" I say. I've got to go to Ragusa. Back to work.

We scramble over more rock walls, taking a roundabout way back to the car. He chivalrously extends his hand at each stony barrier, but I tell him I can manage on my own. We maunder through more fields. Then—the ambush. His big bear paw is parked on my waist, pulling me close. "*La mierda!*" he laughs, Cow shit! I've almost stepped in it, or so he says.

Oooh, bravo! Such earthen wiles.

We pass a pomegranate tree festooned with last year's red fruit, which hangs like Christmas ornaments. "*Mi piace!*" I say, To me it pleases! Just to keep prattling.

"*Come tu piace a me,*" he purrs. Like you please me.

Is this what he had in mind when he said he'd help me with my research?

"Of course it is," Mary will say later. "Americans are so literal. What did you expect?"

I dunno. Not this.

I hurry us into the car. *Phew.* Jig's up. Or…not. Fabio turns on the engine but doesn't move. Out of his mouth comes something weird that—translated directly from the Italian—is, I'm pretty sure, more or less the following: "I have a big desire to make the love with you, little potato."

Never underestimate a Sicilian.

It's high time to dispel, once and for all, this single-minded notion of his that I'm some kind of freewheeling, footloose, happening American woman. I affect the body language of the Pentagon. "What will Enzo think when I tell him you've been talking to me, a married woman, this way?"

"He'll say, 'It's normal. You're a man. Of course you should behave like this.'"

His words are so guileless that I have to believe him. I squirrel them away in my head, so that later I can perform a post-feminist analysis of them, and this is what I'll conclude: His little speech—besides showing what Luigi Barzini calls the "shameless directness of Italians"—is a window into the mind of the Sicilian Everyman.

What I do next is completely un-Sicilian. I look at my watch and say I'm in a huge hurry.

Back on the road in the salty wind, we trade Bush and Berlusconi jokes, discover we both lean to the left. Fabio high-fives me and asks, in his perfectly dogged way, what I'm doing tomorrow, the next day, the day after that. I harden my heart. Busy, *occupata*, every single second until my husband, Kim, arrives, I say. But the truth is, it hurts a little.

We've arrived at Piazza del Popolo. As I gather my things, my beau tries to wangle "just one more walk." He assumes a hangdog look and a fervid tone: "*Ti prego*, I beg you."

You might think I cave, but you'd be wrong. I plant two pecks on his cheeks—the rote Sicilian *arrivederci*—and escape intact. Kudos to me! And end of story.

Almost. I inhale a deep lungful of air and think how eager I am to see Kim. To take him by the hand and show off all the virtues of this Treasure Island—wild asparagus, sharp smells of lemon groves, mounds of blood oranges, artichoke fields stretching as far as the eye can see, a white-tipped Mount Etna, the whole whirling world of springtime in Sicily.

As I watch Fabio's little yellow car buzz around my piazza and disappear out of sight—*Adío! Adío!*— a nagging question keeps playing in my mind, as if a needle's stuck in a groove.

But who'll say I'm beautiful now?

Jann Huizenga now lives in Santa Fe, New Mexico with her husband Kim, but has been spending time in Sicily since 2002. She is an English Language teacher, photographer, and an award-winning writer. Jann has won three Fulbright awards and has taught in New York, New Mexico, and Ragusa, Sicily. She is currently writing a memoir entitled Kissing Sicilians.

SHAYNA MCHUGH

✦ ✦ ✦

A Gringa Learns to Samba

We all have hips, but there
the resemblance ends.

"DON'T COME BACK FROM BRAZIL," MY FRIENDS ADVISED
me, "until you learn how to samba."

"Then I guess I'll never return!" I joked. I had always believed that there were two basic types of people in the world:
those born with the ability to dance, and those born without
it. In my eyes, all Brazilians fell in the former group whereas I
was stuck in the latter. At weddings, concerts, and clubs, being
pulled onto the dance floor was the most embarrassing thing
that could possibly happen to me. I marveled at the people
who moved so naturally to the music, envying the fact that
they always had such a great time dancing. I, on the other
hand, had no idea what parts of my body to move or how to
move them. Everything I did felt awkward. I was secretly hoping, however, that my upcoming semester in Brazil would
somehow magically transform me into a good dancer. Maybe
something in the air or water of South America would inject
some Latin flavor into my gringa self.

Samba, unfortunately, proved to be incomprehensible to
me. I tried to learn and failed miserably. The same thing

happened every time: while I watched the *sambistas,* trying to figure out how on earth they were moving their hips that fast, someone would invariably approach me and ask why I wasn't dancing.

"Because I don't know how to samba," I would explain.

"No problem! I'll teach you," the Brazilian would reply. "It's easy! You just go like this." He would then begin to samba, his feet moving at what seemed to me to be light speed.

"Wait," I would implore. "Where do I step on the first beat? Do I shift my weight forward or back on the second?"

The would-be samba teachers tended to look slightly puzzled at these questions. "I don't know," they always responded.

"Do it slower," I would command. When they did the step in slow motion, I could more or less follow along. *O.K., got it: switch feet on 1 and step forward on 2,* I thought to myself. But when I tried to samba to the rhythm of the music at normal speed, my natural clumsiness prevailed. I could swear that the rapid beat didn't allow enough time for my nervous system to carry the signals from my brain to my feet.

"*Aargh,*" I would groan in frustration.

"You just need to relax," my Brazilian friends repeatedly told me.

I felt especially samba-impaired during the six weeks I spent in the state of Bahia. One Brazilian song describes Bahians as having "God in their hearts and the devil in their hips." It's true: they all danced samba like it was the easiest thing in the world. I was depressed by the fact that six-year-old Bahian girls had more hip-shaking skills than I did. I eventually resigned myself to learning how to clap correctly to the music, since samba clapping follows a syncopated beat that was hard for my non-Brazilian ears and hands to grasp. To the disappointment of my North American friends, I returned from my semester in Brazil with a great deal of admiration for samba but a firm conviction that I was incapable of learning it.

My struggle with samba did not end there. After graduating from college, I returned to Brazil to do marine natural products research. Many of my new acquaintances were samba enthusiasts who got together every couple of weeks for a *samba de roda* (samba circle). I went to these gatherings but stayed out of the *roda*, limiting my participation to clapping and singing. Unfortunately, my friends were not content to let me stay on the sidelines. They sang one song that goes:

> *Sai, sai, sai, ô morena*
> *Saia da lagoa*
> *Sai, sai, sai, ô morena*
> *Saia da lagoa*
> *Ponha a mão na cabeça*
> *Outra na cintura*
> *Dá um bom remelexo*
> *Dá umbigada pra outra*

> Leave, leave, leave, oh *morena*[1]
> Leave from the lagoon
> Leave, leave, leave, oh *morena*
> Leave from the lagoon
> Put one hand on your head
> The other on your hip
> Give a good swaying
> Give an *umbigada*[2] to another

During this chorus, one woman does a samba solo in the center, performing the movements described by the lyrics

---

1. *Morena* refers to a dark-skinned or a dark-haired woman.

2. *Umbigada*, derived from the word *umbigo* (navel), is a movement in which two dancers touch their bellies together. Similar to the way expectant mothers nourish their babies through the umbilical cord, this "meeting of the navels" represents transmission of the energy of the dance from one person to another.

(*Like the Brazilian version of the hokey-pokey*, I mused). As the last line is sung, she exits the *roda* and gives an *umbigada* to another woman, who enters and dances throughout another repetition of the song, and so forth. You can guess what happened: someone gave an *umbigada* to me.

Knowing that there was no escape, I entered the *roda* with my best attempt at samba. I thought I was doing all right— that is, until the part about putting one hand on my head and the other on my hips. While focusing on getting my hands in the right places, I completely lost control of my feet. I tripped over myself trying to get back on beat, but it was too late—I had lost the rhythm, and my steps were all wrong. I'm sure my face turned bright red. When the last line of the chorus finally arrived, I fled the *roda* as fast as possible, bestowing an *umbigada* on the next victim. She glided into the *roda* with a smooth, elegant samba that made me feel like a bumbling klutz by comparison.

I went home that night with a renewed determination to learn how to samba, resolving to practice as much as it took for me to get the step right. The next time I got pulled into the *roda*, I promised myself, I wouldn't look like such an awkward gringa. As I thought more about it, I began to wonder if I'd been trying to learn samba the wrong way. I had recently read an article that drew a contrast between two types of cultures. European and North American cultures tend to center on the mind, which they view as separate and distinct from the body. African and Asian cultures, on the other hand, tend to focus on the body and use it as a starting point from which to relate to the world. Was the source of my problems the fact that I had been trying to understand samba, an Afro-Brazilian art, by analyzing it in a North American manner?

During the next *samba de roda*, I experimented with a new approach. Instead of worrying about counting beats, I simply tried to feel the rhythm. Rather than fussing over which foot was supposed to step where, I let the music guide my movements. I watched the *sambistas* in the *roda* and tried to imitate them without thinking too much about it. As a result, an unbelievable thing happened: I started to get it! My body succeeded where my mind had failed; it figured out the step all on its own. Two of my former attempted samba teachers noticed my efforts and congratulated me, delighted that the gringa had at last learned how to samba. No longer tentative and painfully self-conscious, I even jumped into the *roda* voluntarily—and I loved every minute of it!

There's nothing magical about Brazil's air or water that makes its native people good dancers. It's the fact that Brazilians don't make a distinction between people who can dance and people who can't—everyone just dances. I'm definitely not the best *sambista* out there; I haven't yet learned many of the turns and flourishes that embellish the basic step, and my movements are still sometimes off-rhythm. However, no one ever laughs or *boos* or yanks me out of the *roda* with a cane. The singing and clapping continues just as enthusiastically for me, the awkward gringa, as for the best *sambista* in the *roda*. After six months in Brazil and one *umbigada*, I think I've finally grasped the secret of samba.

Shayna McHugh, originally from Connecticut, has lived in Brazil for more than a year. She loves Brazilian barbeques, samba, and capoeira (an Afro-Brazilian blend of martial arts and dance), but she misses bagels, ice skating, and New York Yankees games.

COLLEEN KINDER

* *

Horns for the Revolution

She becomes a local in her own way.

THE CAB DRIVERS IN HAVANA NEVER BELIEVED ME WHEN I said I wanted to go to Bejucal.

"Bejucal?" They would bark back my destination with a question mark. I'm sure they assumed I had looked at a map of Cuban beaches without my glasses on. Tourists didn't go to Bejucal. They went to Varadero, Cienfuegos, Santiago, or Trinidad.

"*Sí.*" I would arch my eyebrows back at their skepticism. "Bay-Who-Cal." Then I'd nod, loyal to my original pronunciation. After all, I was mimicking the locals of the tiny Cuban town, an enclave of one-story houses an hour beyond the Havana limits. Tucked in a rural fold of the Caribbean's most lengthy isle, Bejucal had nothing to do with the capital of Cuba. That was precisely why I began traveling there.

In Havana, there were roughly three cigar hawkers for every vacationer. Visit a cathedral and you'd field ten offers for salsa lessons, or home-cooked lobster, or pirated CDs, or marriage. It was near impossible to pass through a Havana street without being hissed at, or asked, "Where you from?"

The heckling and sales pitches would tire out any ten-day vacationer. But my "holiday" in Cuba was a year-long public service fellowship. Within a month, I was already aching to disappear. I'd go anywhere in Cuba but a "destination." Bejucal was, by tourist standards, not worth ink on a map.

I heard about the town through a Catholic foundation. There was a nursing home there, run by the Sisters of Charity who were glad to take volunteers. Yes: even American ones. I could stay there if I wanted. In fact, I'd *have* to stay with the nuns. There was no other place for a foreigner to sleep in a town of such negligible size.

The road from Havana to Bejucal is sprinkled with propaganda. The billboards holler at commuters:

We Continue In Battle!
Towards Victory Always!
The Enemy Cannot Imagine Our Unity!
Conserve Electricity

I read them from the window of my collective taxi—an ancient American car kept together by shoelaces and bubble gum. The roadside slogans were familiar by now; they spouted the same rhetoric as Cuba's newspapers, holiday parades, and museum placards.

But as our cab descended into the valley of Bejucal, I saw a strange series of billboards. Five white signs showcased five men in military fatigues. "HEROES OF THE REVOLUTION," announced the billboard preceding them. Full names were printed below their army-green collars, where the fabric drifted off into white space. Judging from the paint's faded hue, these faces had played welcoming committee in Bejucal for decades.

Were it not for the fourth sign, these billboards would have made little impression on me. Grinning like a man with a dirty secret, the fourth hero leapt out from the stern line of comrades. His furry black eyebrows huddled together in the middle, creating a preternatural unibrow. I doubt I was the only passenger in my cab who, when we drove past, shuddered.

My cab stopped at a tiny park, which I later learned was the epicenter of Bejucal. Everyone else rushed out of the cab, so I did, too. Once outside, though, I wasn't so sure where to rush. The fragment of paper in my sweaty hand had nothing more than a cross-section scribbled in blue ink. A stranger paused to help me make sense of this "map," pointing me towards an enormous lime green building: the Bejucal nursing home.

Ambling down the street, I could already hear the difference in Bejucal: silence.

No catcalls. No strangers hissing from balconies. Here, my stiff stride did not invite salsa advertisements. My freckles did not mean I wanted lobster. Here, I would finally get to go on vacation.

The nuns received me like kin, pulling the bags off my shoulders, planting noisy triple kisses on my cheek. I slept in a simple guest room. To reach it, I had to climb through a storage space, where surplus furniture sat inexplicably cloaked in white sheets. The nursing home had a regular tempo: breakfast just after dawn, shortly after the autistic woman on floor two began her ritual "*Que buuuuuuenoooooo….*" A hearty lunch of rice and beans right at noon; meat if we were lucky, eggs when we weren't. In the afternoon, the *click-clack* of domino pieces wafted from the men's recreation room. Dinner came early, as soup, tasting faintly like lunch. Lights went off around eight—if a blackout hadn't already done away with electricity. Anonymous snores followed.

Friendship came easy in Bejucal and felt, for a change, uncomplicated. Though the old folks dropped my first name in favor of "*Americana,*" they greeted me warmly in the corridors of the nursing home. Back in Havana, stepping outside meant first bracing myself to hear the man at the corner bellow: *"¡Llevame contigo! Take me with you!"*

The doorway of the Bejucal nursing home was stocked with quiet old men, holding canes. When I passed, they nodded, seeming to appreciate the minor change in people traffic. There was only one man at the Bejucal nursing home who fancied himself as a suitor. This man did not hawk cigars or teach salsa lessons. Luisito courted me from his wheelchair, where he'd been wooing females since he was an orphaned toddler. Luisito liked to remind me that he'd fit into my suitcase better than any other Cuban: *"Llevame, Coh-lene."* Luisito's torso had an egg shape, as if someone had packed his body into a concentrated ball, like they would clay or snow. Irregular rib bones jutted out from his chest, not satisfied with the narrow quarters. His legs were meager sticks, nearly equal in width all the way down, and could only reach the floor when he scooted to the edge of his wheelchair's seat.

While the stick limbs suggested Luisito was no more than a dozen years old, his hair gave away his age. Tiny white hairs were sprinkled throughout his buzz cut, prominent in the otherwise jet black thicket. Like the Cuban Revolution, which boasted its duration on billboards nationwide, Luisito was forty-six.

His nose and ears had also followed the rules of aging, growing a bit each year until they outsized all other features on his enormous head. Luisito's teeth were large, cartoon-proportioned ivories that his lips couldn't hide without pursing. His eyes didn't quite didn't match, with pupils that floated around without synchrony, trading focus. He had at least a dozen "girlfriends"—mainly nurses and nuns, but one architect, too. Until I fled Havana for Bejucal, Luisito's *novia* club was exclusively Cuban.

The nuns gave Luisito his own room on the third floor. He liked to take me there to point out what stopped working when the lights went out: fan, television, radio—did he mention *fan*? Nothing bothered Luisito more than the electricity quitting. He seemed to think that I, as an American, brought a magic solution to this. ("Is it true the lights never go out in your country?")

In addition to my dozens of adopted Cuban grandparents, I now had a devoted *novio*, who expected to emigrate via my suitcase.

There was just one "resident" close to my age. Ania slept in the guest space, too. There, above the cloaked furniture, she and I had nightly occasion to discover what we shared in common.

Ania, too, had come to Bejucal for a retreat. She came there to detox, after a serious drug addiction. For our own reasons, we relished the asylum of the nursing home, however peculiar it was. And Ania, like me, found plenty of humor in the peculiarities of Bejucal.

Blackouts brought out the kids in us. As soon as the lights blinked out, Ania and I would grab a flashlight and track down Luisito in the dim halls. We would piggyback him upstairs to play pinball on my laptop, laughing so hard the rice and beans in our stomachs burned in protest.

"They think you're here to become a nun," Ania told me one day. I'd just remarked on the glorious quiet of the Bejucal parks, alleys, markets.

"A *nun*? Really?"

Ania had been hearing rumors, fielding questions. "Think about it," she said. "You're living here in the home. You help the nuns take care of old folks…"

Beautiful, I thought.

No one ever broached me with this rumor, and I did nothing to refute it. Assuming the identity of a nun in Cuba came no more naturally than assuming a vacationer's role. I had no habit in my suitcase, nor string bikini either. But playing nun did make foreignness easier for someone who was conspicuously, and often uncomfortably, foreign. Cubans quit mentioning cigars and salsa lessons. In Bejucal, people treated me— ever graciously—as a guest in their country.

I took more confidence in this Cuban community, and they did the same with me. Back in Havana, where living quarters were tight and neighbors were suspicious, Cubans spoke about politics in whispers, with beard mimes and euphemisms I could hardly translate, let alone unpack. In the big lime green nursing home out in the countryside, however, people spoke up—loudly.

The farther a foreigner in Cuba strays from the guided tour, the more the *necesidad* dominates discussion. Middle aged nurses pull the foreigner aside in the pharmacy pantry to tell her what the billboards don't. They know that foreigners come to Cuba with romantic ideas, and they make it a point to snuff out all romance in the word *revolution*.

In Bejucal, there was no such thing as an inappropriate time for politics. Whether we were lifting a frail old lady into bed or spoon-feeding a hungry diabetic, the staff told me how it was in twenty-first century Cuba: stagnant, oppressive, the opposite of easy.

I might have been a pro at rebuffing cigar pitches, but I could not tune out these grievances. The Bejucalis let me pass as a resident in their town; the least I could do was hear what life, as a permanent resident, was like.

It became harder to make the trip back to Havana, to pass the same billboards. I thought time might desensitize me, but the opposite happened. The stale slogans were annoying, then exasperating, more than exasperating, then infuriating. The state propaganda felt wildly inconsistent with the commentary of Cubans—loud and quiet.

Over time, I craved proof of dissent. Public proof. I'd somehow become a complaint box for miffed Cubans, and now I was the one about to burst. If I had to listen to nurses' aides vent about their paltry state paychecks for months, shouldn't the bureaucrats who wrote them?

I mentioned this craving to Ania one night. Nearly a year had passed since I first arrived in Bejucal, an idealistic twenty-two-year-old. I'd gone through a full revolution myself.

"I just want there to be some visible *sign*—any sign—that people here disagree as much as I hear." She and I were lying in our guest quarters. It was night, but neither of us was sleepy. Ania nodded, as if my wish was a given.

"Like the devil guy on the road into Bejucal," I went on, my face screwing up with disgust.

Ania laughed loudly. She knew the devil guy.

"Why should people have to look at that every day? What if he's not their hero?"

He was not Ania's hero. She was, of all the Cubans I'd met, one of the most vocal dissidents. And that night, with no persuasion, she became my accomplice.

The road out to the highway was pitch black. Ania got leave from the nursing home by telling the nuns we needed to take a walk. And we did need to take a walk—for a reason hidden in Ania's pocket, with a red Sharpie marker.

"You have to throw the marker *far* away…" Ania warned. She looked agitated and it was unnerving me.

I knew that I wanted to do this, but I didn't know I had the right to. I was not a Cuban; the Revolution did not impact my life—not beyond this year, at least. And even if my annoyance was warranted, wasn't this a foolish way to demonstrate it?

"Otherwise the dogs will get us," Ania continued.

"The *dogs?*"

"You know, like in the movies." Ania was walking fast. I scrambled over potholes and puddles to keep up.

Right: the dogs. The Hollywood hounds that would bark us down in Bejucal, Cuba.

And there they were: five flat boards, lined up shadow upon shadow, like sitting ducks.

I tried to take calm from the darkness, but taxis kept breaking up the night-black air. A half dozen staggered towards us, casting long beams of visibility, like lighthouses. We must have looked like men relieving ourselves, as we turned to the side of the road and hid our faces.

Darkness, finally, came back. No more cabs from Havana. It was late. It was our chance.

"Now," said Ania.

I jogged to the billboards, hoping this would be over before I could ponder consequences. I counted the signs, until I was standing at the penultimate one. I knew him, of course, for his eyebrows. The devil-hero smirked down at me.

My red marker was uncapped so I could reach up quickly. But when I did, panic struck. I didn't *reach*. The devil-hero was taller than the devil-foreigner. Boosting myself high on my tiptoes, stretching my right arm as high as its socket allowed, I drew. I had no idea if my drawing appeared; the sign felt roughly textured, and I could not see past the furry brows.

We didn't stick around to find out. Ania was darting back to town before I'd even chucked the red marker into the fields, away from "the dogs." By the time we got back to the nursing home, we were too wound up to sleep. The night-shift nurse, a heavy woman infamous for her encyclopedic knowledge of Fidel jokes, humored us with her company.

The next day, I went back to Havana, and Ania went on a walk. She took a friend, and veered their stroll by the Bejucal highway, slowing at the unibrow billboard. There, Ania's friend noticed something odd. Ania said nothing, letting her friend express the shock of seeing the town mascot wearing two thin devil horns.

Before flying out of Cuba for good, I made one final trip to my favorite Cuban resort.

"Bejucal?" a taxi driver eyed me doubtfully.

"Bejucal."

All through the countryside, I sat in quiet anticipation. What mark had the sloppy Sharpie made? A clear sign of defiance? Pathetic bunny ears? Would the sight lend me some closure, or a blush of regret?

My collective cab finally coasted down into a green valley: Bejucal. The town below looked miniature; the billboards ahead, still faint. As we neared, I realized the signs were faint for a reason. Someone had erased them.

They were totally blank: no words, no profiles, no declarations of loyalty to socialism. They'd been stripped bare. All that was left were the grimy, forty-six-year-old shadows of the Revolution's warriors.

Only when our cab zoomed past the fourth blank board did I see it: the pointy red horns had been painted over in white. But this paint stood out like bleached cotton against an old linen cloth: it only accentuated the horns in a fresh, bright shade. Naked and blemished, the signs read like a scolding. I sat in the backseat, holding my ambivalence quietly in my chest. If I mustered any pride, fright cancelled it out. The sight alarmed me, but not because it was surprising, rather because it was real. The Revolution had reacted. *Of course* they painted over our red Sharpie marker. Of course the stain would be stained over, and that soon.

The night Ania and I graffitied Bejucal, only two things changed. The townspeople got a brief reprieve from their devilish mascot, perhaps a needed chuckle, too. And on the national map of the Republic of Cuba, the town of Bejucal was now officially unmarked: a getaway—and a secret—I could keep to myself.

Colleen Kinder is the author of Delaying the Real World: A Twentysomething's Guide to Seeking Adventure and *co-editor of* Confessions of a High School Word Nerd. *She has written for* 20-Something Essays by 20-Something Writers, Salon, The New Republic, Ninth Letter, *and the* Washingtonpost.com.

PEGGY NEU

* * *

Walking Backward in the Land of the Buddha

Failure is to never have tried.

I SAT ON A ROCK GASPING FOR AIR AT THE BASE OF MOUNT Kailash, a remote mountain in western Tibet, which is one of the most sacred pilgrimage sites in Asia. I was trying to cry but was having great difficulty because of the high altitude. As I struggled to catch my breath, I looked up and saw that a man was sitting on the rock across from me staring intently. He had filthy hair and was wearing a dirty robe, facemask, knee pads, and wooden boards strapped to his hands. While it was difficult to discern his expression under his mask, I was sure he was wondering, as was I, what forces had brought us together to share this moment—me, a western Buddhist pilgrim dressed in North Face gear, and him, a Tibetan Buddhist pilgrim dressed in rags.

We both had come to complete the circuit, or *kora*, around Kailash. I was planning to walk around the mountain (which takes three days); he was planning to prostrate around the mountain (which takes three weeks). Both of us were hoping in some way to touch the divine and feel connected to the transcendent energy of the universe, which pilgrims have come to Kailash for thousands of years to glimpse.

Except that I wasn't going to do the *kora*. Despite the brilliant blue sky and warm weather, our guide Anand informed our group that we couldn't continue beyond the first camp because a storm a few days earlier had made the 18,200-foot high pass icy and dangerous. At first we accepted Anand's decision, but as we packed our bags and watched a steady stream of people filing past us up the mountain, we decided to confront him.

I started, "If it's so dangerous, why is every other group going?"

"They're Tibetan," came the reply (translation: not a bunch of wussy Westerners). We pleaded with him to at least try, but Anand was in a foul mood from a night of drinking and was becoming increasingly agitated by our protests. He suddenly exploded in anger and started screaming at us, "Don't you think I want to go? I'm Tibetan, this means everything to me!" (translation: you're Westerners *pretending* that it means everything). With the holy mountain towering in the background, Anand proceeded to stomp off with our porters, leaving us with no choice but to return.

I decided to let the others go ahead and rest on my rock so I could collect myself. I was devastated. This was actually my second attempt to do the Kailash *kora*. I had planned to come the previous year on a very expensive trip led by the prominent Tibetan Buddhist scholar Robert Thurman, but my father became sick, forcing me to cancel at the last minute. I lost a lot of money, and a month later, lost my father to pneumonia.

As I sat on my rock, all those painful memories came flooding back and I felt there must be some deeper significance to my failure to do the *kora*—not once, but twice. Was the universe telling me I didn't belong here? That Buddhism wasn't the right path for me? As I was considering these possibilities, I glanced over at my prostrating pilgrim friend and wondered how I had come to feel it was so important to walk around an icy, dangerous 22,000-foot mountain in one of the most remote places on the planet.

My desire to do the Kailash *kora* stemmed from a growing interest in Buddhism, a love of mountains, and a fascination with places in nature that humanity imbues with sacred meaning—from Native American sacred ground in our own country to the Ganges in India. Kailash and nearby Lake Manasorovar are two of the most important pilgrimage sites in Asia, but are the least visited because of the remoteness. Buddhists believe that Kailash is the mythical Mount Meru— the center of the universe and the source of all life on earth. For Hindus, Kailash is the abode of Shiva, one of three main deities in the Hindu pantheon. Shiva is known as the destroyer, but it's only through his destructive energy that creation can occur, thus starting the cycle of death and rebirth that rules the Hindu universe. References to Kailash as a sacred site actually date back to the ancient Hindu Vedic texts, which are thought to be 3,000 years old.

From a geological perspective it actually makes sense that our ancestors thought Kailash was the center of the universe. The headwaters of four of Asia's major rivers are located in the vicinity of Mount Kailash, including the Yangtze in China and the Ganges in India (in fact Shiva is often pictured with the Ganges River flowing out of his head). The major civilizations of Asia were thus in large part built around these rivers, with their fertile banks giving food and sustenance to humanity since the dawn of history. Just following these rivers to their source could have brought someone face-to-face with Kailash, literally the source of life.

Our trip to Kailash began in Lhasa, which at 15,000 feet is the highest capital city in the world. One of the first things a visitor notices in Lhasa is that Tibetans love to walk in circles. The act of circumambulating a sacred object is actually not unique to Tibetans, but I would venture to say there are no other people on the planet that devote such time, energy, and zeal to the task. They march in force around the Potala Palace (the Dalai Lama's former residence), the Barkor (the old part of town), and every sacred monastery, temple, mountain, lake, or even pile of rocks throughout the land. And all guidebooks warn that a *kora* is always done clockwise. It's considered very bad etiquette to walk counterclockwise—not only do you get in the way, but on a deeper level you feel like you're disturbing some ancient order of the universe.

After several days of acclimatizing in Lhasa we set off for the grueling seven-day trip to Kailash. We spent seven to eight hours every day riding over bumpy dirt roads through some of the most desolate scenery I'd ever seen. We would go for hours without seeing any sign of life—no trees, no grass, no people. Occasionally we'd pass a small town with a teahouse and stop for some soup with a few pieces of grizzled yak meat. At night we either camped or stayed in guesthouses with cold rooms, moldy mattresses, and no plumbing. Several times a day I wondered why on earth I was putting myself through this.

As we got closer to Kailash however, the scenery became more beautiful with deep blue lakes and the snowcapped mountains of the Himalayas. Then, in a moment of great drama, we came up over a rise and glimpsed our first view of Kailash, peeking through the clouds that were remnants from the fierce storm that would leave me on my rock weeping. It was a spectacular sight. At 22,000 feet Kailash is not as tall as Everest but is actually much more imposing. After miles of driving on relatively flat ground, Kailash rises out of the ground like some primitive primal force. It has a broad base and rises to its peak with almost perfect symmetry and it's so solidly anchored that it appears to be connected to the earth's core—channeling, yet containing immense energy from the beginning of time. And it has an intricately faceted surface that gives the appearance of a radiant jewel when light hits it.

The night before the *kora* we camped near the "freedom pole," where pilgrims put up prayer flags before setting off on their journey, and woke up to a perfect day—a brilliant blue sky with a refreshing, cool breeze. Despite the storm and some warnings about the ice, we enthusiastically set off with lots of optimism about making the full *kora*. The trail crossed through a valley and at each of the viewpoints of Kailash there was a pile of stones where people could make offerings, prostrate, and perhaps do a mini-*kora*. We arrived at our camp before dark and settled into a large shared tent while our guide went off to get drunk. We nestled together to keep warm and after a fitful sleep woke at sunrise to see Kailash, a radiant, flawless jewel emanating an otherworldly light that became brighter and brighter as the sun rose.

Then, in an instant, it all changed—the decision not to go, the argument, the stomping off, and me sitting on my rock weeping. And with this turn of events, my absorption in the transcendent energy of Kailash vanished, as if a wall had come crashing down revealing my everyday world of negative thoughts and distractions that Buddhism trains you to avoid. I was at one of the most incredible places on the planet without really being there. I was in my head experiencing waves of anger toward our guide, sadness at my bad fortune, and even jealousy toward all the other pilgrims passing me by.

Perhaps sensing the negative energy emanating from my rock, my prostrating pilgrim friend finally decided to resume his marathon. As I watched him inch his way across the horizon, I vowed that I would not sulk back to town in a funk and ruin my last hours at this extraordinary place. So I got up off my rock and began my seven-hour reverse *kora* back to town. While I don't fully know what transcendent spiritual experience I might have had going the right way on the *kora*, I do know that going the wrong way offered its own kind of awakening—more mundane, more everyday, but perhaps just as powerful.

Almost immediately after starting my return journey, I met a group of Tibetans who thought I was going in the wrong direction because I was con-

> Then it was springtime in the cloudy Himalayas. Nine hundred feet below my cave rhododendrons blossomed. I climbed barren mountain-tops. Long tramps led me to desolate valleys studded with translucent lakes…. Solitude, solitude!… Mind and senses develop their sensibility in this contemplative life made up of continual observations and reflections. Does one become a visionary or, rather, is it not that one has been blind until then?
>
> —Alexandra David-Neel, *Magic and Mystery in Tibet* (1932)

fused. They started waving frantically as if to say, "No, no you're going the wrong way! Turn around! Turn around!" I mimed a sad face and pointed in the direction of the backward *kora* and shrugged my shoulders. Then they grabbed my bag and tried to turn me around while chattering away to each other in Tibetan. It was really tempting to let myself be carried around the mountain by this cheery group of Tibetan pilgrims but I had my ride back to Lhasa to think of. I was so uplifted by their kindness that I continued on the path with a hint of a smile on my face.

Then I bumped into the first of many groups of Indian Hindu pilgrims I would encounter. Hindu pilgrims have the reputation of being the least prepared for the arduous, often dangerous journey to Kailash. Sure enough I came upon this group of what must have been fifty Indian pilgrims of all ages and constitutions.

The group leader greeted me in his chirpy, exceedingly polite Indian accent, "Excuse me ma'am, but why are you going the wrong way, is something wrong?"

I told him there was some ice on the high pass and our guide didn't think it was safe to continue, so I was returning.

"Returning? But we can't return, we've come all the way from Delhi. My aunt has vowed to do this *kora* before she dies to honor her God Shiva." I looked behind him and saw a petite woman in her sixties dressed in a sari and down jacket slumped over the neck of a donkey. He inquired brightly, "Do you think there's any place for us to stay up ahead? We didn't bring camping equipment and we're hoping to find a guest house to accommodate us." Then, as a casual afterthought, "Ma'am, would you be kind enough to give us any extra water you might have. I'm afraid we've almost run out."

I gave them some of my water and told them about a monastery that I heard was putting up pilgrims, and wished them good luck and good cheer. As I continued on I kept the image of the sixty-year-old aunt in my mind. Every time I passed a pile of stones, I placed one on the top and said a short prayer that she and her fellow Shiva devotees would have a safe and successful journey. Trying to imagine myself in her shoes took me out of my own head just a tiny bit more.

The last encounter of the day was with a small group of Tibetan monks. They were hanging around in a jeep at the very end of the *kora*. We exchanged greetings and one of the young monks who spoke English asked me why I was going the wrong way. I sighed and blurted out my whole story. He translated all of this to an older monk who carefully listened, then reached in his bag and gave me a card with a picture of Green Tara, the Buddhist goddess of liberation who helps people overcome all obstacles. Coincidentally, I had just come from a ten-day retreat in India devoted to Green Tara, which had given me a taste of the qualities of compassion and free-dom from suffering that Green Tara embodies. The Lama placed his hands on my head and gave me a blessing that I should not encounter any more obstacles on my journey.

I thanked the Lama, and turned around to see Kailash one last time before heading back to town. As I started walking with my Green Tara card in hand, I began to softly repeat the mantra I had learned in India. And with each breath and each step perfectly synchronized with the rhythms of the chant, I slowly left the sacred mountain behind.

Peggy Neu left her job at a large New York ad agency to travel around the world and reinvent her life at the age of forty-nine. During her two years of travel she worked as a volunteer in Thailand, China, and Mongolia, explored Buddhism in India and Tibet, and had countless adventures backpacking alone through Alaska, Costa Rica, Russia, and most of Asia. She's now back in New York helping nonprofits with marketing and writing about her travel experiences.

ALEXIS SATHRE WOLFF

* * *

Silver Dust

She makes a journey into the ancient ways.

SEVERAL WEEKS INTO MY FOUR-MONTH STAY IN NIGER, I walked through the gates of le Musée National in search of Mamadou Abdou, the Tuareg silversmith who was expecting me.

To get there from my apartment I'd wandered down the dusty Rue de Martin Luther King, often leaping over deep ruts and accidentally stepping in thick brown puddles. Niger had no sewage system or official means of disposing waste, so everywhere sat piles of excrement and waste ridden with infectious diseases. I turned onto Avenue de Gountou Yena, where, in a country whose average temperature hovered in the 90s, I fought goats and camels for occasional patches of shade. Then I took a shortcut through Djamadjé, referred to by my expatriate friends as "the smelly market," where I passed piles of unrecognizable spices, heaps of tomatoes teeming with flies, and slabs of meat baking in the sun, hairy tails still attached. I jetted across Avenue de la Mairie's traffic—Peugeots and Citroens plucked from French junkyards to be reborn as Nigerien taxis—and headed down Rue de Musée, stepping over polio-mangled bodies crawling awkwardly down the street, their writhed hands outstretched to ask for a little change.

This wasn't my first jaunt in the developing world. I'd traveled in Haiti, Nicaragua, and southern Africa, but I'd decided to spend a semester in Niger—the West African nation that was the second poorest country in the world at the time, and projected to be the poorest again as soon as Sierra Leone recovered from its civil war—to prove that I could hack a career in humanitarian work after graduation. Niger, however, was worse than I'd expected—poverty on steroids, as I'd begun to say—and I was beginning to question whether I could handle such a life after all. This doubt beleaguered me during my sociology classes and my work at a nonprofit fighting guinea worm, and I traveled to the *musée* seeking a mindless distraction.

Inside the *musée*, I followed a maze of stone paths that wove me past cages of scrappy-looking animals and one-room buildings with eclectic glass-cased displays. I traveled over a small bridge and then looked up and saw it—the artists' hangar, an open-front structure in which leatherworkers, woodworkers, and metalworkers toiled away at their trades.

As I approached I saw that half the hanger was occupied by several dozen silversmiths working on straw mats, each sitting with one leg on the ground in Indian-style and the other bent up into his chest. A flat-headed anvil was jammed deep into the sand in front of him, and it was on this anvil that he worked, holding his silver steady against it with pliers as he hammered, engraved, or filed. A square leather mat, a jagged hole ripped out its middle, surrounded the anvil to collect the falling slivers of silver. Behind him was a metal lockbox with his tools, and in front of him was a short display table draped with red or black velvet that showed off shiny finished pieces—

knives, letter openers, barrettes, bracelets—all arranged by object in straight, neat lines. As I got closer still I heard a handful of languages—not only the silversmiths' native Tamashek, but also Hausa, Zarma, and French—mixing with the *cling cling cling* of the metal hammers hitting silver.

"*Bonjour!*" an older man called to me. The Nigerian friend of my study abroad program who had arranged my apprenticeship had told him I would be coming.

He was tall and thin, and his skin was wrinkled and worn like that of a well-loved football. His face was small and his top lip protruded further than his forehead, making him look a little like a turtle. With a smile that exposed his crooked teeth, he jumped up from his mat and extended his hand in greeting. He introduced himself to me as Mamadou, then introduced me to nearby silversmiths as his American. I smiled. He would be my Tuareg.

By this point in my stay I'd interacted with members of most of Niger's major ethnic groups—the Hausa guards of my apartment complex, the Zarma men who washed my laundry, the Fulani children in my neighborhood—but not yet a Tuareg. Although hunger and modernity had recently brought some of the nomadic group to the capital, most of Niger's 700,000 Tuareg still traveled by camel caravan through the Sahara Desert.

"You'll make the cross of Agadez," my Tuareg told me in French, pointing to a pendant on a nearby display table.

Tuareg silversmiths, I knew, were renowned for their crosses. Although early missionaries assumed the crosses proved a Christian presence, they're in fact secular: the Tuareg attribute crosses to towns and encampments in addition to names. The most famous is the cross of Agadez, which represents the city in central Niger that was once a bustling trading post and the largest Tuareg settlement.

I appreciated the cultural significance of Mamadou's proposed project, but the cross wasn't my style. A hollowed circle sits at its top, connected below to a diamond with sharp arrows on the side and bottom points. It looks like something goth high schoolers would wear.

My eyes wandered to other pieces of Tuareg jewelry. I spotted dangling earrings I had to have and a chunky chime bracelet I wanted to make. But that I could do later. For now, I'd acquiesce to my Tuareg.

My arrangement with Mamadou was casual: he would be working under the hangar Monday through Friday, and I could join him as frequently or as infrequently as I wanted. Several days after my first visit I returned, plopping down on the space Mamadou cleared for me on his mat and watching him eagerly as he put away his crosses.

Because my language skills were elementary, we communicated through gestures and movements. He motioned for me to follow him to an area in the front center of the hangar where a few rocks glowed with heat, and instructed me to feed the fire by pumping gusts of dry air with an organ-like device, likely made by the leatherworkers nearby. He held a ball of hard yellow wax over the rocks, and I pumped for several minutes until he gestured for me to stop. The wax was sufficiently warm.

Back on Mamadou's mat he handed me a wooden board, a sharp metal tool, and the ball of warm yellow wax. I followed his lead, shaping and sculpting the wax into three rough replicas of the cross before me.

I peeled the three yellow crosses from the board, set them in my palm, and nudged Mamadou to signal that I was done. Grinning, he took my other hand and led me into the sunlight. I walked palm up, carefully, as if carrying a tray of champagne

glasses. He grabbed the crosses and plopped them carelessly—
my heart skipping a beat—on a cement block in the dirt, then
sent me home for the day.

I was lounging in the shade of a baobab tree near my apartment one afternoon during the mini hot season, a few weeks
in October and November when temperatures hover around
100 degrees. It hardly compared to the regular hot season,
which plagues the month of April with temperatures nearing
120 degrees, but the mini hot season affects the country pro-
foundly because it typically overlaps with Ramadan, the
Muslim month of ritual fasting. Between the heat and the
hunger, Niger's already slow-paced life wanes practically to a
halt. Although I fasted only half-heartedly, it was enough. The
tedious tasks of everyday living—bathing, getting food from
the market, washing dishes—proved grueling. I took a break
from silversmithing.

That afternoon I pumped my t-shirt in and out and
scratched the pink spots that dotted my ankles. My hair,
washed only an hour before, was already wet with sweat and
oil. I was tired. I'd lain sleepless in a pool of my own sweat the
night before, using my hairbrush to scratch bites from the
countless mosquitoes that somehow found a way under my
net. I eventually admitted defeat and jumped fully clothed into
the cold shower. Wet and cool, I finally fell asleep only to
awake an hour later squirming in my sweat again.

In the morning the bright sun stole the small amount of
energy that survived the night, and now I sat wondering how
I'd survive until my return flight in December—and what I
was going to do with my life then—when suddenly the space
around me turned dark.

I ran out from under the tree for a better look at the sky. I
didn't understand what could have happened to the sun.

There were no hills for it to tuck behind, no clouds to obstruct its bright rays. But the sky was now orange, and as I stood staring at it, my T-shirt and long skirt flapped like a flag in the wind. I held out my arms and closed my eyes. Sand and dirt crashed into my skin. It hurt, but it was a good hurt...tingling, sparkling, and then itching as it stuck to my sweat.

Then rain poured down and washed the sand away. I smiled and danced in circles, delighted that I'd outsmarted the weather. I thought the sun would come back and my drenched clothes would keep me comfortably cool, at least for a while. Instead, the cold air stayed longer than the rain, and so on the same day sweat dripped from my body, goose bumps popped out from my sunburnt skin.

It was typical of Niger, where none of my expectations were being met.

When I returned to the *musée* a week later, after the heat began to calm, Mamadou's eyes lit up. He put aside his work to stand and shake my hand, slipping on his blue plastic flip-flops and leading me out to the cement block to pick up my yellow crosses, which were now hard.

I followed Mamadou back under the hangar, where we wrapped the yellow cross with a cement mixture and then piled the cement-covered crosses

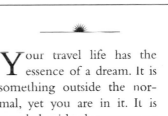

Your travel life has the essence of a dream. It is something outside the normal, yet you are in it. It is peopled with characters you have never seen before and in all probability will never see again. It brings occasional homesickness, and loneliness, and pangs of longing... But you are like the Vikings or the master mariners of the Elizabethan age, who have gone into a world of adventure, and home is not home until you return.

—Agatha Christie

atop one another and added another layer of cement. Mamadou was careful to keep the very top of each cross visible, a yellow dot poking out from gray. Then he led me back to the sunny spot in the dirt, where I again watched him drop my creation.

After fetching my baked cement the next time I returned, I followed Mamadou to a metal table piled with coals. I turned a crank attached to the back of the table, as Mamadou told me to do, and flames rose from the cracks between coals.

Mamadou threw the cement creation into the fire, and after poking it a few times with a metal rod, he reached in his pocket and pulled out a clear bag filled in one corner with silver chips. He dumped the chips into a shot-glass-sized cup made of blackened cement and then placed that in the fire as well. As I watched the glowing silver turn to liquid, Mamadou explained that the wax inside the cement had melted. It occurred to me only then that I'd made a mold. We watched the fire for several minutes before Mamadou instructed me to pour the melted silver into my cement mold, filling the space where the yellow wax had been.

A few days later I cracked the baked cement with a hammer and found three rustic crosses of Agadez inside. I smiled, assuming that I was done, but as it turned out my creations were only rough approximations. Not only did I have to smooth away the grooves and textures left from the cement with sandpaper, but I also had to file each cross into the exact right shape. What was more, I had to do this with a tool that resembled a metal nail file. I pressed as hard as I could, but progress came slowly. Day after day I filed and filed my crosses—crosses that I knew I'd never wear—until my hands ached.

I didn't feel like much of a silversmith, not that I should have after a few months of my part-time apprenticeship. Traditionally prospective smiths work first with wood, then clay, and then only the cheapest metals before finally being en-trusted with silver. Most apprenticeships last a decade, and not all those who enter apprenticeships become smiths. Tuareg sil-versmiths, moreover, are all male—a fact of which Mamadou reminded me once when I imprudently showed up to work in a skirt. He sent me home.

Given my gender and skin color, being allowed to mingle with the silversmiths at all was unusual, and actually studying under one was an extraordinary privilege (one I was probably only afforded because my study abroad program paid Mamadou a small stipend). But it was difficult to remember how lucky I was as I struggled to finish my crosses beside Mamadou, who threw aside perfect pendant after perfect pen-dant. I couldn't help but feel like a failure.

Silversmithing hadn't turned out to be the escape from my worries that I'd intended. Instead it had become an embodi-ment of them.

Weeks and many visits to the hangar later, the silver on my three crosses was finally smooth. It was time to carve designs onto the pendants. Studying Mamadou's work, I noticed that circles and series of short parallel lines appeared occasionally, but triangles appeared most often. The triangle, Mamadou ex-plained, is a common theme in Tuareg design. It's thought to protect against evil.

Mamadou got out his tools: two stamps (a triangle and a circle), a hammer, and a flathead screwdriver. I placed the stamp atop my silver cross and hammered down lightly to leave an impression. It was simple, even for me, but using the screwdriver was another story.

I'd seen Mamadou use it to carve both borders and intri-cate patterns of lines. Holding the screwdriver against the sil-ver with just the right amount of pressure, he rotated his wrist back and forth quickly but slightly, pushing forward, digging a small, straight canal.

Mamadou told me to carve a border just inside the edge of the diamond section of my cross, and I tried, but several millimeters into the task I pushed too hard and rotated my wrist too quickly, slipping off track and carving an awkward line across the diamond. I dropped my pendant on the mat, closed my eyes, and took a deep breath. I went home for the day.

"At last, my American Tuareg has arrived," Mamadou greeted me in French a few days later when I finally returned.

As I lowered myself to the mat, I grinned and continued what had become our ongoing joke, insisting that I was completely Tuareg, no part American—even though I felt anything but. I shook my head when Mamadou tried to hand me a file. Today I just wanted to watch.

Soon an American tourist approached Mamadou hoping to buy a necklace for his wife. He ran his fingers up and down a larger piece Mamadou had pulled from his lockbox. The pendant required a lot of silver and a lot of work, and it usually sold for about 25,000 CFA, roughly equivalent to U.S.$40. I drew circles in the silver dust in front of me as Mamadou attended to the American, engaging in the standard bargaining ritual.

After a few minutes the frustrated tourist turned to me. "He says thirty-five thou.... Is he ripping me off?"

I sat up, folded my hands in my lap, and lied, "Oh no, not at all. They usually go for twice that."

Mamadou wrapped the American's necklace in recycled scraps of an outdated U.N. Development Report, and I returned my attention to the silver dust, pressing my hands palms down on the mat and then lifting them to eye level, turning them this way and then that way so the silver dust sparkled.

As I watched my glimmering hands I forgot everything—my ineptitude at silversmithing (and everything else Nigerien), the burgeoning realization that when Air France flight 731 jetted me back to the land of flush toilets and garbage trucks I'd have to redraft my life's plan, and most of all, the disappointment that the person I wished I were, a fledgling humanitarian, wasn't who I actually was.

When I looked up the tourist was gone. Mamadou was watching me, waiting. He showed me that he had finished my crosses and told me it was time for me to start a new project. He said I could make anything I wanted.

I strolled the aisles of the hangar studying the displayed jewelry before settling on the pair of dangling earrings I'd been admiring for months.

"*Ceci,*" I said in my rusty French. "*Je veux ceci.*"

Mamadou handed me some yellow wax and sent me over to the fire to warm it. As I pumped I wondered how I'd make my earrings. I'd thought only crosses required wax molds.

When the wax felt warm in my hand I headed back to Mamadou's mat, arranging my limbs in that uncomfortable Tuareg position—one leg on the ground Indian-style, and one leg bent up into my chest. I looked at Mamadou with wide eyes and smiled, letting him know that I was ready. He rustled around in his lockbox for a few minutes, his hands eventually emerging holding two metal crosses.

"Copy," he said in French, throwing them down in front of me and gesturing toward my warm wax.

I stared at the crosses. They weren't crosses of Agadez (they were crosses of Tahoua and Iferouane, I'd later learn), but they certainly weren't my dangling earrings.

I shifted my stare to Mamadou, waiting for him to laugh, but he had already returned to his own work. Maybe my request to make the dangling earrings had been lost in translation, or maybe he thought that since so much about me wasn't typical of a Tuareg silversmith, the least I could do was stick to traditional projects.

Wondering what had just happened, I watched Mamadou for a while. Finally, the laugh finally came—but it came from me. *Maybe nothing works out quite as planned,* I thought as I ran my finger through the silver dust on Mamadou's leather mat one last time before picking up my yellow wax, *and maybe that's okay.*

Alexis Sathre Wolff earned a BA in African Studies from Yale University and an MFA in Nonfiction Writing from Columbia University. She is now a freelance writer living in New York City.

RUTH KAMNITZER

* * *

In the Dust of His Peacock's Feathers

*On the road to Murugan, the author finds
the deity in the pilgrims as much as
in the shrine.*

THE CHANT IS ENDLESS, ITS POWER ENORMOUS. IT FILLS
my ears, my blood, carries me forward in this human wave that
knows no containment. It is the India I have always dreamed
existed. And now it has found me.

"Palani? It is nothing interesting madam. Just a small temple. They will just raise a flag at the top of the hill and everyone will go home. Nothing for tourists to see. Better you
come Madurai, we have float festival, very nice." During the
last month of cycling around the Indian state of Tamil Nadu,
my friend Karen and I had passed many pilgrims dressed in
green, on their way to see Murugan, they said, the errant son
of Shiva, at his hilltop temple at Palani. But the man in the
Madurai tourist office had just assured us, nothing to see. Well,
we decided, we would, of course, visit the temple when we
happened to pass through, but there was obviously no reason
to rush.

Then biking along one day, we ran into a human wall that
stretched for miles in either direction. These weren't just the

173

pilgrims in green. This was everyone, and they were all going to Palani. And so now, of course, were we.

Only in India can you bike into a town where you know absolutely no one, and ten minutes later have found a secure place to store all your belongings for the next week and be sitting down to a full feast while entertaining the steady stream of visitors who have come to pay their respects. In our case it was the owners of the local gas company who made us feel so welcome, and their hospitality was so effusive it seemed we'd never be able to leave for the mountain of food amassing on our plates. Eventually our hostess was satisfied that we had eaten all we possibly could, photographs were taken, hands pumped repeatedly in farewell, and addresses exchanged. We ceremonially removed our shoes, wiggled our toes, and set off walking barefoot, with the thousands of others, for the temple at Palani, just over a hundred kilometers away.

The black tar is scorching, and it doesn't take us long to realize why everyone else is waiting out the heat of the day at the side of the road. But Karen has already burned the bottom of her feet almost beyond repair, and excruciatingly painful blisters will plague her the entire walk. Families beckon us from the shade of tamarind trees, where they lie napping on their jute sacks, or eating lemon rice out of banana leaf packages. Others softly sing the names of Murugan while fingering the beads that hang round their necks. We sit with them, and learn the story of Murugan.

Once upon a time Shiva, the great god responsible for the destruction and recreation of this world, was given a golden fruit. The fruit was not to be broken, but consumed in one bite. Being a chivalrous type of god, he gave it to his wife, Parvati, who in turn wanted to pass it on to their children. Shiva and Parvati have two sons—Ganesh, the popular elephant-headed god who adorns the gateways of so many

temples, and Murugan. Not knowing to whom the fruit
should be given, Shiva and Parvati announced a small contest:
whichever son managed to go around the world first would
win the golden fruit.

Murugan at once mounted his peacock and set off, determined to claim the prize. Ganesh, however, being rather stout
and not much one for speed, merely walked around his parents, saying, "You are my world." Needless to say, by the time
Murugan returned home from his transglobal journey, the
fruit was already in Ganesh's belly. Outraged that he had been
tricked out of his prize in such a manner he fled to the hill at
Palani, where the temple now stands. It was there that we were
going to see him.

As soon as the tarmac cools we begin to walk again. There
are truly thousands of pilgrims. It is an indescribable feeling to
be part of something this large, this powerful, this timeless.
Rich or poor we all walk together, all barefoot, all carrying
only a single small bag slung over the shoulder or balanced on
the head. The men wear lungis, a simple cloth tied around the
waist, and the women saris, many of them red and gold. Every
color is a symbol in India, a way of pronouncing something
about your identity, whether it is your marital status, your
region or a pledge you have made with a god. Almost all the
pilgrims wear a *mala*, a string of 108 beads, put on at the beginning of the journey to signify the pledge of the *padi-yatra*
to make the journey barefoot. *Padi* means foot, *yatra* means
pilgrim. This *mala* will be blessed by the temple priests.

We walk, on and on, until night falls, and we sleep, with
countless others, at the side of the road, in fields, in the
homes of villagers who have opened their doors to us, or in
the courtyards of temples. In the morning we rise and walk
again. Never before have I felt so strongly that past and present are not connected by any line, any string, but rather the

past tumbles like a snowball down a hill, an avalanche crashes violently into us, so that its pieces are rearranged but essentially the same. History doesn't repeat itself, it just wears different clothing.

As the only two foreigners, Karen and I are the object of much curiosity.

"*Ingeporinga?*" they ask in Tamil. Where do you come from?

"Canada *poringa*," we answer.

"Kerala?" (A state to the west of Tamil Nadu.)

"No, Canada."

"Karnataka?"

"No, Canada. USA, Canada," we explain, holding our fists up to represent neighboring countries.

"USA. England," they answer, nodding slowly with a look of vague understanding. Another group approaches. "*Ingeporinga?*" It begins again. We estimate that we meet at least twenty people an hour, for at least ten hours of the day (there are some quieter times in the day). If they have all come in groups of twenty, in the four days the walk will take, we will have met, directly and indirectly, 16,000 people. The figure is astounding.

With each passing hour, our line gets wider, longer, stronger. A man walks by, balancing on his head a rooster on a red velvet cushion. It is a gift for Murugan. Another family leads their cow who wears a garland of yellow carnations. She will be blessed by the temple priests before returning home. Women balance brass pots on their heads containing water taken from their village wells and scented with flower petals. It too will be blessed at the temple. Many villagers carry *cavatis*, temple replicas carried on the shoulder. No one can adequately explain to us what they are, and we only see what they are used for when we reach the temple, but they are beautiful nonetheless. Tiny children walk, trotting along to

keep up with their parents who can't be slowed in their
enthusiasm. Occasionally they are whisked up and carried on
the head to save time. I see a couple pushing two children on
a bicycle. There are groups of children who tell us their parents will join them in a few days, and groups of adults who say
they have left their village in the hands of their children.

Karen's blisters are very bad, and she grimaces in pain as
they burst and the tender flesh is exposed to the stony gravel
road. The pilgrims carry her along, one at each elbow, chanting endlessly to keep her mind off the pain. *Subrimanike…Aro-
garah…Muruganike…Aro-garah…Palanike…Aro-garah…Aro-
garah?… Aro-garah.* At first her voice is thin and reedy as she
struggles against the pain, and then she gains power. She
hobbles proudly, head erect, Murugan ahead. I admire her determination and faith.

Sometimes we are adopted by groups of twenty or more,
entire villages. Often they are followed by hired pickup trucks,
carrying extra supplies, food, cooks, and tired children. Those
riding in the back will at times go barefoot, at times wear
shoes, but will not wear the *mala,* a sign of the pledge of the
padi yatra. We rest with them in the midday heat. Karen and I
are fussed over in Tamil, constantly shifted to more advanta-
geous locations in the shade of the truck, while the cooks pre-
pare huge vats of vegetable curry and rice that we eat off banana leaves on the gravel. Then we crawl right under the
truck, spread our tarpaulin sacks and sleep till the sun at last
dips enough for the pavement to cool and then we walk again.
Sometimes we are swept along with richer folk, and we eat
with them in makeshift restaurants at the roadside, where
masala dosa, idly, utapam, and other south Indian specialities are
served to thousands. These restaurants are like factories, the
waiters sweating with profusion as *dosas* fly with lightning

speed, the pails of dhal soup emptied almost as quickly as they are filled. Everywhere we are greeted warmly. Always we feel we are among friends.

For four days, virtually twenty-four hours a day, we are surrounded by Indian people. We fall asleep to them fussing over us, exclaiming over our hairy arms, our strange skin, or admonishing us for not covering our heads completely. They pull up our sheet and tuck it in, so that we blend in more fully with the faceless sexless sleeping masses. For a few hours we escape our identity.

On the third night we sleep in a large communal camp. There are at least 3,000 of us in this field. Oversized speakers scream *bajans*, devotional songs, till past midnight. Miraculously, the noise, which even a week ago would have been unbearable, now does not even bother me in the slightest and I sleep soundly. At 3 A.M. everyone rises as if on cue, and four minutes later their sheets are folded away, saris smoothed down and they are off. Karen and I are left alone in the field, still rubbing the sleep out of our eyes. The road is quiet, the pilgrims walking steadily to try to make some time before the sun rises and turns the black tar into a hot griddle. By draping our scarves over our heads and shoulders and looking down when someone passes we are for a few hours at least, just two more pilgrims on their way to see Murugan.

As we near the temple, numerous paths melt together. The line grows longer, wider, and with each hour more certain. It has no beginning nor end, no definition, not a line but a vector that points from everywhere to Murugan. *Aro-garah…Aro-garah, subrimanike…aro-garah?… Aro-garah!* There must be ten, twenty, one hundred, two hundred thousand of us. No one knows.

On the third day the gypsies arrive by the eastern path. They have a vibrancy that stands out even here, looking exactly the way gypsies are supposed to look; the men with long dark curls escaping colorful bandanas and the women possessed of a mysterious beauty that belies their rags and dirt-smudged faces. Murugan is the errant son of Shiva and so too the god of those marginalized in Hindu society. Now these people of the road are on the road to Murugan and the energy is uncontrollable. They discover us and swarm like locusts and we are carried in their wake.

In the lead is a woman I imagine as the elephant matriarch. Her sari is worn like an afterthought, doing nothing to hide her huge breasts and ass that stick out a mile in either direction. Bangles cover her arms and heavy gold rings sparkle in her nose and ears. She seems about to topple as she limps, very quickly, down the road, her bandaged, bloody feet unable to keep up with her spirit. A beautiful young man, his gypsy eyes dark and smoky, his body lithe and soft, begins to beat a tambourine against his hip. The cry mounts, the songs begin. The woman explodes in dance down the road, and her poor bloodied feet have no choice but to follow. I have never seen an Indian woman dance with such ferocious abandon.

Eventually they stop off at a temple for a free meal, beg some money off us, and we part warmly, with much hand clasping and promises to meet again. I am sorry to see them go.

Coconut stalls now line the road. The machete thwacks as it hits the nut and slices away the fibrous shell until at last the sweet juice runs and the white flesh lies revealed. We drink three or four of these a day, endless sweet tea and innumerable glasses of water from questionable sources. Roadside clinics have now appeared, where doctors dispense free medicine and treat wounded feet, while nurses offer massages. My feet are now almost as bad as Karen's, and I double my appreciation of her stoicism. We hobble together, the lame leading the lame. *Aro…garah?… Aro-garah!*

People from Rameswaram on the southeastern tip of the subcontinent have begun to arrive. Some have spent seven days covering the 300 kilometers, and their pilgrim's bags are even dustier than ours. But no matter where we have come from, we are all going home, and greetings are as between siblings not strangers. And we too have innumerable friends among this crowd. There is a group of six friends in their early twenties. One of them has taken a vow of silence for the duration of the journey, and his friends take the opportunity to arrange his betrothal to me. He only smiles devilishly as the joke is renewed every time we pass each other, dates set, and invitations designed.

The reporters find us. Amazingly enough, among the tens of millions and all that we have seen, we are interesting to them. Ruth and Karen become Ruda and Gareem, laborers who have saved for four years to make this return visit to India. The battle between being honest and trying to make Indians understand that our reality isn't as glamorous as they sometimes believe, lost. Our picture appears the next day in four editions of south Indian newspapers, boosting our already elevated status to new heights.

On the last day of the walk, we meet up with a group of about forty from our village of origin, relatives of the gas company owners with whom we entrusted our bikes. Two of them we recognize. They have covered the 100 kilometers in forty-eight hours, stopping only for a few hours in the night. They have been on the lookout for us, and they greet us now like long-lost friends. Another relative lives five kilometers from the temple, and we are going there for dinner, unannounced but surely welcome.

When we arrive, a well-dressed woman in a beautiful sari opens the door and introductions begin as pilgrim bags pile high in the corner. It takes twenty minutes to trace the lineage back to a common point. While the poor woman is mobilizing the household to feed the masses, the phone rings—thirty-five more are expected within the hour. She is unperturbed. Due to their strategic location near such a holy site, she tells me they receive about a thousand guests a year. I try and picture my mother in the same position. Dinner is obviously going to take some time, so due to our honored status as foreign guests a child is dispatched to the market to buy us *dosas*, which we eat with the women in the kitchen.

Then, unexpectedly, we are on the road again.

It is quiet now, most of the people having settled down for the night. Those last five kilometers take almost two hours, with frequent stops to laugh and argue over who is in worse shape. We imagine the story we will tell, how we hobbled to Palani, arrived at the throne of the great god bent and broken.

The next morning I realize that everything we have seen so far, the days of walking, the chants, the devotion, is only the beginning. Things only get madder.

Pilgrims are arriving by the thousands, and the wide two-kilometer road that rings the temple is fully packed by 7 A.M. The most auspicious day to pay respect to the half-meter-high idol will be tomorrow. We step out of the sleeping area and into the crowds.

I am swept up, the senses pulled in every direction. My eyes glimpse, but don't comprehend, the songs, the fever of devotion, the women whirling madly. Cymbals, drums, anklets of bells, Murugan's name a thousand times, we are almost there and it can't be contained any longer. Huge processions go by, and we fall into their song, our feet still bare following them as we dance down the temple road. A group of about twenty drummers passes followed by the holders of the *cavatis*, presents for Murugan, and in the front the dancers, goaded into trance. Karen is caught and I watch as her hands begin to tremble, her steps become feverish. An old Indian lady sees her too, and holds her hand in caution. She shifts from one foot to the other, like a nervous animal, straining to be let off the leash. She dances, her bloodied feet that made her grimace in pain a few moments earlier forgotten, and they fly as the Indian boys urge the drummers to faster, more dangerous rhythms. I am afraid. The old woman eases her back from the crowd, from the vortex. The procession keeps dancing and we fall back, Karen still trembling. The air is pungent with jasmine, incense, and humanity. The crowd becomes even more dense, and then we pass through the temple gates like a cork. Countless stairs lie ahead but the crowd does not pause. They have walked one, two, three hundred kilometers and the road has not ended yet. The strong don't aid the weak, they carry them. Murugan cannot wait. I see mothers grab their children, fly up the stairs two at a time, grandmothers virtually dragged by a nephew on either side, toddlers bouncing on their fathers' heads.

Yet we too climb, run on all fours. I see the faces around me and I think, how could so many people be wrong? For the first time in my life I seriously consider the possibility that God exists, not as a facet of ourselves but as a completely independent entity. And I am afraid, because if he does exist, if he is Murugan, he's not going to be very happy that I've remained skeptical for so long.

The temple is huge. We have reached the top of the stairs and stand in a huge courtyard, dotted with various places of worship that surround the main shrine. People are going crazy everywhere. I don't know where I am or what's coming next. There is shouting and the crowd parts for a man, naked but for the simplest cloth, being rolled across the filth of the courtyard floor. His hands are clasped above his head, his eyes closed and when the hands of the group pause in their turning of him he lies slumped in exhaustion. In the coming days we will see that it is a fairly popular custom to be rolled around the circumference of the temple, for both men and women. Watch out, we will say to each other, there's a roller coming.

A man walks uphill, hooks in his back pulling a wooden *cavati* on wheels. Another is even more grueling—he walks backwards, the hooks piercing his nipples, in his cart a young boy tied to a stick. Everywhere people are falling into a trance, lashing at the bounds of their bodies. Women dance and thrash, intoxicated with this promise of freedom, in a manner I would never have expected conservative Indian women to act in public. The man beside me, carrying his child, falls into a heavy trance, suddenly lurching madly. The child doesn't even seem to notice. Others rush up and take the child from his arms as the drums begin, the chants start. In the temple courtyard a small space is cleared. The now familiar beat, that builds up so rhythmically, almost then completely breaks down. Two men, a cloth tied around their waists, chests bare, are goaded into trance. They face each other like wild animals whose instinct for preservation has been demented by a long captivity. One has his hands tied behind his back, his tongue forced out and he is so wild I fear he will bite it off. The other man is given a short spear, one end the spade of Murugan, the other a gleaming point. They are released, circle each other, stamping in agitation, and the man with the spear rushes and stabs it through the other's tongue. They jump together in glee, ecstasy, and insanity.

The next day we rise early. Today is the day, the fullest moon, the biggest karmic bonus. The temple road is packed, fired with expectation. We walk the two kilometers in a dense crowd.

Eventually we climb the stairs and enter the temple court-yard. There are three ways to see Murugan: You can shell out 1,000 rupees (about U.S.$30) and be ushered in within half an hour for a relatively peaceful visit, you can pay 100 rupees and wait for up to three hours before you file in with the others, or you can forego the concept of time altogether and sit pa-tiently with the masses in a line already thousands long. We choose the 100-rupee option—you don't want to be too cheap when it comes to God, he's probably mad enough at me as it is, but he would be greedy if he thinks I've got 1,000 ru-pees to spare. The ticket booth has been swallowed and is only identifiable as the dense lump within this larger lump of peo-ple. A helpful man, also going for the 100-rupee option, offers to buy tickets for us. We each hand him the 100 rupees and an extra 20 to assure speedy passage. He emerges ten minutes later, unrecognizable in his degree of dishevelment. But he has the tickets.

By now we have Murugan fever almost as badly as every-one else. The 100-rupee line is already quite long and begin-ning to move, so Karen and I decide why not scale the four-meter-high, wire-mesh wall maintaining order and jump the queue a little. A couple of white girls, surely no one will mind. We scramble up the wire mesh and start down the other side. Men pound at our ankles, scream abuse, try and push us back over the other side—head first. I see the possibility for mob violence and quickly retreat. We go back and stand in the line, wait like everyone else. Murugan again.

Two hours later we shuffle into the main sanctuary. It is so crowded my nose is pressed up against the shirt of the man in front of me, and the air is a strange mixture of sweat and in-cense. The temple attendants keep us moving along at a steady pace, prodding when necessary. The inner sanctuary is dark, and the various statues difficult to make out. There is a small figure on my left, which sparkles a little more brightly than the others but almost too late it registers that this is Murugan, the all-powerful god I and a quarter million others have walked hundreds of kilometers to see. All of five seconds in his presence and it's over, we're back in the sunlight.

The festivities continue. Things are winding down now after the cusp of the moon. Every day the many shrines and courtyards on the hilltop reverberate with music as troupes from different villages perform for Murugan. Music that makes my heart bleed for its devotion, music that makes me cry for the richness of their lives, their love affair with God. Music that makes me wonder how I, in my twenty-six years, could have failed to sense a presence of such magnitude. Always they urge us to dance, and we often do, sometimes self-conscious at the scene we are creating, two white girls dancing to the music of so many young boys, and not wanting to draw attention away from the main event, sometimes feeling perfectly natural, as if we too are offering up what we have.

It goes on and on. Everyday we think we are going to leave something else catches our attention. Finally, on our last night I go to see a singer on the temple sleeping area where we had spent our first night. The place is not as full now, but still there are hundreds of people, and much more garbage. It still smells like a toilet. The singer is an incredibly beautiful woman, her plumpness a sign of her good health. She plays a harmonium and is accompanied by a *tabla* player as she sings in Tamil.

But she doesn't just sing. She recites a poem, the story of a young girl in search of her destiny, and her voice moves so gently between narration and song that it seems the melody is born of the language. It moves, above the crying babies, the suckling infants, the smell of the urine and seems to infect everything with its song. Sitting there, I see that this is the

Tamil's world, that behind everything you will find this ancient song. And I can't believe such beauty exists.

*Ruth Kamnitzer always dreamed of exploring the world and spent
most of her twenties doing so, with a predisposition towards bicycles
and her own feet. She recently returned to university to work toward
a career in environmental management and conservation. She currently lives in Edinburgh.*

* * *

Marrakech Mama

Learning to shed extra baggage
is a mother's dilemma.

MY WORK REQUIRES ME TO TRAVEL FREQUENTLY AND often for extended periods, making me even more vulnerable to self-doubt than the average working or traveling mother. Subtle criticism from several non-working moms in my community about my occasional one- or two-week absences has hit me hard at times. Still worse, I *love* what I do! Combined, all of the above, led me at one point to question almost everything about my role as a parent. Was I a good mother? A good enough mother? Was my babysitter the best available? Did my husband resent the extra work at home while I was away? With every trip, I packed and hauled along such awful extra baggage. Shouldered every mile, along with my duffels, totes, and briefcase, I dragged this heavy load of doubt and reproach. The quiet claws of uncertainty became a constant part of my planning, packing, and leave-taking for years. The pain of separation and concern about my family's well-being clouded the joy of taking off for those new worlds I was supposed to be exploring.

Often my flights would leave very early in the morning. I would tiptoe into my children's bedroom to say my silent goodbyes while they were still fast asleep, inhaling the familiar fragrance of shampoo in their silken hair, nuzzling my nose into their soft, warm necks, and running my fingers over their downy cheeks. Then I would burst into tears on the way to the airport.

The intensity of my goodbyes varied with every trip. I learned that leaving a sick child or being absent for more than one weekend took the heaviest emotional toll. I suffered one of my worst bouts of guilt when my daughters were three and six years old and I went to Morocco for seventeen days on business—the longest I had ever been away from home. But, it was that very trip that ultimately freed me and put my life back into perspective.

For weeks before my departure for North Africa I took extra precautions to keep every microbe away from my children. Compulsively I spent every free moment playing with them. I made endless lists and schedules for my husband and the babysitter, stocked the cupboards and refrigerator to over-flowing, and filled "goodie bags" with simple, gift-wrapped treats to be opened each day I was away. But even my best efforts didn't alleviate my guilt.

Although the pain of separation faded slowly with the excitement of experiencing Africa, I still felt stabs of guilt each day. To comfort myself and stay emotionally connected to home I carried pictures of my family with me everywhere and enthusiastically shared them with waitresses, guides, and travel companions. I safety-pinned my favorite snapshots to the canvas walls of my tent when camping in the Sahara Desert. One day I pulled them out of my backpack to share with a nomadic Bedouin woman and her newborn baby as she boiled water for tea over a wood fire. Together we smiled and cooed over her child and my pictures.

In Marrakech, I placed a framed picture of my daughters on the bedside table in my hotel room, as had become my custom. For years I had performed the same nesting ritual in every new hotel, in every city: I would throw open the curtains for light, mess up the covers on the bed, and ceremoniously place framed snapshots of my children and husband all over the room. Perched on the nightstand, inches from my head, the smiles of my daughters would soothe me as I fell asleep.

I thought of them constantly, and shopping for treasures to take home filled the small amount of free time I had on my first day in the city. In the bustling, colorful alleys of the medina I bargained for tiny embroidered slippers with turned-up toes, leather camels, and

Hawaii was perfect in all the usual ways. The trouble came with the telephone call, the ranch, the food, the policeman. Mostly it was the telephone call.

I'd been on the road for more than two weeks in New Zealand, Australia, and now in Hawaii. I'd been wowed by rain forests, red sand, and burning lava. But then I spent a disappointing morning at a ranch, and afterward, my only bad meal of the trip had left me feeling queasy. Then when I called home my son said, "Mom, you've been gone so long I don't remember what you look like." Just put a dagger in my heart and twist it.

On the way to the airport, I was stopped by a policeman for speeding. By the time the airplane to Honolulu took off, I had turned my face to the window and started to cry. The next day was better. Hawaii is still wonderful. My son still loves me. And I hope I never have a day worse than that.

—Katherine Calos,
"The Phone Call"

exotic dolls. Finally, exhausted from the noonday heat, I returned to the oasis of my hotel room, eager for a few minutes of silence and a cool shower. But, when I unlocked the door I immediately smelled flowers. In a moment I saw them. There, around the picture of my children, fragrant roses had been arranged, transforming the bedside table into a beautiful altar with offerings. But from whom? This touching but mysterious ritual continued for two days. Magically, fresh flowers kept appearing to adorn my children's smiles.

On my last day in Morocco I returned to the hotel late in the afternoon. As I stepped out of the elevator, I heard a rustling in the hall. A short woman with flashing brown eyes and a charcoal-colored bun quickly pushed aside her maid's cart and hurried to greet me. She had obviously been waiting for this moment. Motioning me closer with her keys, she unlocked my door. As I followed her into the room I was once again struck by the sweet smell of flowers. The new offerings were red, white, and pink carnations.

The woman led me to the bedside table where she lovingly lifted the picture of my daughters to her chest and held it tightly. Then she raised the frame to her lips and kissed each girl's photo. I pointed to the flowers, bowed my head, and tried to express my thanks with my hands pressed together in the universal gesture of prayer. Smiling, the woman then pulled a crumpled photograph of her own family from her apron pocket. I took it, admired her four children, then held the picture to my chest and embraced it as she had, gently kissing each child. I reached out to touch her arm in appreciation, and she hugged me closely. As we stood embracing in silent female communion, tears filled my eyes and my throat choked closed with emotion.

Using only gestures and our eyes and smiles, we told each other about our children, and I felt blessed and quietly at peace. This was the true reward of travel: not the places visited but the people who have touched my life. This compassionate Muslim woman reminded me once again that mothers all over the world work, often outside the home, and are thus separated from their children by that work. It is not a choice for most of them, or for most of us. And we are not bad mothers because of it.

In that brief moment of sharing family pictures in a strange city so far from home, I realized that nothing has ever made me as happy or as sad as Motherhood. And that nothing has ever been quite as hard, as intense, or as satisfying.

Occasionally in my travels I experience something that forever alters my life, that brings me back a changed person. So it was in a quiet room in Marrakech. Despite my homesickness, a generous Moroccan mother helped me replace guilt with gratitude forever.

Marybeth Bond is the author of five Travelers' Tales books including Gutsy Women *and* Gutsy Mamas *and the editor of* A Woman's World, *which won a Lowell Thomas Gold Award for best travel book. She traveled alone around the world at age 29, a guilt-free global two year journey. Since then, she has included in her life a husband, two young children, a dog, and dozens of pampered rose bushes. Visit her web site www.gutsytraveler.com.*

KATHE KOKOLIAS

✦ ✦ ✦

The Virgin of Guadalupe

The real Madonna, she is everywhere;
and especially in Mexico.

Fireworks explode all over Zihuatanejo disrupting the evening stillness. The racket will continue most of the night, blaring through our earplugs and blasting into our dreams. After a brief lull (even revelers need some rest), it will become our alarm clock at dawn.

The fireworks and accompanying gunshots herald the annual celebration of Our Lady of Guadalupe, the Blessed Virgin Mary. From December 9 through 12, nightly parades clog the main roads in town. Pickup trucks transport flower-laden icons of Our Lady. Five-piece brass oompah bands, and throngs of candle-carrying worshippers—men in gleaming white shirts, old women walking hand-in-hand, mothers carrying babies, and scrubbed children in their Sunday finery—all follow the makeshift altars. A trail of cars and buses bring up the rear, impatiently waiting to pass the Virgin parades or veering off to imagined shortcuts.

It started in 1529, not long after the Spanish conquistadors invaded Mexico and started imposing Catholicism on the native people. According to legend, one day in December the Blessed Virgin appeared to a newly-converted indigenous man at the site of a temple to Tonantzin, mother of the Aztec gods. The cynical bishop from nearby Mexico City didn't believe Juan Diego when he told of his vision, so the young man returned to the site and prayed for guidance. The Lady revealed herself again and instructed Juan Diego to go up the hill to pick roses where they had never grown before. When he went before the bishop the second time and opened his cloak, an image of the Virgin was superimposed on the lining, and a shower of red rose petals fell to the floor.

Word traveled to Rome and the Pope proclaimed a miracle. The Spaniards built a chapel on top of Tonantzin's temple and soon the two female deities merged into one, but this new Virgin looked different from the one the conquistadors had adopted as their protector when they crossed the ocean to the New World. This Guadalupe had special significance for the indigenous people: her skin was darker, her hair straight, and she was surrounded by the sun, moon, and stars—familiar symbols of Tonantzin.

Like churches all over Mexico, the small outdoor church next to the canal in Zihuatanejo holds a festival on December 12, highlighted by a reenactment of the appearance of the Virgin. Cars parked on both sides of the narrow streets bordering the church create a traffic nightmare. Families fill the sprawling side yard and buy food from vendors—popcorn, cotton candy, and roasted corn on the cob slathered with mayonnaise or chile powder. Babies clutching balloons on strings lose their grip, and howl when the balloons disappear into the night sky.

To be part of the pageantry, the children dress in peasant garments in likeness of Juan Diego. Starting the week before, the market in the center of town sells these outfits, like

costumes for Halloween, except that there is only one choice.
Boys in bleached muslin shirts and pants, and straw hats sport
penciled mustaches. Girls wear white blouses and multicol-
ored woven skirts. Their mothers apply garish rouge and lip-
stick to all the little girls, making them look more like clowns
than peasants. Children line up to pose on a scruffy donkey in
front of a painted cactus landscape while a photographer snaps
their picture to record the event.

Later that night in my apartment a few blocks from the
church, I stare at the sculpture of the Virgin of Guadalupe that
I bought in Michoacán and placed over my bed. Woven from
the reeds that grow along the shores of Lake Pátzcuaro, she is
nearly two feet tall and is framed by a starburst of dried
grasses. Her countenance is radiant, her crowned head tilted at
a benevolent angle, and her hands are folded in prayer.

She moves me in a way that I don't understand. I am not
Catholic and have never been religious, but I do think of myself as a spiritual person. My hope is that if I keep searching,
perhaps one day I will find a system of beliefs that will fit with
who I am, that will feel as comfortable as my worn blue
chambray shirt that I wear on chilly mornings. Over the past
three decades, I have been drawn to feminine images of the
divine, from the ancient goddesses of Old Europe—rounded
clay figures found in caves, their pictures painted on walls—to
the pantheon of goddesses of ancient Greece, each with her
own particular attribute—Athena for wisdom, Artemis for
courage and strength. But none of them have touched my
heart. With the Virgin of Guadalupe I feel a connection, a
deep longing for the Mother.

I make collages from prayer cards of Guadalupe that I buy
from vendors in front of churches, their stalls filled with
rosaries, crucifixes, and pictures of Christ praying in the
Garden of Gethsemane. I surround her picture with handmade

paper of deep blue or purple, and draw gold stars and a quarter-moon around her head. These icons fit in tarnished tin frames that I hang in my bedroom. On the frames I glue *milagros,* small metal charms—petitions to the Virgin by those seeking divine intervention. The type of *milagro* that is selected depends on the nature of the person's difficulty. Troubles with health or love, with family, vehicles or animals all have corresponding figures—miniature arms, legs, hearts or heads, children, cattle, trucks. Fashioned out of silver or gold-toned tin, they are tied with a red ribbon. The devotee pins the *milagro* next to the Virgin's icon in the church alcove, kneels in prayer and asks for her help.

I seek her out as I travel around Mexico. I look for the Virgin with her sweet face and tender smile. Unconditional love flows from her. Her hands open gracefully in forgiveness, with the power to heal all wounds of the past and present. She wears a mantle of blue with bright stars. A crescent moon graces her like the Great Goddess of ancient Crete. The golden sun shines over her shoulders, a reminder that, like her counterpart Tonantzin, the Aztec Goddess of Heaven, she is the Queen of the Cosmos.

The Virgin of Guadalupe is all over Mexico. She *is* Mexico. She is in the churches, often overshadowing the image of her son. She is in roadside shrines, in a corner of a living room, in a backyard amidst hibiscus bushes, banana trees, and laundry drying on a line. Her icon hangs on the walls of restaurants, and she graces the narrowest neighborhood *tienda* that sells a few groceries. She rides regally on the dashboards of buses. She adorns the back of a t-shirt, a tattoo on a muscular forearm—*Dulce Madre,* Sweet Mother. Both believers and non-believers have attested to seeing her likeness on the wall of a crowded subway station in Mexico City, and in other locations as far away as Chicago.

Beyond her role as Mother of Mexico, Guadalupe has crossed borders with the global migration of Mexicans in search of a better life. These emigrants transport her wherever they go, carefully packed with their belongings. They carry her picture in their wallet as they would a beloved family member, and place her in shrines in their new homes and businesses.

No longer the meek Mother of the Son of God, the Queen of Heaven has evolved over the past several hundred years. She has led revolutions, emblazoned on the banners of the indigenous people and *mestizos*—those of Spanish and native blood—inspiring them to fight off their oppressors. She is the Giver of All Life and a role model for anyone who longs for freedom, for liberation of the body and the soul. The Virgin stands for purity, independence, and strength, and has become a symbol of the feminine spirit in the Americas. Her image has been chosen by both the pro-choice and the pro-life movements to represent their values in the bitter battle over women's reproductive rights. The quintessential loving Mother embraces all her children.

Guadalupe, you are the guardian of our dreams, protector of our hopes.

I write in my journal:

Dear Virgin, Can we talk—woman to woman, mother to mother, wife to wife?
How do you do it, day after day, year after year?
How can you always be so patient and loving?
Don't you ever get tired of listening to everyone's troubles?
Come sit beside me and tell me your story.
And I'll tell you mine.

Dear Lady, I surrender to your love.
I am your child.
Give me the courage to do all that I am meant
to do.
Let all that comes from me be grounded in love.
Fill me with hope.
Bring me peace.

Kathe Kokolias is a writer and photographer living in Colonie, New York and Ixtapa, Mexico. She has traveled in Mexico, South America, the Caribbean, Spain, Greece, and Italy. Her articles and photos have appeared in various publications in the U.S. and Mexico, and two essays aired on National Public Radio. This story was excerpted from her travel memoir, What Time Do the Crocodiles Come Out?

CATHERINE LEM

✦ ✦ ✦

A Conversation in the Dark

Communication doesn't need
a common language.

WE HAVE BEEN SEARCHING FOR OUR HOTEL FOR OVER AN hour. Clutching a travel guide in one hand and a map in the other, Jessica and I huddle under a small umbrella squinting up at the unintelligible street signs.

We are in Prague just for this one weekend, a weekend to escape from our studies in Vienna. We are here just to be somewhere new, but our lack of planning as we grabbed a guidebook and a change of clothes and ran to catch the last train has caught up to us once we are unloaded one cold and rainy evening in Prague. Somehow we had expected Prague to be more like Vienna, with tourist-friendly maps and smatterings of English here and there. But as we leave the streets usually trod by tour groups and go off in search of an increasingly obscure motel advertised in our book, we realize that we are in trouble.

The night is getting darker as the rain lashes around us in the wind, somehow evading our umbrella and aiming straight for our eyes. It has gotten so dark that we have to stand right below the street signs to make out the Czech script and compare it to that on our map. For a long while we stand on that corner, staring blindly into the night through our dripping eyeglasses and debating whether we should go back near the tourist area and splurge on a hotel-room that is out of our price range but easier to find.

I hear the shuffle of footsteps nearby and turn to see an umbrella approaching, its owner hidden by the dark. My heart starts to thump as I considered our position—two young girls in a strange city alone in the dark.

"Is that a man?" I ask Jessica. She wipes her glasses and squints towards the figure and shakes her head.

"I don't know. I don't care, let's ask for directions," she begins to wave, "Hello! Hello!" The umbrella spots us and changes directions, coming toward us. I hold my breath until I can make out the hunched body of a small elderly woman shuffling toward us. This woman embodies all of the images in my head of old Europe. Her gray hair is pushed up underneath a brown scarf, framing her deep wrinkles and laugh lines. She wears a gray sweater that looks itchy but warm over a black skirt that goes down past her stockinged knees. Her shoes resemble little brown buckled boxes. She has a look of being left in the dryer too long that reminds me of Sophia from the old TV show *Golden Girls*. As she gets closer she breaks out into an almost toothless smile. "Hello! Thank you! Can you speak English?" Jessica asks.

The woman cocks her head, "*Blaho vecer.*" Jessica tries again, hello, can you understand English?... The old woman just smiles at us and begins to laugh, her solo tooth shining in the streetlight. "Ah, foreigners. *Tehe ar odesly?*"

"Foreigners, yes! We are foreigners! Can you help us?" I ask as the wind begins to pick up, ripping at the map in my hand and spraying us all with cold water. Jessica and I begin a dance of charades, indicating the motel's name in the book and pointing to the map, doing the universal confused shrug. The old woman watches us for a minute, clapping her hands and chuckling. She takes a quick glance at the book and begins to laugh more, shaking her head.

She takes my hand, still laughing, and we begin to walk. We go a slow turtle's speed through the wet streets of Prague. The old woman begins talking to us in a slow, slurred voice. We cannot understand a word she is saying, but her tone is soothing. She may have been talking about a million things, but her words wrap around me as we pick our way in the dark and I imagine she is telling me of her life, of years filled with children and strife, love and wisdom.

After a half an hour I turn to Jessica, "Where do you think she is taking us?"

Jessica jumps as my words interrupt the rhythm of our stately pace against the woman's voice. "I don't know," she answers as we continue on. The old woman lets out a girlish giggle at the sound of our strange words, and then she continues to speak. Her voice rises as she emphasizes some point, falls to an occasional whisper as she grips my hand. I can't tell if she is talking to me anymore or if she is talking to the night, using her words to fill the dark. Then she falls silent, and looks at Jessica and me with expectation.

I feel it is my turn to talk, and I begin to tell the old woman about my life in Vienna. How I am there to learn about the turning point in Austria before the world wars. I tell her about how I love Europe, how my whole self tingles with the discovery of a new café or while watching small children play in flower-laden courtyards. I speak of a lost love who I had wanted to share my travels with, and about how the beauty of light and rain dancing along cobbled roads makes me wish that I could explore new places forever. The old woman listens carefully as if she can understand every word. She smiles when my voice laughs and nods slowly when I turn morose.

Jessica goes next, talking about what she wants when we graduate from college. She tells about her mother and her boyfriend, and as I walk along with the woman's fragile hand within my own I stop listening to Jessica's words and turn my ears towards her sounds. We cross streets and alleys, the rain falls harder and softer and stops. I'm wrapped up in Jessica's voice and the old woman's shuffle, forgetting all about the map soaking in the puddle in my purse and the lost motel and the fear of the dark in a foreign city.

Then the old woman stops. Still smiling she points across the street to a small building, our hotel. She pats my hand and turns to touch Jessica's. Then with another beautiful smile she waves and walks away. She becomes just an umbrella and then fades away into the night.

Catherine Lem fell in love with travel on a high school tour of Italian cathedrals. Although sick of cathedrals, she contracted a bad case of wanderlust. Since then she has lived in Italy, Austria, Malaysia, and China, and traveled through Mexico and much of Europe. Currently, Catherine is traipsing around Africa, finishing her master's work in global health, and fantasizing about where the road will lead her next.

MARISA PEREIRA

* * *

Fasting in Paradise

Denial is the mother of pleasure.

ALL ROOMS WERE EQUIPPED WITH A COLEMA BOARD, allowing a safe gentle irrigation and cleansing of the colon. Filtered water was piped into the bathroom faucet—no more hauling buckets to the room for the twice daily coffee enemas. I was advised to do a pre-cleanse "fast" before my arrival at Spa Samui by eating mostly raw foods, salads, fruits, lots of vegetables, and to do a liver flush twice a day. A concoction of olive oil, lemon juice, garlic, ginger, and cayenne pepper, the liver flush was supposed to help my system be prepared for the seven day cleanse. I not only did not do the liver flush, but I also indulged in daily chai teas, curries and delicious fried delights such as *samosas* and *pakoras* during the last four months I spent in India prior to coming to *Koh Samui*.

I arrived at a tropical Thai paradise, slightly overweight, possibly with a few parasites from eating street food and an additional layer of dirt on my feet that would not go away no matter how much I washed them. Temple visits and meditation at ashram halls required bare feet on surfaces often covered by a film of ancient dirt that seemed not to leave devotees' feet easily. I had been taking care of the layers of dirt in my soul at temples and ashrams, now I planned to take care of the excesses in my bowels.

Spa Samui offered two types of resorts. The Beach Resort with thatched roofing and small bungalows was situated by the beach and the Spa Village Resort with large, air-conditioned bungalows was perched on the hillside with a direct view of the beach a few kilometers away.

Helpful clerks at the Spa Village Resort spoke fluent English and welcomed me in a beautiful reception area with satellite dish and comfortable sofas. Health magazines and books covered the surface of an enormous wood center table. There was also a health library attached to the reception area, and the resort offered dozens of classes and services including daily massage. I was ready for pampering. After checking into my beautiful room—a rustic, panoramic bungalow designed in old fashioned Thai teak wood, including a king bed and antique dresser, telephone and remote A/C—I headed to the restaurant. The spa boasted it was the best vegetarian restaurant in the island. I glanced at the menu. An extensive list of fresh and many raw dishes made me salivate and I hesitated about the seven-day Clean-Me-Out program I planned to do. I ordered raw vegetable lasagna served with macadamia nut dressing and Caesar salad, a fresh "softy"—frozen creamed mango topped with honey and cinnamon sauce and a raw fruit pie for dessert. It was like dining at my favorite San Francisco raw restaurant on a Thai island! My bowel movement would sure get regulated after a few days in this place, I thought.

After my delicious meal, I skimmed through the menu again. Rejuvelac Salad—cabbage, onion, and carrot shredded together and marinated in acidophilus; *gang phet saparot*—

pineapple chunks in coconut milk curry with veggies and tofu; raw energy balls with figs, walnuts, pecan nuts, and spirulina; fresh green drinks…yum, yum, the list was long. Then I looked at the seven-day Clean-Me-Out program: Intestinal cleansers, herbal nutrition tablets, and detox drinks taken five times daily, two colon cleansings at our personal colema board in the room, one flora grow lactobacteria capsule, veggie broth, and a packet of herbal laxative tea to be consumed during the week. The parasite Zapper, a small box that produced a 2.5 kHz (2500 pulses per second) output with copper handle endings was optional. It is known to kill organisms such as bacteria, protozoa, and other parasites like giardia that are susceptible to the frequencies of electromagnetic energy produced by the Zapper. This technique was new to me and I wasn't sure I needed it.

In case you are wondering about the colema board, here is how it works: one end of a board of about six-by-two feet is placed on top of the open toilet. A five-gallon bucket sits two to four feet higher than the board where the individual lies face-up. The bucket is filled with filtered water and coffee that flows down by gravity into the colon through an enema hose inserted into the butt hole. The water and waste flows directly into the toilet. It is sort of a home colonics and it lasts forty-five minutes to an hour. Repeated sessions are supposed to eventually break the old encrusted toxic waste loose from the lining of the colon. The coffee is known to give a good flush to the kidneys and help induce the toxins out of the body.

The Clean-Me-Out program is based on Richard Anderson's "Cleanse and Purify Thyself" book and it had been brought to the spa by a Californian who moved to Thailand. Anderson, a naturopath, describes a profound divine experience in his book, wherein a female divine being filled him with information. He states that purification is a guaranteed entrance into heaven and that people who are willing to purify themselves shall have the help of God's mightiest messengers and, if necessary, legions of angelic beings. I did not know what to think of the religious statements and the promises seemed far-fetched but I remembered the physical benefits were positive when I went through this cleanse before. I was sure my colon and intestines would appreciate a break from the bombardment of grease, caffeine, and excess food I had been putting them through for the last months.

As I remembered, my body was weak at first, sometimes I felt nauseous from the release of toxins and not much energy to do anything. But at the end of the cleanse, I felt an incredible light feeling, my eyes and senses were clearer and my energy level increased. Spa Samui seemed to provide me with a perfect setting for a cleanse but I still could not decide. Did I want to forgo eating for a week, and follow the strict daily cleansing routine? It was a hard decision to fast in the midst of such good food and to endure lack of energy in such a paradise.

I missed feeling light with energy and I could use losing a few pounds. In addition, I was curious as to how I would endure a fast with the temptation of so many edible delights and decided to take on the challenge. So, I signed-up and paid in full for the week's program in case I felt tempted to change my mind.

Koh Samui is a popular Island on the East coast of Thailand, surpassed only by Phuket in popularity. There was a lot of environmental degradation and development, including boutique spas like the one I was staying in. Deforestation and pollution generated by resorts damaged mangroves; the demand for coral souvenirs and irresponsible dive leaders who allowed customers to use harpoon guns put the 450 million-year-old coral reef at risk of destruction. The chemicals used to feed the prawns in their breeding pools and ward off disease washed back into the swamps, damaging not only the mangroves but also the water used for irrigation, drinking, and washing. I was glad that eating prawns was not in my plans but I had mixed feelings about being a contributor to the island's degradation by supporting spas and their fancy accommodations. I wondered if I would be happier in the smaller coastal villages, still untouched and not catering to tourists.

On the other hand, Spa Samui offered pampering and "new age" activities in a tropical setting that were hard to ignore. The spa recommended the Five Habits System to Longevity: cleansing, breathing, food combining, exercise, meditation and peacefulness, and it presented several possibilities to achieve it. Yoga, tai chi, and meditation were offered daily, in addition to a wide menu of services including massage and ozone therapy.

The Thai massage came in many flavors including wild mint oil, lemon grass skin toner, and tangerine ladies massage. They were ministered with precision and softness by the five or six smiling masseurs ready

---

L ast year at this time I was traveling in Laos. I spent my birthday and Christmas in the riverside village of Nong Khiaw. Food was scarce and I was lucky to be able to find a bowl of noodles. I was feeling one of those lonely pangs of homesickness one sometimes gets on the road, often during holidays, wondering what my friends and family were doing.

Just at that moment this small girl ran up to give me a beautiful pink flower, a gift from the universe. She didn't want anything in return, just handed it to me with a grin, and ran away. It's the most wonderful birthday gift I've ever received, and I still look at it taped in my journal, a reminder, that sometimes the simplest gifts are the most precious.

—Alison Wright,
"A Simple Gift"

by the mats on the long wood deck by the fruit trees. They pulled, stretched, and pressured points in my body and then applied my choice of oil to suit my skin. The herbal steam room with thirty-two Thai herbs filled my nostrils with pleasure and drew out impurities in my body. The aloe vera bodywrap smoothed out my skin and the ozone therapy helped me recover the oxygen lost in my lungs after breathing pollution and dust while in India.

The many amenities and distractions helped me not to think of food. The tropical swimming pool filled with purified water and natural salts instead of chlorine looked like a natural pond with moss edges and rock formations, and the adjoining decks were perfect spots to sunbathe and relax.

I watched up to four hours a day of Dr. Bernard Jensen's videos on nutrition, exercise, cleansing, and physical well-being. *Silica is the nerve force, magnetic energy. We are an electro magnetic being—alfalfa and watermelon are good sources of silica and potato peelings the best.* Dr. Jensen was amusing and knowledgeable. *The lymph system is composed of 80 percent sodium which keeps the joints young. Sodium is found in high quantities in whey from the liquid in yogurt, raw goat milk, and black figs.*

When I was not feeling nausea from the cleansing, I got into a golf cart and headed to the beach, three kilometers out at the Gulf of Siam. I enjoyed swimming in the salty water, breaking the waves, and doing a few laps—I was always prepared with my swimming goggles and hat—I loved the exercise. Sometimes I got a massage at one of the stands on the beach, other times I just hung out and drank freshly picked coconut water while I watched tourists dine at the restaurants by the beach.

The resort offered a Chinese tea ceremony in the afternoons, lead by Master Khong in a beautiful garden. The time I spent there helped me keep my eyes off the restaurant with its delicious dishes. It also gave me the chance to socialize with other guests, most of them of English descent, expatriates living in Hong Kong and Indonesia. We sipped the tea slowly listening to Khong's explanations about the teas' origins and properties. It was a three hour ritual and two tiny vessels were used by the guests: one long and one round—the long one was for sniffing, and the small round one for drinking. Master Khong used two little tea pots, one for brewing and the other for serving. This technique avoided the bitter taste of over-extracted tea. So delightful!

Unlike the Japanese tea ceremony, the Chinese one was more focused on the tea than on the ceremony itself—what it smells like, tastes like, and how it compares with the previous tea served. The only rule was to turn the long sniffing cup down when we had enough of a certain tea. This simple rule allowed me to stay in my body rather than my mind. We started with white tea that was poured into my long sniffing vessel. The delicate buds endowed with fine white pubescence did not have much of a smell, and I noticed a soft light taste as it quickly made it into my round drinking cup and down my throat. *Oolong is lightly fermented,* Khong would say as he poured the tea from the tiny pot into my long vessel, which I then poured into my round drinking cup after a quick sniff. Each serving was a couple of swallows of tea and my mind danced with expectation of what the next round would smell and taste like. Maybe this was the surrogate I found for my cravings for real food. The medicinal properties of these fantastic teas deal with issues such as tooth decay, digestion, fatigue, cancer, heart disease, and, of course, longevity. I loved sitting around sipping these precious teas and chatting with the expatriates. Johanna, an Englishwoman who lived in Jakarta with her husband, the owner of an export business, came to Samui once a year. Nelly and Julie, originally from

Australia, lived in Hong Kong for ten years. They were co-workers in the restaurant marketing business. I learned all about the best places to eat in Hong Kong in case I decided to stop there on my way home. They also came regularly to lose weight so that they could continue indulging in the best Chinese cuisine in their adopted home country.

Our days consisted of taking detox drinks, herbal supplements, coffee enemas, swimming, watching Dr. Jensen's videos, getting massages, and socializing with the guests. The pampering was great—one time I arranged for a masseur and a pedicurist from the beach to come to the hotel. Although I asked them to come at different times, they arrived together and insisted they could work on me at the same time. The pedicurist even found a way to speak with someone on her cellular phone while on "duty." It was so hilarious to see her filing my nails while the masseur stretched and massaged my leg, I did not care.

My last (and second) meal in this beautiful peaceful place was a breakfast of fresh papaya, dusted with goat cheese crumbs and topped with bee pollen, seven days after my arrival. My eyes were clear, my mind fast, my skin vibrant, and my feet finally clean. In a final touch, I purchased the optional parasite Zapper and held onto the copper endings for an hour a few times during the last days. I wanted to ensure I continued my travels solo. The large amounts of food I was eating before the cleanse could have been an indication that there were more than one of us getting fed.

Marisa Pereira took a yearlong sabbatical from her job with the government to explore the world and intensify her spiritual practices. She traveled through Europe, Southeast Asia, India, Thailand, Australia, New Zealand, and Japan doing pilgrimages, staying at ashrams and zen monasteries, climbing mountains, and occasionally indulging in a tropical spa. She found the world to be wide and large; a vastness, that to her surprise, caused her to switch the monastery walls and spiritual search to an ordinary life with a lover, a home, and a non-vegetarian diet. After 365 days on dusty roads around the world, she returned to her state government job in San Francisco where she lives and writes about her travels. She is originally from Brazil.

* * *

Fast Train to Paris

It's never too late to enjoy
that delicious spark.

I'M ON THE TGV—THE FAST TRAIN TO PARIS—TRAVELING with my husband, Brian, and my five-year-old daughter, Lily. It's the last leg of a two-week vacation through the French countryside, which began in the southwest region known as the Dordogne. There we spent a week with friends, sightseeing, swimming, napping, wine tasting, and feasting, and then the three of us took off on our own driving tour, heading east toward the Riviera.

All that second week, I felt as if we were on a bus and truck tour except the show on this tour didn't move, we did—losing our way in the Cevanne mountains and tiny Provençal villages, stumbling onward into hidden hill towns, consuming everything from delicious roadside tavern cassoulets, to four star, five-course dinners featuring organ meats. Our escapades were great fun, but by the time we descended into Nice to board the train, I was exhausted, and I knew I'd be just fine so long as I never saw another gallbladder floating in cream.

Sitting on the train to Paris, I sink with relief into my seat. Lily sits next to me, looking out the window. Brian is one row in front of us and across the aisle, sipping a glass of red wine and reading *The London Times*. As the train pulls out of Nice, I too look out the window, drinking in the beauty.

The train stops next at Cap D'Antibe, and I watch a young man in his late twenties sit down a few rows ahead of my husband, facing me. Normally these days, I pay little attention to young men; after all, I'm married, a mother, in my forties, and I live in Hollywood, California, where youth is a major commodity and heads don't easily turn unless you're a "10" in your twenties. True, everyone from my peers to the cashier at my local Trader Joe's (whom I love because he cards me when I buy a bottle of wine) assures me I look great for my age, but since I met my husband on a blind date over fourteen years ago, turning heads has held little fascination for me. That sport and vanity belong to a previous chapter in my life, a time when I was searching for the kind of love and attention I now have in abundance.

Still, this is going to be an extended train ride, so to amuse myself I rest my eyes for a moment on this slim young man with piercing dark eyes and elegant Roman nose. My exhaustion lifts as I become acutely aware of his long, dark ponytail, his prominent sideburns accentuating high cheekbones and chiseled chin that, together, complete a striking if not absolutely pretty picture. I pick up my dry literary novel and attempt to read so that my fixation on this young man isn't too obvious. Much to my surprise, when I glance up for one more peek, I catch this attractive young Frenchman checking me out.

I look over my shoulder to see who's sitting behind me, but the seat is empty. I look back at him and he smiles. I quickly bury my head in my book, but of course I'm not reading. I'm thinking about Brian sitting one row in front of me, completely oblivious. He wouldn't in a million years believe me if I told him a man almost half his age was flirting with me. I don't quite believe it either.

Twenty years ago, when I was riding slower trains through Europe, I sped from one adventure to the next; while Henri, my French boyfriend, pouted alone in Paris, I hiked the Swiss Alps, sunbathed topless at the Cote D'Azure and later, at the Italian Riviera, played football and other games with wild Italian boys. Finally I took pity on Henri and hopped a train back to Paris. I was cute and young and I traveled light—no husband, no five-year-old. On this trip, no one makes the mistake of calling me *Mademoiselle*; I am *Madam*, and every other moment I am "Mom," "*Mom*," "MOM!"

Behind my book, I close my eyes and see myself at twenty-four. I have perky breasts and a flat stomach. Henri and I are dancing on a balcony under a Paris sky to music playing somewhere deep inside his house. I press my body against his, and we kiss as a full moon rises. He pulls away to look at me, and says, "We do very well together." I smile, pull him close, and whisper, "Yes, we do," and our lips touch again.... "Mom!" My daughter yells into my ear. I startle awake.

I escort Lily to the snack car because she's hungry and "needs" something sweet. As we trundle through the cars, I feel sluggish and pudgy. Too much *fois gras* and *duck confit*, I sadly acknowledge. As I lay out plans for the diet I'm going to start when I get home, I'm not even thinking about the young Frenchman, but there he is, standing right behind me in line. I assume this is but a coincidence until he smiles at me without even a glance at my adorable little girl.

I smile back.

Wow. Is he actually interested? Could I possibly still have some allure? I can't let this opportunity for adventure pass me by—can I—maybe for old times' sake?

As we wait in line, I strategize. After I buy a bag of milk chocolate wafers for Lily, I'll turn to Dark Eyes (that's what I decide to call him) and whisper *attendez ici*, (wait here, at least that's what I think it means), but of course that won't matter much, we'll hardly be speaking. I'll lead Lily back to my husband and ask him to watch her while I "freshen up." I'll return to the snack car, motion Dark Eyes to follow me, and I'll lead him to the lavatory—no, no, too small, too smelly—I know, remember that movie, what was it—where Frank Sinatra and Janet Leigh fall in love between train cars? That would work. O.K., I'll race back to the snack car and motion Dark Eyes to follow me through a door that says *N'ouvert pas*, but we'll open it anyway, and there we'll be, between the cars...

And then what? I can't even begin to imagine. Twenty years ago it was all so easy—spot cute guy on train, smile, sit down, talk, coffee and cigarettes when we disembark, a good-bye kiss or, if he's interesting, an afternoon making love in his humble-if-oh-so-romantic *atelier*. But now, now that I have Dark Eyes out there between the train cars, with my husband and child a train car away, what next? Do we simply start making out, whispering into each other's ears, "*Je t'adore*?" Do I throw myself on him? Do I help him unbuckle his pants, pull up my skirt? This is crazy. The conductor could come by, or my daughter could come searching for me when Brian accidentally falls asleep. Then what? I imagine Lily gazing through the window, seeing her mommy's thighs wrapped around Dark Eyes' hips. And let's not even think about the condition of those thighs. No! I won't think about Lily or my thighs. I won't think about anything except that I want this—and no, it's not suitable for The Family Channel. Yes, I unbuckle his pants, yes I pull up my skirt, yes I press against him, and yes he wraps his arms around me, and yes I feel him inside me, and yes I devour his mouth as he devours mine, and yes all the passion that exists within me wells up and, Oh God—the motion—of—the train—has never been—more acute—never more—exciting.

I jump as someone taps my shoulder. I turn, my eyes blinking rapidly, attempting to regain focus. It's him, Dark Eyes. My knees begin to quiver. The train slows to a stop, and Lily grabs my leg, trying to recover her balance. I know how she feels. He points to the man behind the counter. It seems I'm holding up the line. I hastily pay and turn back to Dark Eyes. "*Excuse moi,*" I say, embarrassed—for various reasons. "No problem, Madam," he says, a glint in his eye. Oh God, is he psychic? I blush and turn away.

My daughter and I head back to our seats. Dark Eyes follows. We sit, and as he passes, he leans toward me and whispers into my ear, "*Bon journai.*" "*Merci, vous aussi,*" I mumble demurely, as I look into his eyes before he straightens up and moves on. I watch him walk down the aisle, and as he sits, I see him greet a pretty girl who has taken the seat directly across from him. They begin an animated conversation. Instantly I feel abandoned—forgotten. What does she have that I haven't got— besides a defined waistline?

I look over at Brian. I have to laugh; he has indeed fallen asleep, his newspaper scattered on the ground at his feet. Lily finishes a drawing, places it on my lap, and says, "Look, Mommy, look." I admire her work and give her a hug. She hugs me back hard, then kisses my cheek before beginning her next fete de accomplishment. My heart melts, as does my need to relive my youth. I pick up my book and find the place where I left off—I decide it's not dull, just challenging. The train begins to pick up speed, and over the intercom the conductor informs us that from here to Paris, we have no more stops.

Cheryl Montelle is a Los Angeles-based writer whose stories have been published in the online magazine, DivineCaroline.com, and in the anthologies, Deliver Me: True Confessions of Motherhood, Raging Gracefully, *and* Cup of Comfort for Mothers To Be. *She has also been published in* Fresh Yarn, Seven Seas, On The Bus, Rattle, Moth, *and* Spillway. *She is a member of The Los Angeles Poets and Writers Collective and presented a self-published collection of short stories and poems called* My Life and Paul McCartney *at the UCLA Book Fair through the Collective. Cheryl also performs her stories at spoken word events around Los Angeles.*

SERENA RICHARDSON

⋆ ⋆ ⋆

Castle Beds

She wanted to be eighteen again,
but a lot was lost in translation.

"I WANT A CASTLE BED IN THE TOWER," I ANNOUNCED
to *Luciano, waving the brochure. How romantic!"*
    "Top or bottom?"
    "Excuse me?"
    "A 'letto a castello' is a bunk bed."
    "Oh. Um, listen, don't tell anyone I asked you that."
    "Absolutely not."

I shifted the weight of the pack a bit to get some circula-
tion back into my shoulders and moved deeper into the meager shade provided at the train station. This plastic backpack,
an imitation leather item abandoned at the school's lost and
found, was an important prop to this adventure of mine.
Without it, and forced to use a conventional suitcase, I would
not have been able to complete my fantasy. Now I stood,
alone, a forty-five-year-old woman in the scorching August
sun, impersonating a vagabond teenager roaming the Italian
countryside looking for adventure. What a gas.

A garbled voice came over the loudspeaker and I could detect a shiver of anticipation in the crowd. We were three and the train, one of the few to actually stop at this one-platform station outside of Padova, must be arriving. Montagnana awaited.

Treviso, my new home near Venice, was an hour away, yet it felt as if it were on a different planet. There I was a student on a break from school, the proud owner of a maroon one-speed and learning how to be a girlfriend, all over again. It had been over twenty years since I had so shaken up my life, twenty years of stressful, life-consuming, back-stabbing, yet familiar, corporate work in California. Having left all that behind and in a virtually unknown language and land, everything was different.

Here I existed in a bubble as I slowly adjusted to life, I suspect, in part, a result of the protective fretting of Luciano, my brand new Italian boyfriend. Just beyond this bubble of security was a gray hazy world, which I could just make out, but couldn't yet process. Like the first days at elementary school, everything looked bigger, the distances farther and other people smarter. Who knew what was happening on the second floor; I was still trying to figure out homeroom. For me to venture out alone, one floor up into the next grade so to speak, was a monumental undertaking.

Luciano had helped organize this trip by making the reservations and worrying. He could not join me, nor did I really want him to as it was important for me at this point to be alone. After six weeks of my depending on him for pretty much everything, and six weeks of intensive Italian classes, I needed to get back some of my familiar independence. I wanted out of the bubble, and to take this new language out for a spin.

I stepped out of the grubby station and surveyed the broad blank boulevard that began abruptly in front of the cracked cement steps. I began the long trek to the walled city ahead of me, an aging Dorothy entering Oz, clad in khakis and tennis shoes. The gates, which once withstood invading Longobardi and Visigoths, were open and expectant. Hopeful even. My guidebook billed this as one of the few completely fortified towns in Italy and in fact, it was magnificent. I turned left after entering and walked the few paces down the winding cobblestone street lined with deep porticos and sparse shops. The road ended as promised at the tower embedded in the wall, and at the reason for my choosing Montagnana to begin with. For housed in the tower above the gates, which open onto the road leading to Verona, is a youth hostel, complete with winding stairs, bunk beds, and the answer to my nostalgic quest for solitary adventure.

The wooden door creaked open and a young man looked up from his magazine. I stood there, allowing my eyes to adjust to the cool darkness of the castle, in my dorky shorts, tank top, and shit eatin' grin.

"*Io ho un prenotazione,*" I said in my lousy brand new Italian.

"*Sì. Nome?*"

"*Serena Reech-ard-sonn.*"

"*Eccoci qua.*" Here we are.

He rattled off a few sentences explaining, I am sure, the rules. I understood precious little except that I could expect to be alone in the room that night and that I could use the ticket he gave me for breakfast in a local bar. The most important stuff. He handed me a skeleton key large enough to counterbalance the weight of my pack and I headed for the women's dorm, lurching up stairs that spiraled through the medieval tower. I peered through the narrow openings designed, without a doubt, as a place from whence to shoot arrows. Now, they were just openings for the welcome breezes that shot through them in puffs like a carnival game.

The women's dorm room occupied an entire floor of the tower, with windows on three sides and a dozen sturdy metal bunk beds. The lofty ceiling was braced with beams in which 500-year-old ax marks could be seen. I leaned out the window and closed my eyes. The late afternoon light fell on my face with welcome warmth; the sun, fat and red in the sky, having done its damage for the day was slipping behind the trees on the road to Verona. I liked saying that: The Road to Verona. I imagined a group of riders setting out on that road below the castle, nothing but farmland and danger stretching between this walled village and the promised romantic city at the other end.

Later, lying in the top bunk of the empty room, I flipped open my phone and called Luciano. His voice, tinny and small in the crappy phone, was pleasant to my ears. We spoke little, but I missed him, the distance softening my edges. I said goodnight and lay on the bed gazing up at the massive beams. Outside the side-show windows, I could hear the occasional incongruous passing car on the road to Verona. Otherwise, silence. Surrounded by empty castle beds, I was truly on my own, the "real" world forty feet below me and a million miles away.

I awoke early tingling with excitement and feeling eighteen years old. I had grand plans for the day: a short train ride to Este and then a hike to the medieval town of Arqua Petrarca. I reread the passage in the guidebook, "walkable in about an hour by the back road." With my ridiculous bag packed for the day, I swirled down the stairs to earth. The manager was at the reception and in our salutations he asked about my plans. When I cheerfully explained my destination, his wide, affable face froze.

"You cannot walk that road."

Being a stubborn woman, I took this as a challenge, not a friendly warning. "Sure I can. The guidebook says it is a lovely walk. Don't worry!"

He shook his head, waved goodbye and, perhaps not expecting to see me again, turned to the guest book to confirm I had paid up for the night.

The town of Este is famous for its ceramics, not a trace of which I saw in the otherwise pleasant town. But while I wandered its streets, the manager's warning kept playing over in my head. I looked again at my map and rethought the adventure. Darn it. Resignedly, I tracked down the bus station and purchased a ticket for Arqua Petrarca. Then, assured by several passersby that I was at the correct place, I stood expectantly, and alone, at what appeared to be a widening in the road and nothing more. A bus arrived and slowed as the driver peered out at me. I looked at him expectantly, but I guess I wasn't interesting enough as he gunned the engine and disappeared down the road in a cloud of exhaust.

I stood there for almost an hour, mulling over the whole idea. Had I misunderstood some key information? More often the norm than the exception, when I did understand something everyone was surprised, especially me. And maybe the charming town of Arqua Petrarca was not my destiny. Perhaps I didn't really need to go there. When one is alone, the luxury of internal conversation is a deliciously absorbing and time consuming one and I jumped when a bus roared up with its doors already open. Startled, I stepped up and said, "Arqua Petrarca?"

"*Sì,*" the driver grunted at me, closed the door and pulled hard at the steering wheel. Wow. I was on my way.

My fellow passengers on the crowded bus swayed from the leather ceiling grips. I was surprised that the bus was so full.

Why were all these people going to this little town? I began
to have suspicions. Moments later, when we pulled into
Monselice, I knew why: I was on the bus to Padova. I moved
to the front and spat at the driver, "You told me you were
going to Arqua Petrarca! Why did you mislead me with such
blatant mendacity! Have you no respect for my desired destination? You are a disgrace to your country and bus drivers the
world over!"

Well, O.K., I am sure it was more like: "Arqua Petrarca no!
You lost time me. True not. Where now he go?" But I must
have expressed the seriousness of my situation enough to
make him feel bad as he scrambled to suggest alternative solu-
tions, none of which I understood, but I was not going to
Padova. "Let me off this bus!" I said imperiously. The doors
swung open and I exited into the dust.

This anger carried me off the bus, through Monselice, and
to the outskirts of town where the rage petered out and I
looked up for direction confirmation. I saw a sign with an
arrow: ARQUA PETRARCA 4 KILOMETERS. I can do that, I
thought. Just to be sure, I waved down a passing man dressed
in a coat and tie, carrying a briefcase. It struck me as odd for
someone to be walking the weed-lined road dressed for a
board meeting, but he probably thought similar thoughts of
me for he too paled when I asked him for directions.

"You cannot walk that road!"

I sighed. There was no turning back now. "This is the way,
correct?"

"*Sí.*"

Thanking him, I hitched my backpack into place and
started out. The countryside was beautiful, wide and open,
with oceans of corn baking in the sun. I was eager to be on
my way.

Thanks to the bus driver, I was now approaching my destination from a different, albeit closer, starting point. However,
I soon discovered the reason for everyone's concern. With absolutely no shoulder on the road, I had to leap off into the
high grasses each time a car whizzed by, going way too fast for
such a small road if you ask me. I imagine I provided entertainment for the drivers, but I could see the promised hills getting closer. I kept going. After a kilometer of dodging death,
I took a long pull on my water bottle and turned onto the
long stretch of road leading to the base of those hills. Here
there was no traffic at all for they were resurfacing the asphalt,
a more hideous job in the oppressive heat I cannot imagine.

The surface of the road shimmered in the heat and I could
see mirages of swimming pools, cabanas, and pool boys in the
distance. These turned into incredulous construction workers
in torn, sweat-ringed t-shirts, sitting on chugging, hot, tar-
laying machines. My water was disappearing alarmingly fast as
I slowly placed one sticky foot in front of the other, furious
that I was providing, yet again, entertainment during what was
usually a boring day of repairing tarmac. I pulled my hat down
farther on my head and began to think in survival terms. Did
I have any food? Could I suck water from the vegetation along
the road? What was that buzzing in my ears? What were the
early signs of sun stroke? I imagined them finding my corpse
sometime in September, face down in the tar, with my
pleather backpack melted to my body.

With an inch left in my water bottle, I reached the end of
that road. The construction workers, disappointed that the
show was over, shrugged and returned to work. A new sign
appeared: ARQUA PETRARCA .80 KILOMETERS. Hmmm. Why
such an odd distance? Nothing made sense. The road went up
now and suddenly there was a slight breeze. One foot in front

of the other, around the bend, uphill, again. Were I not on the verge of throwing myself in front of the next passing car, I might have noticed the stretch of fertile farmlands in swirling ribbons of gold and green expanding below as I climbed. And then abruptly, a sign swam before my sunburned eyes: WELCOME TO ARQUA PETRARCA in three languages. I had arrived in the damn charming town.

Pleased to have survived, I never stopped moving. Glancing left and right at the few sagging medieval stone houses, I walked straight to a miniature park where an old man stood in a rumpled white shirt, watering the sturdy flowers. He wordlessly handed me the hose, having most assuredly seen victims of the guidebook before. I drank long and deep. The water was tepid, but as I bent over in the sudden shade with water moving over my face, I felt life surging back into my limbs. Panting a thank you, I handed back the hose and he, with a grin, pointed in the direction of the ice cream shop. The guy was reading my mind, but I had to do something else first.

"Tickets for the bus to Este?"

"Next to the ice cream shop." He smiled again and said, I think, "See you later."

Twelve minutes and two ice creams later, I was standing at the "bus stop" which consisted of a rusted chair in the grass. Across from me at the only intersection in town sat the gardener, along with two friends, in a row of similarly rusted metal chairs leaning up against a stone house. He waved at me and smiled. His friends waved.

"*Buona fortuna!*" they called.

"*Grazie. Arrivederci,*" I answered.

I had spent all of fifteen minutes in a town I risked my life to reach. Had I ignored the words of warning from the outset, I could only blame myself and the guidebook for my folly.

Now, I could pin it on the two bus drivers who had put me in this predicament, so I felt better. With a full water bottle and fortified for what was sure to be a long journey back to Este, I stood and gazed at the entire town in front of me. O.K., now that my heat-swollen brain and feet were returning to normal shape and size, it was indeed a pretty village. Suddenly a bus roared through the narrow street and came to a screeching halt before me.

"Este?"

"*Sí.*"

I took him for his word. What else could I do? My cheering section watched me enter and take my seat in the blissfully air conditioned bus. I turned to wave and then hung on as the bus careened around the hills I had just labored to cross. We screamed across the fields, and twenty minutes later, the bus pulled into Este. It had taken me three hours and a year off my life to reach what took this driver twenty minutes to cover.

I limped into the hostel in Montagnana and the manager looked up, not disguising the surprise on his face.

"Well, hello! How was it?"

"Great! Beautiful. But perhaps not worth the walk, really."

He nodded in silent agreement, giving me the dignity to stagger up to my loft without further comment.

I peeled the pack off my back, stripped down to flip-flops, and ducked into the vast communal shower one floor down. This being eighteen again was wearing thin. Especially when I noticed that another woman had arrived and I no longer had all twelve beds to myself. But after a shower and fresh t-shirt, I felt ready to wander the streets in search of a glass of wine and something *tipico*. Later, sitting under a breezy portico with a glass of the local pinot grigio and a plate of prosciutto di Montagnana wrapped around sweet local melon, I felt pretty darn cocky. I dug around in my bag for a black felt-tipped pen, took out my guidebook and carefully crossed out "Arqua Petrarca, the gem of the Colli Euganei." There, gone.

Yes indeed, I was in charge of my world.

Serena Richardson is a freelance writer and English teacher originally from Northern California who is now living in Mareno di Piave, a village in Italy about the size of an Oakland strip mall—but with more history. She writes of her life in the Veneto and indulges her delusion of being a photographer.

KATHLEEN HAMILTON GÜNDOĞDU

✶ ✶ ✶

Measuring Cups

Sisterhood comes in all sizes,
shapes, and ages.

"*Dios mío!* Mom, get them out!" I felt like I was being manhandled by an octopus. Yelling and trying to dodge groping hands, I knew I was cornered with no place to go.

The dressing room was small to begin with, and with four matronly women squeezed into it with me, it was downright claustrophobic. This was not my idea of a vacation—half naked and crammed into a cubicle with only a piece of light-weight cotton hanging down serving as a door. Please let this be over soon! I thought.

"Now Honey, just behave. They know what they're doing. It will be over in a few minutes and we can go to the pool," my mother casually replied as she continued to browse through the racks of the lingerie store. My already fragile teen body image was being assailed, as my breasts kept getting prodded, pulled, pushed, measured, and thoroughly examined by more people than I cared to have them exposed to.

What had brought me to this? I wondered. Why, of all places, did my family have to choose Acapulco as our annual

Thanksgiving destination? We were the only American family I knew that each year decamped here for an extended stay instead of staying in Texas and having a nice, normal Turkey Day. My friends were home getting ready to enjoy a bird and all its accompaniments, but tonight we'd have our usual holiday meal. Every year it was the same thing—red snapper served with beans and rice and flan for dessert—eaten while watching the cliff divers tempt fate with each leap of faith into the surging surf below at la Quebrada. It took me a long time to understand exactly what Thanksgiving was about. For years I thought it had something to do with Pilgrims jumping off cliffs like lemmings. No wonder kids at school thought my family was weird. After the dressing room experience, I really was looking forward to my usual watered-down piña colada with dinner. That might well be the high point of my day.

Acapulco in the '60s was still a beachside village. There were two large hotels in town—the Presidente on the beach and the pink and white bungalows of Las Brisas spread out across one of the hillsides above the sleepy village. We stayed at the Presidente only once. My mother was terrified of the lizards that crawled out of the drainpipe when anyone showered. The scorpions that wiggled under the doors leading out to the beach were another deterrent. After nights dodging the wildlife in the rooms, we vowed to never stay there again. The layout of Las Brisas suited our family much better. My parents had a bungalow to themselves, as did my brother and I. The bungalows were grouped in twos up and down the hillside, with a small private swimming pool between every two cottages. The added plus of staying there were the pink and white jeeps provided to guests as a courtesy for trips around town and the surrounding coves.

The fact that Las Brisas was rumored to be a getaway for a few Hollywood jet setters wanting to soak up the sun and have private rendezvous with or without their spouses was another draw. We would check the large main pool in the morning for celebrity sightings, but always came away starless. Acapulco was not yet a destination for the masses of gringos that would one day descend. This was a getaway for families from Mexico City. The bay had no cruise ships disgorging tour groups or private yachts vying for space. Instead, there were a handful of small fishing boats and the occasional Mexican Navy ship docked for a few days. In fact, there were usually only a handful of foreign tourists in town—most came for diving in the still shark-infested crystal clear waters of a nearby cove or for deep-sea fishing further off the coast. Many of the gringo tourists were moneyed, wanting to be off the beaten track, but with some degree of comfort. Mexican families drove here over the mountains, risking the roads that washed out in the rains, for a getaway from the hustle and bustle of Mexico City. This was still an exotic destination for foreigners, with an airport consisting of a Quonset hut next to a tarmac strip that was about an hour drive along a two-lane road across a mountain. Sometimes the trip to the airport could take longer, depending on how heavy the donkey cart and truck traffic was that day.

My mother had a love for all things Mexican. At home in San Antonio we spoke English and Spanish. Our maid, Juanita, moved from northern Mexico to Texas, and spoke only Spanish, so we learned Spanish with a northern accent from her. Our living room,

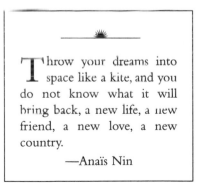

Throw your dreams into space like a kite, and you do not know what it will bring back, a new life, a new friend, a new love, a new country.

—Anaïs Nin

dominated by a huge brass Aztec calendar hung above the fireplace, reflected my mother's love of Mexico. Flanking the fireplace were two large brass candlesticks bought in Mexico that were more suited to a cathedral than a ranch-style house. The exposed roof beams, painted Pepto-Bismol pink, added to the tropical feel of the décor. The bar off the living room was my father's rendition of a border bar—complete with papier-mâché parrots hanging from the ceiling, a slot machine, and a painting on black velvet of a topless woman we referred to as his "blue-eyed Mexican."

In Texas, our home was often the setting for a full-blown fiesta around the backyard pool, complete with a mariachi band blaring away while guests from all over Mexico mingled and sipped margaritas. Many of my parent's friends were wealthy Mexican landowners and bankers who jetted into San Antonio by private plane to pick up the latest fashions and whenever they were in town they dropped by for a visit. Professors and their families from the University of Mexico campus in downtown San Antonio were also frequent guests. My mother took classes on Mexican culture and history at the university, all given in Spanish. On weekends, if I were lacking anything better to do, I would join my mother and sit in on classes with her.

Living in south Texas, Mexico was an easily accessible place for vacation—whether in the mountains, deserts or beaches. We lived just outside San Antonio; a city immersed in Mexican culture, and had Spanish and English idioms inter-woven into our speech. I grew up hearing stories of witches who changed into animals, spells cast against foes or to bring love, the Virgin of Guadalupe appearing to peasant children, and of conquistadors who tried to conquer ancient, refined cultures with brutality. Mexico was an important part of our lives as we spent large parts of the summer exploring cities and villages in the interior. We often drove through the desert to reach Guadalajara and Guanajuato. The monotony of the dry, brown northern desert was only broken by the sudden appearance of a brightly garbed child by the side of the road holding up an iguana, tortoise, or large brown desert rat for sale. I never did find out if these were meant for pets or dinner. My parents, knowing that I would want one as a pet, always refused to stop to investigate. Trips to Mexico City and Monterrey were taken in a private plane that my father co-owned, with my mother sitting in the front, acting as translator between air traffic control and my father, who had only learned very basic Spanish.

Thanksgiving weekend offered my mother yet another chance to visit Mexico. Airfares were low and my brother and I were allowed out of school for a couple weeks, promising of course, to bring our books along and do homework to turn in on our return. My teachers thought that it was wonderfully exotic and exciting to have a student who traveled to a place they had only seen in the movies. A little over four hours by air and we were away from San Antonio and basking on the beaches. Little did they know that we weren't hobnobbing with movie stars. Instead, my brother and I played in the streets, parks, and beaches with the local children. Because we knew our way around town, and knew how to take taxis and buses, we were allowed to roam as we wanted, the only requirement that we be back at the hotel and dressed for dinner. We were often to be found lying on the beach under the palm frond palapas, drinking warm sodas bought from passing vendors. The shopkeepers remembered us from each year and measured our growth as if we were long lost relatives. A sort of extended family grew up from our visits. My parents knew that my brother and I could be let loose to roam as we wanted because everyone would look out for us. If there was a problem or emergency, the village was small and my parents could be found quickly. So, for the most part we were left to spend our days as we chose swimming at the beach, flying kites with local friends, and nosing around the shops to see if there was anything new that we just couldn't live without.

At home we were each in charge of packing our own suitcase for the trip. If we forgot something we could probably buy what we needed on arrival. On this trip, however, I forgot to pack undershirts and found out that girls in Mexico didn't wear undershirts. My mother and I searched the shops around the *zócalo*, or plaza, but to no avail. The dusty plaza stores offered a collection of jewelry, fruits and vegetables, shoes, clothing, and trinkets. After sitting under one of the many palm trees shading the *zócalo* and sipping watermelon juice, we went into the lone lingerie store. It was midday, and many people were home for siesta, but there still were a few women out shopping for goods for the evening meals they would soon be preparing. It was my packing oversight that brought me to my current dilemma. My breasts, much to my thirteen-year-old chagrin, had been slower to develop than many of my friends', and so I still wore undershirts. But, after discovering that they were not to be found in Acapulco, my mother and the saleswomen in the lingerie shop decided that it was finally time for me to graduate from undershirt to my first bra. This decision drew whoops of laughter and comments of encouragement from the sales force about the rate of growth of my soon-to-be breasts. Suspecting that something interesting was happening inside, other women came in from the *zócalo* to see what the fuss was about. Fifteen or more women of all shapes and sizes surrounded me. An elderly woman dressed in black cackled with delight at the spectacle of this shy teen-aged gringa being fitted for her first bra.

Taken to a tiny changing room in the back of the store I was quickly divested of my shirt. Measurements were taken as I was poked and prodded by all interested onlookers. Predictions about my growth were pronounced as I stood semi naked and embarrassed. "Not to worry, I was the same way, slow to develop on top," one woman told me. "And now look at me! *Dios mío*, without support they would hang to my knees!" She laughed, grabbing her breasts and jiggling them for emphasis. A woman yelled across the room, "With those breasts you could feed an entire village, my sister!" "She has nine children! She did feed a village!" another voice chimed in. The room was filled with laughter at that comment. I was amazed that middle-aged women could act this way. My mother certainly would never grab her breasts in public. Mesmerized, I could only watch and listen to this display of female camaraderie that I had never experienced before.

The realization slowly set in that for these women this was not just a form of entertainment, but they were involved in a rite of passage. "Geez, the first bra must rank up there with first communion," I thought. As my mother continued to browse, the women compared notes on their breasts—development, ailments, aches and pains. Every one of these women had been a young girl shy about her body too. They knew what I was going through at the moment, and through their stories and actions they showed me that they understood and cared. In their eyes, I was entering womanhood, and they, as *comadres*, or co-mothers, due to the fact that they knew me from our yearly visits, were witnessing together my rather slow advancement into their world. They were here to cheer me on and encourage me. Teen angst slowly gave way to fascination with these women. My mother, continuing to browse, listened in on the conversations, but didn't join in. "Is she uncomfortable with her body like I am?" I wondered.

After measurements were taken and approved of by all concerned, the selection of an appropriate bra ensued. My mother, who was not one to discuss body parts or functions easily, had thought that we could quickly come in, find an undergarment, and go back to the pool. However, she too began to catch some of the excitement of the moment as she helped sort through the undergarments brought to her for final inspection. "Too frilly, too stiff, too much support, not enough support" she said judging each one brought to her. Each was carefully examined before being put in either the "maybe" or "reject" pile. "Ay, I remember when I was your age. The world waited for me," sighed one old woman. "*Es verdad,*" said another, "all too soon though we were wives and mothers. Now we watch our children and grandchildren grow and dream of their futures."

A brassiere was finally found that met everyone's exacting requirements. It was made of soft cotton with light padding and a minimum of lace. "The padding will give encouragement to your breasts to grow more," clucked a middle-aged matron. Before being allowed to put my shirt back on, though, I had to model it for everyone. "*Ojalá,* God willing, you are now a señorita, no longer a *niña,*" sighed a crone dressed all in black. Smiling back at her I wondered if she was remembering her youth.

My mother paid for the purchase as the women hugged me to their breasts and pinched my cheeks. "Just wait until next year," one woman laughed, "you'll be back needing a much bigger size!" "Yes, my dear, you will soon have bigger chi-chis to try and keep out of the hands of boys!" giggled another matron. The women adjusted their clothes, rewrapped their woven rebozos around their shoulders, and wiped away the tears of laughter. Dignified, proud, and once again solemn, the women were ready to go back and finish their errands. Who would suspect that these women were jiggling their breasts and laughing so hard they cried just moments before? My mother shook hands with them all and thanked them for their help.

I watched as we all left together, a group of women of all shapes and sizes going about their business. I realized that I didn't feel embarrassed anymore. Instead, I felt proud to have been included in such a group of women. These women were joined by a common experience, and they had just included me in it. I saw women who know who they are and who are comfortable with their body image. "*Ojalá*," I thought to myself, "I hope one day I'll have the confidence they do. I hope I can measure up to them."

Kathleen Hamilton Gündoğdu, a displaced Texan by choice, has been a chef, roofer, secretary, bookkeeper, international meetings planner, editor, fundraiser, textile dealer, and writer. She has traveled the world extensively, often with her young son in tow. She is currently a contributing writer for numerous magazines, including Hali, Modern Carpets and Textiles, *and* Time Out Istanbul, *as well as being a correspondent for* Today's Zaman, *an English-language newspaper in Turkey. Her stories are included in the anthologies* Tales From the Expat Harem *and* Mexico: A Love Story.

GALE RENEE WALDEN

* * *

Pilgrimage to Jackson

*The South is America's dreamland
and unconscious.*

THERE ARE SECRETS IN THE DEEP SOUTH. IT'S SOMETHING I've always known. Secrets a Yankee can't know and yet still wants to consider. The moss seems to go up and down: how can something do that at once? Nothing really right can do that at once. How can a place live inside another place and still be separate? There were more than one of these riddles to solve in my childhood and some of them involved my own South Side neighborhood of Chicago, a place that my mother referred to as the Old World.

In 1962 we had moved from the central Illinois prairie into the city and it did seem as if we had entered another world. Many European languages mingled on our block. The babushka women swept the outside sidewalks every day; and there were vendors who pushed carts up and down the street calling out their wares for sale, but if you walked half a block to 63rd Street, you could see the modern world beginning in the storefront shops: there was Pixie's Café, which served olive burgers; there was a card shop with little blown-glass animals and cards and Slinkies in the back that the owner let kids play with while the moms shopped. The shoe shop on 63rd Street was called Jack O'Day's. The guy who ran it had the name of Jack and sometimes he would put himself in the huge shoebox he kept in the middle of the floor and jump out at us. Bill was the butcher and twice a year, dressed in white, he brought over a quarter of a cow to put in our freezer.

Most of the Polish, Irish, and Lithuanian immigrants in our neighborhood had the Catholic Church in common; my father was a Methodist minister, and that more than anything else defined us to ourselves and to our neighbors. On Saint Patrick's Day, the Protestants dutifully wore orange to school, a color, which even when you are very young, is not flattering to light skin and additionally, even in the public schools, dotted us as minorities in a sea of green.

If the South was a foreign country far away, Catholicism was the foreign spiritual country living next door. The Catholics had Saints and a Jesus who refused to leave the cross even at Easter. The Catholics got to choose fourth names when they got confirmed: names of a saint they admired, and they could keep these names secret from the rest of the word. My friend Karen chose Bernadine, a choice I didn't understand aesthetically but that I was jealous of anyway. Nothing about Methodists was hidden, nothing about us was secret; if the Catholics were involved in mysterious rituals where wine (real wine) actually turned to blood, the Methodists were, well, methodical. The gospel was to be read and the lessons applied to the world in which you lived, in the time period in which you lived. The liquid at communion didn't even change to wine but remained grape juice. The stained glass windows where angels floated through the air with trumpets were pretty much the only concession our church made to a spiritual world that somebody interested in Peter Pan might want to inhabit.

As I grew up, I got tutored in Catholicism through a combination of saints and open guitar masses and the television show *Dark Shadows,* which all the Catholic kids watched religiously. But I was dependent on literature to inform me about the South.

Eudora Welty's place in my imagination was a mystery even to me—I'd read the work of Flannery O'Connor much more thoroughly than that of Welty. O'Connor was working with both my mysteries: the South and Catholicism, a merger that mystified even people within those respective populations. I had to return to the work again and again and yet the only image I ever had of O'Connor was symbolic, a peacock more than she herself, perhaps a testament to her Catholicism, where there isn't necessarily distance between metaphor and actual thing.

Eudora Welty was a Protestant, more ambiguous about her use of symbolism.

Tonight a sheared slice of moon has us mad to talk and watch as it makes its way over the great hill of the sky.... Drinking kava makes us want to tell stories. I knew we would tell stories eventually.

As we tell our stories, the beach fills with life, with passing shapes lost in mist, and with color. The sand underneath us becomes the vast and timeless desert of North Africa. The trees above us creak and moan like the trees on the coast of India. A wind blows up from New Zealand. Wind chimes in Burmese villages whisper through the woods. Puffs of clouds off in the distance and over the ocean become the Himalayas, the Andes, the Urals, the Italian Alps. The people we describe in our stories come to life and sit here with us at the fire. Tales are spun and woven deep into our souls. We listen spellbound, anticipating and dreaming of these places far away, these beautiful mysterious places.

—Laurie Gough, *Kite Strings of the Southern Cross*

There was something mythic about her, but simultaneously familiar and intensely human.

It was she who allowed me, even at the heights of feminism, to consider the courtesy title "Miss" when referring to someone over eighteen; she who allowed me that much access into the South. When she died on July 23, 2001, I felt a profound sense of loss as if something large had passed not only from the world, but from my much smaller world. The PBS eulogies and newspaper obituaries inevitably compared her to Chekhov as a master of the short story and then went on to report on who was attending Katharine Graham's funeral (who had died two days earlier). I started to wonder about who was attending Miss Welty's funeral. I called the Millsaps College English Department and was told an open funeral would be at Galloway Methodist Church in Jackson the next afternoon. I decided, uncharacteristically quickly, to take the fourteen-hour trip south on the Amtrak, which if Amtrak was on time (a big if) would get me into Jackson in time for the funeral and in time to return to Champaign on the five o'clock train. I would be in Jackson for five hours. When I called my parents to tell them I'd be out of town for a couple days and where I was going, my father said, "Galloway Methodist? That was one of the churches." I hadn't thought about the arrests for many years, and hadn't even located them in a specific city, but I knew immediately what he meant, and I paused. "You should go," my father said.

In the early 1960s, my father, Don Walden, was becoming increasingly involved in the Civil Rights Movement, which was breaking out mostly in the South. It was still a foreign country, still far away from us at that point, but on World Communion Sunday, October 6, 1963, three students from Tougaloo College, two black and one white, were arrested as they sought to enter Capitol Street Methodist Church in Jackson, Mississippi for morning worship. The story made national news, and because this was a worldwide church, and because a Tougaloo College Chaplain named Ed King had requested outside help, a lawyer and four Methodist ministers, my father included, drove down to Jackson in a station wagon. It was the beginning of a journey which ended with all four ministers incarcerated in the Jackson County Jail, and the lawyer, Lee Rayson, calling on two prominent New York attorneys, William Kunstler and Arthur Kinoy, to fly down and to argue that the case be tried in federal rather than state court.

The ministers had been warned they would not be welcome. On Saturday they met with local pastors and argued their case for an open church. They were told they would be arrested if they tried to accompany the "visitors" to church the next morning. The next morning twelve people (the four ministers, seven Tougaloo students, and a Tougaloo professor) were arrested at three churches, including Galloway and Capitol Street Methodist Churches. Bail was set at $1,000 for students and $500 for pastors and professors.

Back home, I was six and none of it made any sense to me. My father was in jail. Our parsonage was right next to Chicago Lawn Methodist and in back of us on 63rd Street was a Chicago Police station. "Your choice of redemption," my mother had said the day we moved in, standing in the back alley, her arms extended in benediction toward both the jail and the church.

I had seen the drunks, the handcuffed people going into the police station; I had heard the fights and the guns going off which no one would ever talk about. Though my mother tried to tell me that my father was in jail for doing something good not bad, back home in our neighborhood, letters starting arriving, some from the South, most from within Chicago, some of them nasty and threatening, some of them more considered, almost all of them using the word "meddling." I felt the beginnings of what I now know to be shame, but at the time couldn't label.

My father returned home a week later. The Methodist church had posted bail money and I thought maybe that would be the end of that. But it wasn't. It was the beginning of something else. Bill the meat man said, "That's the last time you'll get any of my cows," and the woman in the gift shop hid the Slinkies when we came in and Jack never again jumped out of the shoebox at us. After that, only certain people let their kids play with us. And, in 1966, after Martin Luther King marched in our neighborhood, and the American Nazi party came in to march against him along with many of our neighbors and there were riots and cars overturned and gun shots, and King later said he had never experienced such hatred; after the ministers in the area had opened the doors of the churches symbolizing welcome and sanctuary; after the rocks came through the windows of the parsonage, lobbed by people who used to be friends; after the children had to be sent away for a while because of threats; after we moved to an integrated neighborhood; after Martin Luther King was shot and I saw my father cry for the first time; after he said, "I've had enough" and asked for a transfer to an all black church; after one morning in church when a white person came into the sanctuary in this black neighborhood in this black church and I ran to my mother terrified and furious to demand, "what's he doing here?" and she said, "probably worshipping," and I said, "but he's white," and she reminded me that so was I; after the Methodist church did not take a strong stance against the escalating Vietnam War; after my father temporarily but for a good long time left the ministry; after all that, we went to Disney World. Which is in the South.

I may be the only child in existence to have resisted this trip. But to my mind the South was where all the *Afters* started and my personal fantasyland was in the *Before*. But as a child you go where your parents take you and we flew down to Florida not only to see Disney World, but also to pick up a finned 1961 Chevy Impala from my grandfather. Driving back through Georgia and Tennessee, on two lane highways, shanties to the side, people on porches waving bandannas at us in our old futuristic car, the South felt exotic and dangerous and permanent, as if once you stood on one of the porches, you could never leave. I was glad to be moving, glad to be contained, glad to be headed north.

But at ten the night after the day Eudora Welty died, I boarded the Amtrak and fell into the sleep that is particular to the train, a rocking sleep, punctuated by long deep whistles, by trees and churches and convenience stores floating by you in what appears to be a dream. When I awoke at seven and looked outside, I knew we had passed over into the South. Outside there were swamps and moss and inside my hair had started to curl itself into ringlets and maybe even grow.

By the time I was in college, the nontexual sources from which I had taken my images of the South were: the Allman Brothers eating a peach on a porch and the movies *Deliverance* and *Cat on a Hot Tin Roof*. The rest of my references were from books: *Their Eyes Were Watching God* by Zora Neale Hurston, *To Kill a Mockingbird* by Harper Lee. All of the short stories of Flannery O'Connor plus *Wise Blood*, *As I Lay Dying*, by Faulkner, *The Member of the Wedding* by Carson McCullers, and the story, *Why I Live at the P.O.*, by Eudora Welty. I had read other of Welty's short stories and, later in college, read her novel *The Optimist's Daughter* and the memoir *One Writer's Beginnings,* but it was *Why I Live at the P.O.* that I incorporated into my imaginative Southern world.

The obvious reason for this choice was that the story involved mail (which I am fond of) and that it was funny. It was an unusual humor: slapstick mixed with the absurd mixed with dry wit—Uncle Milty meets Monty Python. But there was also something more complex: a turn at the end like in a sonnet. There is a point in the story where the character of Sister, who has left her seriously dysfunctional family to go live at the post office where she works, says that she wants the world to know she's happy and if her sister Stella-Rondo should come to her on bended knees, and "attempt to explain the incidents of her life with Mr. Whitaker," that she (Sister) would simply put her fingers in both ears and refuse to listen. Sister has, until this point, been to my mind one of the more reliable narrators of events in this family of eccentric characters but she loved Mr. Whitaker herself, and her stubbornness contrasted with her deepest desire leaves the reader questioning the reliability of irony. It is not completely unlike the turn at the end of Faulkner's *Absalom, Absalom,* where Quentin replies to Sheve's question about why he hates the South: "I dont hate it,… I dont. I dont." To the sophisticated reader, this declaration seems a textbook case of denial, and the reader loftily can say, "Me thinks thou dost protest too much," but part of the riddle is an off-chance the denial might be true, that nobody is privy to the deepest part of character, not the character and not the reader and perhaps not even the writer. It is this particular layering that seems resolutely Southern, this particular layering which makes me question my own perceptions of geographical character.

In my real life, after the Florida trip, before this trip to Jackson, I had only been south again twice, and both times I was extremely aware of racial and regional protocol. I flew into Atlanta in 1994 for a convention and because I had recently seen *Gone With the Wind* for the first time, I was especially self-conscious when it occurred to me in the airport that my tapestry luggage looked an awful lot like a carpetbag. But Atlanta is a cosmopolitan city, nothing like the pillaged Hollywood set, which anyone not as faithful to their imagined cities might have guessed.

A couple years later, I drove to Memphis to write on Elvis impersonators at Graceland, among the handicapped Elvi and the Vietnamese Elvi, I was most aware of the black Elvis, who looked so much like Elvis reversed, with the same features but dark skin and white hair and white sideburns, that the white photographers dubbed him "the negative Elvis," as if he was a photograph yet to be developed.

That is another way I knew, even on the train, that we had entered the South: the picture of race was different. In the dining car I sat near a blond woman who was actually wearing jewels on the Amtrak and who called the black waitress "doll" over and over again and everyone involved seemed to accept this with good cheer and with what appeared to be a genuine fondness and I again felt like I'd entered a world where I didn't understand the rules. In Chicago, this same encounter would not have been likely to engender fondness and might even have caused a fight.

In Jackson, the train station was in the process of being seriously renovated, but I found a washroom and changed into a beaded vintage dress from the forties, and the highest shoes I could walk in because that seemed like appropriate attire; there was a fashion differential in my imaginative South that I wanted to match.

The street outside the train station was a street in decay, and yet behind the decay were remnants of a more elegant downtown. Across from the train station there was a skeleton of the Edwards Hotel and the façade was gorgeous, even in ruin, perhaps because of the ruin, with vines growing out of verandas and iron balconies suspended on crumbling brick. To the left of the train station, underneath the train viaduct, I saw, as if looking through a window, a neighborhood of damage that lacked even decaying beauty. It was a window into blight, a porthole into a past that keeps rotting, an opening that people turn their back to in order to walk in the opposite direction toward the newer buildings and the newer downtown. This was the direction I walked also.

The Galloway Methodist Church looked a little like the White House, replete with stone steps and pillars. Although I arrived early, there were already people milling about. I found a childcare center in the basement where I dropped my bag and then wandered about the church. It was huge and I walked around once before settling in the balcony to listen to music piped out of the big organ. As the church filled up, I noticed that there were indeed black people in the congregation. The Galloway web site, in fact, advertised itself as a church for all, although its history section skipped from 1959 to 1969 with a perfunctory understatement, "There was some civil rights upheaval." The service itself was so resolutely Methodist that I felt at home; the prayers and hymns of my youth were so deeply familiar that I also felt the pain of the church divided against itself, much in the same way my father must have felt about it thirty years ago.

Bishop Clay Lee gave the sermon. If you've listened to many sermons in your life, you know it's an art form, not unlike poetry. And this guy was one of the best I'd heard; he not only managed several telling and humorous anecdotes about Ms. Welty, but also spoke more eloquently about the purpose of fiction in life than I'd ever heard any academic do. It also occurred to me as he recounted the years of his friendship with Ms. Welty that he was probably there, on the other side of the divide, when my father was arrested.

Lee compared Welty's examination of people to New York Yankee great Yogi Berra, saying, "In 1963, Berra was told he would be the team's manager the next season and spent that season observing the players and their moods." Continuing on, Lee made a connection between Berra and Welty through Jesus, saying, "Isn't that what Jesus told us to do...not to look for the obvious in people but for what's inside them? And wasn't that really the talent of Eudora Welty? She helps us not only to understand ourselves but each other."

Like a good poet, a good preacher encodes, and I don't think it was insignificant that Lee referred to the year 1963 via a non-racial reference, and one that was a stretch of sorts. Eudora Welty, who lived in Jackson almost all her life, had herself said in interviews that it was a year when many times she picked up the telephone to strangers asking her why she hadn't spoken out more, or written more against the atrocities going on in Mississippi, to which she replied, "It's not the type of writer I am. Whatever wrongs there are, I want my stories to show them as they are, to let them speak for themselves." The only time she ever wrote out of anger, she has said in *One Writer's Beginnings*, was on the night Medgar Evers was murdered in Jackson. The story entitled "Where is this Voice Coming From?" was written in first person from the murderer's point-of-view. Ms. Welty went on to state that she didn't know if the story was "brought off"; and that, "I don't know that my anger showed me anything about human character that my sympathy and rapport never had." Whatever moderation Ms. Welty showed, it wasn't enough for some, and the week of her death an internet "Nationalistic" web site which celebrates the deaths of all civil rights workers, cheered her death also, and criticized her for not leaving the Galloway Methodist Church along with fifty percent of the congregation when the church finally integrated.

After the service, I had time to go to the cemetery and I was joined in my walk by a woman who taught at a college in Jackson. I told her portions of my story, and she told me about writing in Jackson and we got lost. By the time we arrived at graveside, in a cemetery caretaker's truck, whatever service held there was finished, although the coffin was still suspended in air. I saw the first person I recognized, a Southern writer whose work I admired and we spoke briefly. And when I saw Bishop Clay leaving, I took a deep breath and actually ran after him. People surrounded him, but he turned toward me and took my hand as I introduced myself. I told him how much I enjoyed his sermon and then I said, "My father was one of the ministers from Chicago arrested here in 1963," and his face actually fell with kindness. "I was in Philadelphia," he said (which I first thought was in Pennsylvania but later learned he was speaking about Philadelphia, Mississippi, a town itself given to church burnings in those years), "but I remember it well.... It was a difficult time." There was something in the way he said it that made me think it was for him, too. "Thank you for coming," he said, "and thank you for coming up to me."

The story of my journey made its way around graveside, and as I was leaving, a woman approached and introduced herself as a relative of Ms. Welty, and said, "Eudora would have loved that you came," and it was one of the better things anyone has said to me in my life.

A reporter and her friend offered me a ride back to the train station. "You dressed perfectly," the reporter told me and the other woman said cattily, "Did you see what Kay Gibbons was wearing?"

Back at the train station (which during renovation was a trailer) the train was late, hours late, hadn't even left New Orleans, five hours away. Almost everyone in the trailer was black, except for myself and one older heavyset woman, hair in curlers, cane in hand. I was nervous here somehow; I felt like we were in the midst of a Flannery O'Connor short story, in some waiting room and that someone might suddenly say something untoward, causing somebody else to throw something. I didn't want to be the person who said the thing that caused the throwing and I was silent until a man across from me introduced himself as a music professor at Southern Illinois University and said, "I knew you were a teacher too," and we forged some alliance in the trailer waiting room which had nothing to do with race but everything to do with class or at least education. Because I had once been in music school, because his daughter attended the university at which I teach, we were deeply involved in the game where two strangers try to figure out the person they know in common. It is a game much like connect the dots. We appeared to be getting close when on the other side of the trailer someone loudly asked, "What else you have in you?" and I looked up and over and saw a pleasant-looking, middle-aged black woman questioning a younger woman who had a baby in her arms and three small children at her side.

"What else you have in you?" the woman repeated. "Indian?"

The younger woman smiled and nodded.

"I could tell by your hair," the woman informed her. "I have Indian in me, too, from my Granddaddy. And I think I have some French in there someplace, too. We're all mixed."

She turned to the woman beside her and repeated her question, "What else you have in you?"

Everyone seemed to take this conversation as mundane, something to talk about waiting for the train, and I got the same topsy-turvy feeling I get when I look at that moss that hangs up and down. That maybe everything wasn't secret here, maybe it was even more open.

On the Amtrak, an attendant with dreadlocks told me he could tell I was a good spirit, and professed horror when I said I'd never been to New Orleans where he lives, he said I'd love it, said he lives in the Old Slave Quarters. "It's very spiritual," he said, and at the same time I was thinking, how can that place be spiritual? I was also thinking, O.K. maybe I'll go.

When I got home, I told my father about meeting Bishop Clay Lee. "I remember him," my father said, "he was considered something of a liberal." When I later read in Charles Marsh's book, *God's Long Summer*, that Bishop Lee too had counseled strongly against the church visitors, my father sighed and said, "Well as Dick Gregory said, being liberal in Mississippi in those days meant lynching from a lower branch."

But in truth it meant more than that; there were many Mississippi ministers who went out on a very different limb, and many who left the state or the ministry, as well as those who wavered longer than they should have. The Gospel that offers redemption and change doesn't always necessarily offer it quickly, or without consideration of personal history and regional politics. In subsequent research after my trip to the funeral, I felt happy when a parishioner in Philadelphia recalled hearing, in 1964, a white minister speaking on the radio urging a stop to the violence after a bombing of Mt. Zion Methodist Church and it turned out to have been Clay Lee, and also chilled when it turned out on June 21, 1964 that Michael Schwerner, James Chaney, and Andrew Goodman stopped to change a tire in the parking lot of the First Methodist Church of Philadelphia (Rev. Lee's church) and it was in this parking lot that they were arrested, an arrest which led directly to their murders.

None of it is easy territory to negotiate, going back and forth into a history that wants to be forgotten into a present that is still trying to determine where all the bodies are buried.

The ties that bind aren't always of Christian love, but can be forged through literature, or through chance meeting and they are messy.

What I do know is that at that graveside, I felt a loosening of something I hadn't forgiven. When I introduced myself to Bishop Lee, the part of my character who now attempts to enter the layers of the South was introduced to the character who, sure of geographical innocence, only wanted to hover above that story—a self who has been stating for many, many years: I do hate the South. I do. I do.

Gale Renee Walden has been published in Prairie Schooner, Fiction, *and* Mid-American Review. *She was the 2002 winner of the Tenth Annual Boston Review Short Story Contest for her story "Men I Don't Talk to Anymore." Gale teaches in the low residency program at University of New Orleans.*

ANNA BRONES

* * *

The Tuesday Pineapple

The simplest transactions
anchor the memories.

"QU'EST-CE QUE TU VEUX CHÉRIE?" WHAT DO YOU WANT
dear? The large woman in a long skirt and sweaty, red tank top
asks. Her hair is pulled tightly back into a bun. Wisps of coarse
hair stick out from beneath the tight elastic

"*Bah...je prendrai des ananas comme d'hab.*" Umm...I guess I
will take pineapple as usual. It's funny that we are having this
interchange; she knows exactly what I am after.

"*Tu vas les manger aujourd'hui n'est ce pas?*" she questions
with a twinkle in her eye asking me if I am going to eat them
today. She already knows the answer.

It is Tuesday morning. I am standing in the daily market
of Capesterre Belle-Eau, a town physically located on the
southeast side of the island of Guadeloupe and symbolically
located somewhere between France, the Caribbean, and the
middle of nowhere. This is what I do every Tuesday morning. My weekly routine, not only to buy the week's practical
vegetables and two pineapples that will quite impractically be

consumed in one sitting, but also to stand in a space where I feel safe and relaxed.

In a village where I am one of the only tall, white, blonde women, the safety and security of the market is welcoming. Here there is no cat calling or whistling from unknown men proving their machismo. In a society warmed by the sun, men are often "overheated" and remarks go as far as *"tu es délicieuse ma belle,"* You are delicious my beautiful. Even local woman are commented on in a vociferous manner. A male friend of mine tried to ease my frustration when I once mentioned my dislike of the uninvited "hello beautiful" that I hear so often. *"Mais ils ne le disent qu'aux femmes belles!"* But they only say that to women who *are* beautiful. His thought was nice; he had genuinely tried to make me feel better. I was not reassured.

Here in the market however there is no macho-inspired *"bonjour ma belle"*; there is only the softness of *"qu'est-ce que tu veux chérie?"* which feels as gentle and loving as if it came from my own mother. Instead of my usual hurried pace, used to dismay possible admirers, I for a few moments raise my eyes from the ground to look around me. Here my only interchange is between this Guadeloupe woman and myself; she a motherly figure, her hands cracked from working in her garden and I, the somewhat insecure, white English teacher.

I do not even know this woman's name, nor does she know mine; by definition she is a complete stranger. She welcomes me however; greets me with her warm smile and my cherished pineapples, like a plump grandmother holding a tray of freshly baked cookies to an anxious five year old. The effect is calming. As she sits on her well-worn stool, putting together bundles of thyme, parsley, and green onions, she embodies maternal essence.

"Et ton chéri, il va bien? Il travaille aujourd'hui?" She is asking if my "sweetheart" is doing well. He must be working, she

adds, noting his absence. She is referring to my boyfriend who graciously made the move here with me, knowing perfectly well that we would feel stuck in the middle of nowhere and that I would be uncomfortable in the male dominated society.

The two of us usually come together, a young white couple in a Guadeloupe market full of old farmers and fisherman; clearly out of place, and even more so when I come alone. After a step inside the open-walled building and towards the selling space of my "market mother," this ceases to matter. She knows that I belong; Tuesday is my day.

The first few weeks in town we were assumed to be tourists on vacation from France; since Guadeloupe is a French overseas *departement*, there are many of those. When Tuesday morning evolved into a weekly pilgrimage, she realized we were not merely on vacation. Since then she has opened up. After a two week vacation away from Capesterre Belle-Eau we returned only to hear "*Je pensais que vous etes parties.*" I thought you two had left. There was a twinge of happiness in her deep voice realizing that she had been wrong.

With a bag of tomatoes, a bag of cucumbers, and her popular bundle of thyme, parsley, and green onions in my canvas market bag, she knows there is only one thing left: my pineapple. The object that grounds me to this new place that I call home, and causes me to appreciate the tropical sun and rain that fluctuate in a natural dance nourishing the earth. Through the fruit that she so carefully chooses for me, I find something that I love about this society. The sun-soaked ground is not only home to overheated, overfriendly men, it is also home to a maternal warmth that is available to anyone, no matter where one is from.

The purchase feels like an indulgence every time, mostly because I know that I am incapable of eating only part of it. Fortunately, she often sells me two pineapples for the price of one, noting that a small section of both of them may just be a little too ripe and possibly brown and that I should chop that part out. Sometimes both fruits are devoured in an afternoon.

These pineapples are nothing like the round, green, spiky fruits that make their way to fruit stands and grocery stores north of the tropics. They are skinny and narrow, elongating at the top where the dusty green leaves jet out in a bold manner. *Ananas bouteille* they are called in French: bottle pineapple. A dark yellow at the base fades to a softer tone in the middle and finally to light green at the top; blended watercolors left over on an artist's palette. These pineapples have no barcode-imprinted sticker, they are in their original form; authentic like their vendor.

The market is my solace. For a few short minutes the rest of the world turns off and my senses are only capable of noticing the fruits and vegetables that lie around me, spread out on canvas sheets like offerings to the gods. I am alone in a cool, white building overlooking the sea with only the sounds of voices discussing the state of bananas and the morning's fish catch surrounding me.

My watch reminds me that it is time to leave; a trip to the supermarket for more substantial goods calls before the midday rush. I am forced to leave my Tuesday morning temple. I leave my unknown woman, who on some level provides me with enough maternal energy to make me not miss that of my own mother's, far away from this island. She smiles as I leave. I realize there is no need for names between us. I know that she will remain there on her well-worn perch, a calming constant in the everyday uncertainty of my daily life here, and most importantly, she knows that I will buy pineapple on Tuesday.

Anna Brones is a seasoned traveler passionate about culture and adventure. She lived in Guadeloupe for seven months while teaching English, during which she discovered her love for fresh pineapple and bananas and also learned that she prefers cold weather during wintertime.

✦ ✦ ✦

Waiting to Die

She experiences a very different
approach to life's end.

"You want to see the bodies?"

"Madame, you want to see the fires?"

"*Achi,*" I replied, because for a while I thought that meant "maybe." Now I don't think it means anything, literally. It doesn't translate into anything. I guess it really means I'm a clueless white girl muttering a meaningless phrase that sounds similar to "good" in Hindi which is "*acha.*" So I still say *acha* a lot and people seem to like it. Or, more likely, they just like white women. The non-literal translation of *acha* is "please take a moment to admire my breasts" because it seems like people think I say that a lot. Or they think I say "I am white and therefore love seducing Indian men, please brush my ass as you pass."

"Come, I show you. No money."

"No money," I repeat firmly.

"No money," he insists.

No money? Really? I had at least been around long enough to be skeptical of any free offers. Especially here in Varanasi, where spirituality is for sale on every corner and the white people are hot to buy it. Maybe he sensed some vague spiritual connection with me. I did have my head shaved to the skin, Indian straight-razored to be exact. I felt like it gave me some strange street cred. Like I must be deeply spiritual or else totally insane to throw away my feminine features so callously. Having your head shaved seems to make you look like you're good at things even if you're not. It just means you have balls, which I guess deserves a certain amount of street cred in itself.

I said again what I think means "maybe" and he heard "good" and started to walk, motioning for me to follow, and for some reason I decided to follow him down a dark winding alley. At home I would probably not follow a strange man down an alley on the promise that I would see bodies, but I didn't mind leaving the bustle of the main streets, overcrowded with hordes of cycle rickshaws and cows. Besides, he was really old and about a foot shorter than me, so I figured I could take him. He had big haunting eyes, like so many Indians, and wore a slightly tattered button down shirt and similarly worn brown pants and flip-flops. His hair and bushy mustache were gray. I hiked my flowing skirt a bit and followed him as he deftly dodged the massive piles of cow shit. I almost lost him while stopping to watch the monkeys leap through a tangle of wires from a tattered overhang to another rooftop. The children we passed playing in the alley stopped their games to stare in half suspicion, half delight at my strange white face.

A group of men turned a corner carrying a body over their heads on a bamboo stretcher with a bright red-and-gold cloth draped over it. They swept past me as I clung with my back to the stone wall and were gone in an instant before I could absorb the feeling of being in the presence of a dead body. I stared, slack-jawed, in astonishment and the group of men who happened to be lazily staring at me chuckled at my shock.

"Body," my little old man commented matter-of-factly with a slight smile and a head tilt. Life and death coexist more happily here than in the West. There is no one to keep the dead away from the living, or the shit away from the food.

Wandering on through the lanes, the stone buildings were browns, whites, grays, but also warm yellows, dusty pinks, and cool blues. Most were plain and boxy, but an occasional one had ornate arches and detailed decorative roofs, left over from the glory days of the Raj. They were usually two or three stories and all sloppily connected. The ground was also sloppily connected and strewn with random steps and holes. The narrow little streets twisted sharply, revealing a tiny Hindu shrine or a vendor tucked into dark shops that were literally a hole in the wall. Some had giant scales for weighing something unseen, others huge smoldering cauldrons, others had beautiful silks floating into the alley on the hot breeze,

---

So beautiful have been the days of this year. I have seen a love that would be one with the humblest and most ignorant, seeing the world for a moment through his eyes. I have laughed at the colossal caprice of genius; I have warmed myself by heroic fires and have been present at the awakening of a holy child.... My companions and I played with God and knew it.... The scales fell from our eyes and we saw that all indeed are one and we are condemned no more. We worship neither pain nor pleasure. We seek through either to come to that which transcends them both.... Only in India is the religious life perfectly conscious and fully developed.

—Sister Nivedita
(1867-1905)

others tiny Ganeshes or wooden toys. Some called to me, "Madame! Have a *loook*! Looking is free!" All stared as I passed.

Inside the little shrines idols wore their orange marigold garlands in various stages of decay and the incense snaked into the alley, filling it with an eerie haze and a potent smell. Wading through the thick hot air of the holiest city of Hinduism was like a weird dream. I started to feel the spirits I never thought I believed in. Gradually the incense faded into the familiar sticky stench of cow shit that was in turn replaced by the smell of a different smoke. It was drifting from the river and enveloping us as we ambled on toward the source of the smoke.

"Da bodies. *Looook*." He pointed.

There they were. Bodies, maybe seven or eight, burned on little piles of wood and their smoke filled the air. They burned all day and night my guide explained with a head wobble, "all the time burning." We had emerged from the maze of alleys on to the ghats. All along the Ganges, the holiest river in India where the water is fabled to have come from the feet of Shiva, are exotic cone shaped temples and steps leading down into the water. Some are bright pinks and yellows. This was Manikarnika Ghat, the burning ghat. Here all the temples were dark and loomed menacingly over the river. The smoke was overpowering and made my eyes burn behind my oversized sunglasses.

"Dis way, Madame," beckoned my guide, my last connection to the world I had known before stepping back into what seemed to me like Biblical times. The dusty scene reminded me of the illustrations from *The Bible in Pictures for Little Eyes* that had mesmerized me during long hours of church as a child. If I was stuck in a time warp this guy might be my only way back out.

He led me toward a larger concrete building lined with stacks of different kinds of wood used for the burnings. We crept up a dark flight of steps and came out in a big, open concrete area with a roof, like a covered porch. It looked out onto the river and was totally empty except for the old women on the floor.

"They wait to die," he commented nonchalantly.

They looked just like I would have expected someone waiting to die to look: scraggily gray hair, emaciated, draped in faded robes. One woman reached out and clutched my hand. Her robe was so loose I could see her sagging breasts and prominent ribs beneath it. There was almost nothing left of her but giant sad eyes. They crouched on the floor watching with a powerful stillness what would be their fate in a matter of days, maybe weeks. She didn't say anything, just squeezed my hand with her bony fingers. They were begging for money to buy enough wood for their bodies to be burned. I squeezed her hand back and put some rupees in it. We both returned our gaze to the bodies that she would soon be joining.

I kept thinking about my great grandmother Mabel back in her Alabama nursing home. Her left leg was amputated and a machine did her breathing for her. Although she got to watch *The Price Is Right* at an unreasonable volume while she waited to die, she wouldn't have had to wait nearly so long in India. Instead of the concrete floor she had an adjustable bed and carefully monitored food and temperature. And everything was kept wrapped and sterile, and the walls were a crisp stark white. Death is denied for as long as possible. It's well concealed and carefully wrapped when it does arrive.

"Loook, a child," said my guide. "They do not burn. Too pure."

The boy would later be weighted down and sunk in the river from a boat. The same would happen to pregnant women and holy men.

The old lady and I watched silently as a young boy was

dipped into the river strapped to his bamboo stretcher. The thin gold cloth clung to his body and face, revealing the sallow outline of his cheeks. I drew in my breath sharply, as they gently pulled the cloth away from his face. It looked like a doll's face, still perfectly formed, but stiff and pale. The men of his family gathered around him and poured the holy water into his lifeless mouth with small clay bowls. The women don't come to burn the bodies. "They make too much cry," explained my old man.

At another pyre a body had just finished burning and the men closed the ritual by dousing holy water over the ashes. They formed a motley assembly line from the river to the body and passed a clay pot from one to the other, filling and emptying it several times. A frail little old man stood closest to the pyres and dutifully poured the water onto the body. He dressed in white robes and had his head shaved as signs of mourning. He must have been the husband or father or brother of the dead. As is the custom, for the final pot of water he turned away from the body and threw the pot over his shoulder so that it shattered into many pieces. The pieces of clay and the ashes and the holy water all lay together. He lurched forward as if it took all his strength to push the pot from off his sunken shoulder and onto his beloved. The other men took both his arms and helped him stand. Very slowly, he walked away without turning back.

It occurred to me that the sound of the pot shattering was the first sound I had been aware of for a while. I had been so immersed in the sights and the smoke that the breaking of the pot was so loud in my mind it was as if it woke me from a dream and reminded me that everything I was watching was real and was happening right before me. Hot tears streamed down my cheeks and mixed with the salty sweat covering my face and body.

I felt like I was tripping. Like the place was ripping through me while I sat motionless and let its power consume me. The incredible beauty and awful hideousness of life and death, totally raw, washed over me. Sickening and gorgeous. In the same vista, smoke billowed up from charred bodies and just beyond it little boys in their underwear playfully jumped off ledges into the river, splashing and squealing with delight. Steps away from the mourning families several beggars stood knee-deep in the water and panned for gold from the fresh ashes. They quietly scavenged for bits of riches. Gold teeth, nose rings, maybe a toe ring. No one seemed to notice or mind. Those bathing for cleanliness intermixed with the ritual bathing sadhus, the frolicking boys, and the cows calmly cooling off in the brown, murky water. The women, fully dressed, waded down the steps and into the murk, gossiping with their bright saris clinging to them. The men, however, were free to strip down. I got caught staring at one having his morning bath. He made direct, awkward eye contact as he vigorously lathered up his ass with both hands beneath his loose underwear. I jerked my head to the next image, a little boy scurrying toward us with a kettle roughly as large as he was.

In India, I happily replaced my coffee addiction with chai and was excited to hear him yelling, "Chaichaichai! Chaichaichaichai!"

"Chai, Madame?"

Still wiping tears from my face with my sweaty palms, I smiled at the barefoot little vendor.

"Please. *Teen*," or three, in Hindi.

Even in the stifling heat I loved the sweet, milky hot tea. I bought a three-rupee cup for myself and one for my guide and another for my old woman waiting to die. He grinned at me, poured from his giant kettle, and hurried off leaving us with the delicate clay cups. I held the cup in both hands and closed my eyes, letting the sweet steam cover my face and the smell of black tea replace the smell of burning bodies. My old woman nodded once slowly in acknowledgment and we sipped together, still watching the parade of life and death pass before us. It was the best chai I'd ever had. I didn't know what to do with my little clay cup when I was done. Should I take it back to the boy so he could use it again? Or should I give it to the old woman? She didn't seem to have a lot of possessions. I handed it to her warmly, if a little confused. She took the cup from my hand and threw it onto the ground, where it shattered. Her thin lips spread into a wide toothless grin as its sound broke the silence and woke us both up inside.

Christina McCrory is a nomad masquerading as a grad student in speech/language pathology. She grew up in Alabama, got her B.A. at Louisiana State, and started grad school in New Orleans, until Hurricane Katrina hit and gave her a chance to take another year off and travel to Mexico and India. She has returned to New Orleans and is giving grad school and semi-permanent residency another shot.

PAT WALKER

✦

Taking the Cure in Bulgaria

*A cleansing holiday needn't
bust the budget.*

A SELF-CONFESSED SPA JUNKIE, I'VE BEEN SLATHERED WITH bright blue clay during the infamous turquoise wrap at the Golden Door. I've been blissed out by hot stones placed between my toes at The Orchid. I have huffed and puffed my weight-loss way up hills at the Oaks in Ojai. I've tried every mud bath in Calistoga and even splurged on the overrated champagne facial at the Sonoma Mission Inn. So when I decided to visit Bulgaria on the recommendation of some travel savvy friends, I couldn't wait to check out Bulgarian health spas. I was in for a big surprise. Serious spa goers in Bulgaria don't come to knock off a couple of pounds or get their pores cleansed—they come to cure what ails them. And *the cure* is mostly in the water.

With more than five hundred natural mineral hot springs throughout the country, Bulgaria's therapeutic spa treatments involve either drinking, soaking, or swimming in the water, and are said to cure many modern-day ailments: kidney stones, rheumatoid arthritis, chronic colitis, eczema, bronchitis, varicose veins, asthma, obesity, chronic constipation—even sterility. Oh, and did I mention cellulite?

This magic water is clear, colorless, and almost flavorless. Out in the Bulgarian countryside, it shoots out of rocks or bubbles up in muddy pools. In the cities it pours out of ornate spouts in the main square or trickles from fountains near the public baths. And it comes out hot. Hot enough to burn your fingers. I drank so much of it—cooled off, of course—on the "more is better theory" that I later needed a curative treatment for a very bloated stomach.

Nearly five thousand years ago, the water must have intrigued the early inhabitants of the area, as villages and towns sprouted up around the hot springs. Legend has it that in 200 A.D. invading Roman soldiers stopped to bathe their wounds in the warm, soothing springs near what is now Hissar. Later the Roman emperor Diocletian constructed a fortress around Hissar, and built splendid villas and ornate marble baths, creating the first Bulgarian health spa. The crumbling fortress walls and ancient marble baths are still there.

In the twentieth century the Communists would build huge, block-style hotel spas around the mineral water (and mud) where Bulgarians could enjoy a spa holiday for just a few leva. After the fall of Communism, many locals can't afford the new hotel spas and have to make do with public baths or take their families to bathe *au naturel* in the rural hot springs.

Whether they live along the Black Sea or in remote villages in the mountains, Bulgarians take health and healing very seriously. The spas I visited had complete medical staffs: a doctor, several nurses, and a variety of skilled body workers and trained masseuses. Treatments for the *cure* are referred to as balneology.

Hotel Augusta in historic Hissar was my favorite spa, partly because the staff was so enthusiastic about the commercial possibilities of their spa, and partly because the road to Hissar winds through the famous Valley of the Roses, the source of pure Bulgarian rose oil, which is much sought after by cosmetic companies. It is a romantic drive through serene pastures, orchards of flowering fruit trees, and fields of lavender.

The Hotel Augusta is typical of Bulgarian spas undergoing privatization—management remodels when it can afford to. So the swimming pool, the first section to be revitalized, is right out of a posh Hawaiian resort. The hotel itself, built during the Communist era, is dark and dreary by American standards. While the lobby was decorated in dark brown velvet, with unlighted chandeliers (to save money), my large suite with living room and small refrigerator was done in cheerful bright yellow and green.

From my deck I could look out over the valley. Just the sight of the lush green rolling hills below a ridge of purple mountains lowered my stress level. To me, the air in Hissar smelled like sunshine and felt like silk against my skin.

Boyan Manlev, my guide through a Bulgarian-based tour operator, accompanied me to the spas. At first I thought this was odd, but most Bulgarians speak little English, so as it turned out, Boyan was a big help. Unfortunately he knows more about my medical history than he ever wanted to.

Dr. Ianna Hristozova was the head doctor at Hotel Augusta. A short redhead with a wide smile, she greeted me warmly but scolded me for not planning to spend at least seven to ten days taking the cure. "We will do what we can in two days," she said. "But no promises." Recently, she explained, a Texas couple had stayed for a month. "They were here for chronic constipation," she said seriously. "They went back to America very happy."

After a long interview about my medical history and a quick check of my blood pressure and a tongue inspection, I was sent off to meet the head nurse, also named Ianna, who would start a cure on my lower back. Nurse Ianna, a trim thirtyish blonde, is married to one of Bulgaria's top archeologists. She told great stories about some 4,000-year-old Thracian tombs recently found nearby in a farmer's field. She talked a mile a minute in broken English.

My first treatment was an underwater Chinese massage that left me limp. While I reclined in a huge hospital-green tub of warm water, Ianna used a fat green hose with an intense spray of water to massage the acupuncture meridians of my body. Then it was back to my room for a nap and several glasses of mineral water.

Two hours later she took me upstairs to a sunny room for my paraffin treatment—hot paraffin poured into a hopsacklike bag and applied to my back for forty-five minutes. I could feel the warmth of the paraffin seep deep into my back. Afterward, she handed me another glass of water. I couldn't remember ever having been so relaxed.

The next morning, after a brisk walk around the grounds and a chilly swim in the pool, I met with a wild-haired masseuse, for a holistic aromatherapy massage. The essential oils used in aromatherapy are believed to relieve a wide range of stress-related disorders, skin disorders, even PMS. In a state of total relaxation, I slid off the table smelling like juniper, lemon, and coriander.

I had found the Chinese massage session so relaxing that I somewhat guiltily indulged in another one before we headed for Sandanski and the spa at St. Vrach, where I had heard of a miracle machine that eliminates every woman's greatest enemy: cellulite.

Sandanski is near the Greek border and boasts a balmy

Mediterranean-like climate. It is easy to see why the long-term Communist dictator of Bulgaria, Todor Zhivkov, built one of his residences here. Opulent, with white marble staircases, massive windows, views of the valley from every room, and its very own lake, Zhivkov's residence is now the hotel St. Vrach.

It is pretty much as he left it thirteen years ago. You can rent his very own sprawling presidential four-bedroom, four-bathroom suite for about $250 a night—complete with a room for your bodyguards. The suite is so big it occupies the whole top floor of the hotel and includes a conference hall with fireplace and a kitchen.

Perched on a hill and overlooking unspoiled farmlands and quaint villages, St. Vrach was my idea of paradise. Although the dining room was huge and formal, Boyan and I took our meals with the other guests outside on a terrace overlooking the lake. At St. Vrach there are no sounds except birds chirping, the occasional quack of a duck, or the rustle of the warm evening breeze through the trees. The resort town of Sandanski, about a ten-minute drive away, is more lively.

But I didn't care about nightlife. I was more interested in the cellulite cure. Dr. Georgy Iossifov, medical director at St. Vrach, reminded me of a small-town pediatrician. Tall, white-haired, and in his late sixties, he exuded warmth and kindness; I instantly trusted him. After a brief exam he outlined a program, but shook his finger and gave me my second scolding, saying he could not do much in two days, that if I was serious about curing my back and lumpy thighs, he would need ten to fifteen days.

My anticipated cellulite treatment consisted of several small suction cups placed on my thighs and back. A small whirring machine regulated their motion. It felt like several hands playfully pinching my skin. I lay face down in the treatment room with sunshine pouring through the windows, thinking about what crazy things women do. Later I soaked in a red algae bath in the dictator's private bathtub.

The spa at St. Vrach is in transition. The new management has ambitious plans. Current treatments include programs for increasing life span, reducing weight, curing asthma and other respiratory system troubles, and stopping smoking.

Or you can have a program tailored to your needs. Dr. Iossiffov was proudly planning to host a group of Danes the following week, who would be bathing in red wine. Spa staff had rigged tubs that looked like oak wine barrels. I laughed. I, who had just taken a bath in red algae, could not believe that anyone could sit in warm water and red wine, but the doctor said the Danes took this very seriously and that red wine could possibly prevent skin cancer.

Lulled into a blissful stupor by the balmy air, sunshine, and treatments, I entertained fantasies of living at St. Vrach permanently.

And we had not even hit the Black Sea, which is considered Mecca for European spa junkies. Of the numerous Black Sea spas, the Hotel Dobrudja in Albena (north of Varna) is probably the most famous. And the most serious. It's so serious they call it Medical Center Albena. Treatments cover everything from aging, stress, obesity, and neuritis, to neuralgia, arthritis, rheumatism, and sexual dysfunction. The large fitness center has the latest equipment. The spa also offers cosmetic services that include the latest trendy skin peels.

Bulgarians highly recommend Dobrudja. I met with the head doctor, a specialist in aromatherapy, who gave me a tour of the facilities. Treatment rooms were rather basic. I was intrigued by the warm beeswax treatment and, of course, the electrical and light treatments for cellulite. The spa's staff of sixty can perform up to two thousand various procedures a day.

Unfortunately, I did not have time to try treatments at the Dobrudja. This tall, imposing hotel overlooks the white-sand beach and glittering sea. The coastal air, incredibly warm and sultry, is probably an important part of the medical center's *cure* rate.

There are many stories about Americans who have come to Bulgaria hoping for a cure. Americans seem to come to Bulgaria when all other treatments have failed. At St. Vrach, a high-powered New York businessman came for asthma treatments. It took seven years of visits, but eventually he was healed. As for me, although two treatments on the cellulite machine did not cure what ailed me, I departed Bulgaria with no sign of stress in my body, with a radiant complexion from drinking all that water.

Last month a friend and I spent what should have been four glorious days at a famous-name spa in Arizona. What a disappointment. Some $3,500 and several trendy treatments later, I left feeling that the good-looking, well-trained staff didn't really care what I got out of it. No doctor scolded me. No one asked about in-depth health issues. My friend and I received very little personal attention. I figure we could have flown to Bulgaria and taken *the cure* for a full fifteen days and *still* had money left over.

Over the years, Pat Walker's involvement in the aviation industry took her all over the world and she ended up in some pretty strange places. At a Special Operations Forces conference in the Middle East, she met a group of Bulgarian businessmen who encouraged her to visit their country. She did not have a clue where Bulgaria was. One thing they insisted—she had to try the spas. A year later she found herself in Bulgaria and discovered a wonderful, quirky country and was soon blissed out by the friendliness of the people and spa delights. Pat is now the owner of The Cultural Explorer, a cultural and philanthropic travel company.

KELLY   SNOWDEN

* * *

Woman in the Land of *Wa*

A cross-cultural experience takes root.

IN JAPANESE THERE IS A WORD, WA, WHOSE MEANING IS difficult to translate. Its denotation has morphed over time to encompass larger things than mere "harmony," which a glance in the dictionary yields. This is like calling Fuji a mountain, when to the Japanese it is an awesome volcano, a place of pilgrimage.

Wa is harmony, but it is a forced harmony. In the pursuit of *wa*, individuals submerge their own selfish goals in favor of a larger group objective. The word has mutated so much that it has come to mean the Japanese culture itself at times, a placid lake on the surface with everyone's individual needs buried underneath.

I didn't know the word when I arrived in Tokyo in the midst of a stifling summer, but I saw its effects everywhere. Trains ran to the minute, the homeless never pleaded for spare change, and even the seediest neon alleyways were considered safe. Everything was smooth, and I endeavored not to cause any ripples.

I traveled from Tokyo to Wakayama, where I would spend the next year as the first foreigner to live and teach English in the rural mountain village. During my ride from the airport, I rehearsed how I would introduce myself to my new boss so as to demonstrate the proper respect. Don't look him in the eye. Don't get up from your bow until he does. Don't let his bow go deeper than yours.

When the time came, we were in a windowless, cramped room. They called my name and he came forward, a slim man my father's age with eyes like saucers. I hinged at the waist and concentrated on the linoleum. Then I heard him chuckle lightly. I peeked up and spied his offered palm resting in midair, unshaken. Then I laughed, too.

During my first weeks, the faces of my coworkers at the board of education emerged from the haze of foreign novelty. Fatherly Maeda, who was the only Japanese man I ever met who cooked for his wife. Sporty Hiraku, who owned a motorcycle and taught his two sons to say "May the force be with you!" whenever we parted. And my boss, who let me pick overflowing baskets of plump strawberries from his crop. They initiated me into the world of karaoke, *taiko* drums, and finally, *enkais*.

Enkais are office parties, but in Japan they serve a purpose more important than mere socializing. They are what allow *wa* to function in the office. For one night, the social hierarchy of the workplace is drowned with alcohol. With a literal pop of the champagne, the pressure is momentarily released and secretaries can rail against CEOs, underlings against top management. The next day all is forgiven, if not forgotten.

My first *enkai* was on a steamy weeknight at the only place available in town, a tiny inn. I pushed tempura around with my chopsticks and pondered how early I could leave without appearing ungrateful. The party grew louder and fuller, and I was about to ask for a ride home when my boss sidled beside me and began to chatter in Japanese, his face ruddy with drink. The conversation began as playful until I realized he had come to air some frustrations of his own.

He asked me if I had noticed that American women were different than Japanese ones, that they were bigger in certain places. He asked me if I was going to stay true to my boyfriend. Then he asked me if my pubic hair matched the hair on my head.

I felt as if my bones were melting, as if everyone in the room had heard our exchange. Lucky for me, my coworker Maeda had. I fled to the restroom after my boss's comments, and Maeda was in the hallway when I came out, offering me a ride home. During the entire drive he apologized for his own boss's actions. I waved my hand in the air as if to brush the matter aside, but it remained.

The next day at work everything was normal, calm. I sulked at my desk,

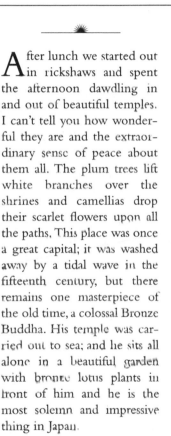

After lunch we started out in rickshaws and spent the afternoon dawdling in and out of beautiful temples. I can't tell you how wonderful they are and the extraordinary sense of peace about them all. The plum trees lift white branches over the shrines and camellias drop their scarlet flowers upon all the paths. This place was once a great capital; it was washed away by a tidal wave in the fifteenth century, but there remains one masterpiece of the old time, a colossal Bronze Buddha. His temple was carried out to sea; and he sits all alone in a beautiful garden with bronze lotus plants in front of him and he is the most solemn and impressive thing in Japan.

—Gertrude Bell,
Letter (1898)

and my boss even lugged over the dictionary and quizzically pointed to the word "homesick." I was disturbing the *wa*, not playing by the rules.

I grew up with stickers stating "This Insults Women" always at the bottom of my schoolbag, ready for plastering on offensive magazines and pictures. Yet I couldn't bridge the gap between that slogan and my experience. I sat quiet and excused myself to go to the bathroom when it turned personal. My boss never laid a hand on me outside of awkward public hugs during my year there, but he regularly approached me at *enkais*. He told me he had dreams about me. Once, he called me in the middle of the night to leave the only words he ever said to me in English. He told my answering machine: "My name is Nishikawa. I love you."

I complained to the governing council for my county, who informed me that I could move to another school, another tenuous foreign home. I declined.

He may not have touched me, but Nishikawa molded me nonetheless. I began locking my door and car in a village where people left keys in ignitions. I felt as if I grew smaller on my walk to work, becoming something too tiny and inconsequential to merit any attention. I dressed as if the chill of fall were upon me even while the trees remained green and plentiful. And I became *wa*.

I ran every day, feverishly and for hours. My journal overflowed with vehemence. Friends listened quietly as my voice cracked over the phone. These same friends would never recognize my Japanese self, a withdrawn girl who rarely smiled but never scowled. My focus was to teach the children of the village English, and I set all of my bitterness aside for it, displaying a serene front. I was beginning to understand why Japan may have a low rate for homicide but not for suicide.

The day I left, several friends came to see me off at the airport even though it was a two-hour drive from my adopted hometown. There was Tamago, my tireless drum teacher who gave me fabric to make my own kimono. There was Miyoko, the doctor's wife who tried to cure my homesickness with lavish dinners every Tuesday. Last was Nishikawa, who hugged me in the airport like he told me he had in a dream.

I left them behind a glass partition and have shamefully not written to a single one. I have long internal dialogues with them at times, trying to explain in a common tongue why I have left Japan.

Except for Nishikawa. I owe him no explanation. But I think of him, too. When I shrink from a passion because of a fear of attention, I think of him. When I suppress unpleasant feelings but can't explain my motivation, I think of him. And these thoughts remind me that the *wa* didn't stay behind a glass partition at the airport. It came home with me.

Kelly Snowden lives in Brooklyn and is an assistant research editor for Food & Wine magazine. She is secretly addicted to television and tries to curb her habit by not paying for cable. So far this approach has failed, as she finds herself inexplicably watching Judge Judy *or* Wheel of Fortune *with embarrassing frequency.*

ANDREA G. FISCHER

⋆ ⋆ ⋆

Killing Me Softly

When a Very Bad Idea isn't.

"THEY WILL KILL YOU, YOU KNOW."

The Turkish travel agent tells me, "You are killing me softly," but he says it as casually as if he were a waiter announcing the specials for the evening, as he hands me my plane ticket from Istanbul to Tehran. While certainly qualifying as a unique sales pitch, this was not the first time that I had heard some variation of this theme.

When I first told people I planned to travel to Iran on my own in 2001, most looked at me as if I were announcing my plans to vacation underneath a highway overpass. In fact, I did not actually know the reason I was going; I simply knew that I had to go. And since, even to me, this sounded like the set up to a Very Bad Idea, I offered explanations that I thought would be acceptable to most people: that I was interested in the history or in the culture of the country. All of which were true, and none of which were really the reason.

But, if anyone had doubts about my sincerity in going to Iran, they had only to see what I went through to get a visa.

The Iranian government is notoriously stingy in granting visas to three categories of travelers: independent travelers, single women, and Americans. I happened to be all three.

After several months of bureaucratic gymnastics in the U.S., I arrived in Istanbul, Turkey, where I was to pick up my Iranian visa. There I was told my visa authorization number was invalid. Several days, many international phone calls, and repeated treks to the Iranian consulate later, I finally received my new, and allegedly valid, visa number. I hurried to the consulate only to find the doors closed. I tried persuading the guards to let me in, but to no avail.

Alas, bureaucracy is a bit like quicksand; it is best not to directly struggle against it, but look for a branch, a hand, or anything that will pull you out, and when you spot it, grab on with all your strength. Determined not to leave empty-handed, I slumped against a wall and did not move. Finally, after a half-hour of this, one of the guards took pity on me and unlocked the doors. I had hold of my branch.

That was how I found myself on a midnight flight from Istanbul to Tehran, watching an overhead monitor track the plane's progress. I watched with both excitement and apprehension as the black flight path arched across the map until it touched, then crossed, into Iran.

Tehran is not, to put it as politely as possible, a city that will likely ever grace the glossy cover of a travel brochure, as the chance of getting black lung disease is not typically considered a selling point for tourists. The pollution does not look so much as if it had arisen from the city, but rather, as if it had been poured from above and was settling in for the duration between the unevenly-spaced teeth of the city's concrete buildings.

The first thing I did in Tehran was purchase a manteau, a long, loose trench coat type of garment that, along with a head scarf, satisfies the requirements of *hejab*—the Islamic dress code that is required for all females over the age of seven in Iran. While women may also wear a chador—a black, all-encompassing tentlike cloth—most women, especially in the cities, choose to wear a manteau.

I purchased a plain, dark blue, tea-length manteau made of a light cotton fabric that, in an apparent nod to the secular fashion of the 1980s, had shoulder pads sewn inside and a scooped neckline. I put my hands through the cuffed sleeves that hung slightly below my wrists and into the pockets.

Nearly everyone that I met in Iran asked me what I thought of *hejab*. "It is hot," I answered as diplomatically as I could. And it was. At the end of the each day in the hot desert of southern Iran, I found a constellation of salt across the back of my manteau from my evaporated sweat. It also proved to be, at times, a source of comfort. As my internal compass points aligned roughly with "lost," "hopelessly lost," and "curled-up-in-the-fetal-position lost," the sight of a group of women in their chadors, moving together with a common cloth liquidness like a school of fish, was a relief, their presence a guarantee of both safety and assistance.

And although I had to comply with the requirement to wear the *hejab*, there were other restrictions whose practical enforcement was more lax. One of these was that Americans traveling in Iran must be guided at all times.

I was able to skirt this regulation by telling my guide that I had to visit the family of a friend I had in the U.S. My guide insisted on getting his friend, a cab driver, to drive me to my make-believe destination. To my surprise and relief, there was actually such an address. However, as luck would have it, the fake address turned out to be a house that was, like much of Tehran, undergoing major reconstruction. Scaffolding hung over much of the house and several windows were missing.

The cab driver looked at me doubtfully and asked, "Are you sure this is the right address?" I assured him it was and got out with a cheery wave. But, he did not leave, as he had been given instructions to see me through the door.

I fussed and fidgeted with the straps on my backpack, carefully adjusting straps for which I never had any use, but whose precise length and location were now of utmost importance. After several minutes of meticulous backpack grooming, the taxi driver finally gave up and left.

I waited a few moments and then took a cab to the bus station. I decided to take whatever bus happened to be leaving first. It turned out to be a bus going to Esfahan, a city approximately seven hours south of Tehran.

There is a difference in the travelers who chose to come to Iran. Without exception, none of the travelers I met were under twenty-five, and all seemed to have come to the country at some crossroads in their life, as if drawn by some force to a country that is itself at a crossroads, both politically and culturally.

I met one of these travelers while walking back to my hotel in Esfahan one night. I had noticed a tall, thin man walking at a respectful distance beside me. It was difficult to see more without turning my head. The edge of my headscarf prevented any sort of discrete glances.

It turned out we were both staying at the same hotel, and we spent that evening talking and drinking tea in the hotel's courtyard. Jasper had come from Amsterdam on a motorbike. He planned to thread his way through the cities and villages of Iran and continue to Pakistan. He was also struggling with questions about the future of his thirteen-year relationship with his girlfriend, who had remained in Amsterdam.

I found myself easily telling Jasper things that I had not said out loud before. Although I had graduated from law school and had a job that many would envy, I felt as if I had stayed too long on a train that I'd already known was heading in the wrong direction when I boarded. Somewhere far behind was a love of words and writing that was abandoned in the ease of floating from one "good" decision to the next.

When we parted at the end of the evening, we went to our separate rooms, our own personal borders clearly drawn and agreed upon.

During the following days in Esfahan, I often found myself ruminating on the fact that it was summer in Iran, and wearing a coat, pants, and scarf outside seemed like something you'd do on a dare, not on a daily basis. Then one day I am struck by an idea—if I wore the manteau without my shirt underneath, I would still technically be in compliance with the rules of *hejab*.

When I emerged shirtless from my hotel, I immediately began to imagine that everyone knew I was naked from the waist up. Thanks to my nervousness and dwindling confidence in my ability, should I be caught, to parse the fine semantic difference of being "technically in compliance," this arrangement soon proved to produce as much as sweat as the original.

I had just returned back to fully-clothed sweating when I was approached by two Iranian girls, Maryam and Nazi. This was not the first time, nor was it the last time that I was approached by strangers on the street. Although the Lonely Planet guidebook to Iran advises "Bring a book. Bring lots of them," to combat the dearth of organized entertainment or nightlife, I soon discovered that due to the overwhelming and generous hospitality of Iranians, of all the pieces of advice for me to have taken to heart, this was the most ridiculous.

Maryam and Nazi invited me to their home for lunch. Their house, like many other houses I visited, was hidden away behind a large, solid wooden fence, beyond which was a lovely garden. Once inside the house, the girls took off their manteaus and chadors and insisted that I do the same. I silently thanked whatever god may be applicable to a situation such as this that I had put my top back on.

After a meal of *khoresht-e fesenjun* (chicken in pomegranate sauce) shared on a cloth spread out on the floor, the girls told me I was welcome to stay with them as long as I wanted. I politely declined their invitation and told them that I had to go meet Jasper at the Si o Se Bridge, or, literally, the Bridge of 33 Arches.

If I had announced my impending plans to sew my hand to my forehead, I think fewer questions might have followed. Is he Iranian? No. Is he your boyfriend? No. Where did you meet him? I tried to explain.

The girls wanted to accompany me. They were afraid that I would be late, so they helped me with my head scarf, their hands swooping gracefully like birds, arranging my scarf and fastening the large, flat blue buttons on my coat. Each of my hands was taken by one of the girls, and together we set off running toward the bridge.

Out of the corner of my eye I spotted a group of Komite, or religious police. They jumped out of a jeep, surrounded a man and began to beat him with what looked like night sticks. If the girls noticed it at all, they did not give any indication, and I followed their lead. We did not slow down. The bridge, with its smooth arches skipping over a dry and cracked river-bed, was just ahead, and we kept running, hand in hand.

If acquaintances had fears about not being able to find the particular proverbial ditch by the side of the road in which many were certain I'd be left in Iran, they didn't need to worry—they had only to follow the trail of books that I was leaving behind. I left behind history, politics, language, and religion, but kept poetry—specifically a book of poems by the mid-fourteenth century Persian poet Hafez.

Hafez is so beloved in Iran that it is said that more copies of Hafez's work are sold in the country than copies of the Koran. Hafez's poems are like a literary kaleidoscope, each rereading of the deceptively simple words seems to reassemble differently, revealing something new.

It was from Hafez's tomb in the city of Shiraz that I was returning when I spotted Jasper's motorbike parked outside of the Hotel Estaghle, where I was staying. Although I was surprised, it was pleasantly so. When we had parted in Esfahan, it had been with an exchange of email addresses and a warm handshake. I had not expected to see him again.

We spent the next days in Shiraz meeting for breakfasts of hard-boiled eggs, carrot jam and toast, and visiting the city that Hafez is said to have only left but once in his life. Among the places we visited was the Bogheye Shah-e Cheragh, or shrine of the King of the Lamp (the brother of the eighth grandson of the prophet Mohammed). Only women who have chadors are allowed inside, but it is also possible to rent one at a small expense, and in my case, a bit of personal dignity. The chador that I rented was white with tiny patterned flowers, and when I draped it over both my manteau and backpack and I looked vaguely like Casper the friendly Muslim ghost.

Nonetheless, it worked to get me inside the shrine, where hundreds of thousands of small, mirrored tiles lined the walls and ceiling, giving slivers of reflections back in a fractured brilliance. A sheet separated the men's and women's sides, and an Iranian took me through both sides. Although I was hesitant to follow, not one of the men, who were deep in prayer, voiced any objection to my presence.

At the tomb, I watched a woman cry, the black ink of her chador spilling around her. Traveling is a bit like painting a picture by negative space; you become defined by what you are not; what you have not experienced, and it is also, at the same time, a gradual chipping away of those spaces. That could have been me. It still might be me. I might be you. You might be me. I found myself envious of the comfort that she was able to find there.

When we returned to the hotel, Ali, the young desk clerk, asked us if we wanted him to get us some vodka. We said yes and gave him eight dollars for two cans of black-market vodka. That night, on the roof of the hotel, we sat on a mattress covered with a worn, soft faux animal print blanket, and Ali brought the vodka out on a thin blue plastic tray. We brought our glasses together in a toast and drank.

Well, almost.

Immediately after taking his first sip, Ali turned his head and spit it all out in a spray of not-veiled-at-all disgust. He had never had vodka before, he told us. It turned out that my Dutch companion was likewise, also not a fan of vodka. As a firm believer in the manifest destiny as applied to alcohol, I finished my drink and then the rest of both of theirs. This solution proved to be satisfactory to all.

At some point, Ali politely got up to leave. We urged him to sit back down, to stay, but he feigned that he had to go back to work. Although Jasper and I were not together and found ourselves often telling people this, our disavowal of a relationship only seemed to reinforce people's belief, including Ali's, that we were romantically involved.

Earlier that afternoon, while Jasper and I had been walking through the trees at Bagh-e Eram (Garden of Paradise), an elderly gardener had grabbed at Jasper's hand and then at mine. At first we were alarmed, but we quickly relaxed once we realized that the gardener simply wanted to let us know that we could hold hands in his garden. That was not an occurrence unique to Shiraz. Throughout the country it seemed that love, or, at the very least, the desire for it, was marching through on tiptoe.

I first heard its gentle footsteps in the mountains north of Tehran while waiting for a telecabin that winced its occupants up Tochal Mountain. When the operator asked the young man in front of me if he wanted a specific color of telecabin— for there were dusty yellows, blues, and reds available—he laughed and said that he did not care what color the cabin was, so long as the windows were tinted. He was with a girl and it was clear that they were not married.

All over the country, its foot tapped impatiently in the confessions of young Iranians who told me about their boyfriends and girlfriends who their parents didn't know about. Ali, too, had a girlfriend that his parents did not know about. Love may not be able to conquer all anymore, but it appears to be a worse biological threat than anthrax could ever be; stubborn, hopeful, and infectious.

That evening, I found there was no one that I could confess what I was feeling to when the night ended too quickly. Hafez was there though, and I read his poems until I finally fell asleep.

When I visited the original city and citadel of Bam, which was built in the twelfth century, I stayed for hours without seeing another person. Its vast six-square-kilometer collection of clay and straw skeletons of homes had, at one time, contained between 9,000 and 13,000 people. Walking through the abandoned metropolis was like walking through a Hiroshima-like tracing of another people's existence; it was at once beautiful and ghostlike, both unsettling and familiar.

I came back from my trip exhausted and ill from a mysterious illness that had plagued me since Esfahan, and which had made it increasingly difficult, if not impossible, for me to retain any liquid or food. I fell into the bottom bunk on top of the covers. Many hours later, I woke up to see a familiar face; it was Jasper squatting next to my bed, a concerned look on his face and a hand on my shoulder. Somehow, it seemed, we had found each other again.

When I got up, the owner of the guesthouse, Akbar, was serving dinner on the large courtyard that overlooked a sunken garden. The table and bench where we ate were surrounded by hammocks that Akbar—and guests, too, if they so desired—slept in during the hot summer months. During dinner, Akbar, a former English teacher, said that although he was free to leave Iran, he chose not to. He could not imagine a better existence than what he had created there. With the smell of honeysuckle floating in on the cool evening breeze, it was impossible to imagine any falseness in that statement.

Akbar's teenaged son, Mohammed, whose laugh seemed as if it was trying to break free of its bodily host, taught me how to properly pronounce the infamous "*Marg bar Amrika*" or "Death to America" slogan, which could be found stenciled on walls throughout the country. It was graffiti, though, that was bereft of any real menace. Its careful practiced perfection betrayed its originator as being someone less motivated by unbridled hatred than by a government paycheck. It had no more malicious heft to it than Mohammed's contagious carbonated laugh.

Later in the evening, when the other travelers had broken apart and regrouped in smaller knots about the courtyard, Akbar stopped me on my way back from one of my numerous trips to the bathroom, to speak with me alone. He did not

sk me, but rather told me, that he knew I came to Iran for a
ason. I told him that was true, but that I did not know why.
kbar, with his large, thick, square glasses and one leg crossed
er the other, waited patiently for me to find my answer.

thought back to the cold January day in Chicago on
which my mom went with me to the post office to mail my
first attempt at an Iranian visa. She had also been there years
earlier when I was mailing job interview thank-you letters,
and I could not help but wonder, while we stood in line that
second time, whether she was aware of the careful unraveling
of a sweater that was occurring. I know I was not. It wasn't
until I was thousands of miles away, on a trip that everyone
had warned me against, that my choices, my desires, however
wrong everyone else may think they are, however wrong they
may eventually turn out to be, are mine to make.

And I knew what I had to do when I returned. I would
quit my job and begin again, this time to write. And I did, albeit very slowly, glacially even. But it was there, the movement, and this time, it was mine.

*Andrea G. Fischer is a freelance writer who once while traveling at-
tempted to drink a cup of salad dressing, believing it to be a new and
exotic beverage. Although she would like to believe that this was an
isolated incidence brought about by unfamiliar surroundings, she has
proven to be equally adept at embarrassing herself domestically. When
she is not writing, she can often be found in San Francisco's Mission
District, enjoying a round of Ranch Dressing with friends at the
local bar.*

ASHA PATEL

* * *

The Gift

The best are indeed free.

IN A TEAHOUSE IN THE BACK STREETS OF GION, MY MIND remains congested, muggy, and drowned in the polluted rivers of pessimism. It is a far cry from the clarity which I had hoped travel would provide. And I am sure that life will continue to show me her course—one over which I have no control but still feel I ought.

I flew, Hong Kong to Singapore, having no time to exploit the free internet and other services at Changi International Airport before being swiftly hauled onto a connecting flight that would bring me here: to the home of bullet trains, technological advance, strange foods, and Shinto temples, where beneath the concrete jungle of buildings, lurks a scurry of life steeped in cultural traditions and a way that is authentically Japanese. In fact, so Japanese that after seven months of solo travel across the globe, I experienced the most extensive cultural shock suffered throughout my journey. I am in the big T: the capital city of Tokyo, which I had presumed to be relatively international. Yet, I found myself in a linguistic jam, where the tools of communication and comprehension were beyond my reach. While of course this reduced functionality to a minimum, I endeavored to have fun with it. In response to the service with a scowl that was sometimes received, I began to sport a grin that would have been the envy of any Cheshire cat—to which the reactions were varied and amusing. Some suddenly found fascination with their feet as they abashedly looked downward, some reciprocated with shy reserved smiles of their own, while others just became further enraged by this strange smiling *gaijin* and overtly displayed their annoyance by a deep furrowing of the frown.

At first appearance, Tokyo is an atomistic society, awash with individualism. But underneath this cloak pumps the lifeblood of social cohesion, where the atoms are stuck together forming the molecules of Japanese society— something solid, and seemingly impenetrable. I was grateful to have a friend in the city to guide me around and act as interpreter in my endeavors. Though our friendship was not without its own communication problems.

In Yokohama, I went to the Hundred Steps, at the top of which lives a Japanese belle, Oyuchisan, who is the theme for artist and pet, and the admiration of tourists. One of the pleasant events of my stay was the luncheon given for me on the Omaha, the American war vessel lying at Yokohama. I took several drives, enjoying the novelty of having a Japanese running by the horses' heads all the while. I ate rice and eel. I visited the curio shops, one of which is built in imitation of a Japanese house, and was charmed with the exquisite art I saw therein; in short, I found nothing but what delighted the finer senses while in Japan.

—Elizabeth Cochrane Seaman, *Nellie Bly's Book* (1890)

Yuichiro and I were acquainted from our time spent living in France, three years ago, since which time neither of us had used French extensively nor daily. Given that French was our only common language, the pair of us frequently ended each day with brain-ache from the search for vocabulary.

I continued to struggle with this; the attempt to integrate, understand, and infiltrate the cultural barriers as all aspiring nomads do, and yet, there was something implicitly futile in this endeavor, as I was to discover. I headed out of the city and into the more isolated regions of northern Honshu; somewhere, in the middle of nowhere, where even solitude had a hard time being found. I sat, sandwiched between the endless murky gray of the sea, and the sky. The amalgamation of anxiety, homesickness, and unfamiliarity were compounded by the apparent remoteness of my existence, which altogether formed a perfect recipe for dejection and entrapment. Emotions drifted through me, mirroring the movements of the ocean, coming and receding; just as the sand was thrown out onto the shore, and then reclaimed just as swiftly by the powerful motions of the undercurrent. I sighed. A fast-forward button would have been appealing, but I didn't want that, not really, for there was a deeper understanding that the abundance of the moment was overflowing with the lessons I needed, enabling me to observe the lithesome quality of the illusion and having the courage to enjoy it; to revel in the very nature of travel, as it presented itself in an array of plentiful, albeit sometimes unpleasant experiences. And unpleasant they were. As I walked back to my accommodation in the pine forest, a sudden sense of urgency led me to pack up my belongings and head back to the chaos of the capital city. So, hoisting onto my back all twenty staggering kilos of the pack that had become akin to a spare limb, I relaxed as I waded through swarms of people and navigated my way through a maze of intersecting train lines. And I smiled as I realized that it was not in silent moments of yoga on the rooftop, nor mountain views, nor even Shinto temples in which insights were to be found; it was in those chaotic, stressful times when I just threw my hands in the air and let the fate-filled moment run its course. It was then that I realized my struggle to conform was futile, for it was from within me that a sense of home, a sense of belonging was to be found.

Arriving at Sendai, I stood on a platform, basking in the glory of this realization while admiring the impeccable station, the respectful staff, and the gleaming white *shinkansen* as they glided silently into the station and departed within seconds of their allocated timeframe. Mesmerized by the soporific effect of these thoughts and clockwork motions, I unexpectedly became aware of a presence by my side. I turned around to drown in deep chestnut pools, as beautifully brown as the falling autumn leaves. The eyes belonged to an old face, aged by experience rather than time. They gazed at me, affirmatively. As I surrendered to the unfathomable space within, there emerged a smile, a little hesitant at first, but extending to a beaming, penetrating grin that reflected all that was within me; a distant, forgotten self that transpired in that moment as his eyes held my gaze. And so it was that I finally found home. Not in the familiar confines of my own country, but a deeper, more definite sense of belonging that is available when one opens her heart to the infinite possibility that life is.

The return to home in my own country, which was about as smooth as the upside of a cactus, provided the perfect juxtaposition to this experience, enabling me to savor the sweetness of that day, which lingers evermore. And so it is that the ebb of life continues to flow, and beautifully illustrate that I have evolved, transformed by that wonderful gift we call travel.

At age twenty-three, with an ever persistent itch to travel, Asha Patel's heart and mind hinted at retribution if she did not satisfy demands to explore the unknown. So, after graduating with an LLB. Bachelor of Laws from the London School of Economics and a diploma in French Law from the University of Strasbourg, she quit her job in a London-based management consultancy firm, stuffed a few belongings into a pack, and left. Asha's most prized possession, her journal, was always in her hand.

Index of Contributors

Acknowledgments

Many people have influenced me and my work on this book—courageous friends, singular strangers, and most importantly my mother, who always believed in me and thus taught me to believe in myself. Thanks to Dad, as well as Mom, for taking us on long car trips across the USA, giving us roots and wings, and exposing us to the world beyond Ohio.

I have been inspired, advised, encouraged, and soothed by my patient, supportive husband, Gary Sheppard. I have been tolerated and forgiven my absences in mind and body by my heart's great joy, my daughters Julieclaire and Annalyse. Simply, sincerely, thank you.

Some time ago, on a journey over the Himalayas from Tibet to Nepal, I developed a friendship with two wonderfully crazy, entrepreneurial writers, James O'Reilly and Larry Habegger, the editors of the Travelers' Tales series. Under a tropical moon on the shores of the Pacific in Mexico six years later, we began and ended the evening, as we had so often before, sharing travelers' stories. During our chats we decided to work together on an anthology about contemporary women travelers. Heartfelt thanks to James and Larry, friends as well as the series editors. My gratitude to Susan Brady and Christy Quinto who kept us all organized and on time during production, and to Lara Endreszl for her hard work at every stage of production.

Finally, my deepest appreciation to all the women who are included in this book, for giving us new stories to live by and strengthening our resolve and courage to step out the door.

"Pulling the Trigger on a Trip" by Susan Van Allen published with permission from the author. Copyright © 2007 by Susan Van Allen.

Additional Credits

About the Editor

Marybeth Bond has not always been a Gutsy Woman. At summer camp, when she was ten years old, she was nicknamed "Misty" because she had a bad case of homesickness. Not one of her counselors would have predicted a traveling future for her. However, several decades later, Marybeth has hiked, cycled, climbed, dived, and kayaked her way through more than seventy countries around the world, from the depths of the Flores Sea to the summit of Mount Kilimanjaro. She studied in Paris for four years, earned two degrees, and had a business career in marketing.

At twenty-nine, she took off again, this time to travel alone around the world. These two years of travel changed her life. She met her future husband, an American, in Kathmandu, Nepal, and she returned to begin a new career as a writer, consultant, and lecturer. Since then she has given lectures around the world at such venues as the Explorers Club and Asia Society in New York.

Marybeth's first book, *A Woman's World,* is a bestseller and won the Lowell Thomas Gold Medal for Best Travel Book from the Society of American Travel Writers Foundation. It is an eloquent collection of women's writing that paints a rich portrait of what it means to be a woman today.

Marybeth was a featured guest on *The Oprah Winfrey Show*, with her book *Gutsy Women.* As a nationally recognized travel expert and media personality, Marybeth has appeared on

CBS News, CNN, ABC, NBC, FOX TV, and National Public Radio. She was the "Smart Traveler" radio host for the nationally syndicated Outside Radio show and the travel expert/columnist for the Travel Channel on ivillage.com, a women's online network. She was also the "Travel Expert" for CBS's *Evening Magazine*. She is currently the Adventure Editor for *travelgirl magazine* and the Spokesperson for AAA, Northern California. Follow along with her at www.gutsytraveler.com.

Marybeth has two children and a husband, and lives in Northern California. She travels as much as she can—with her family, her friends, or alone.

OTHER BOOKS BY MARYBETH BOND

A Woman's World

A Woman's Passion for Travel

Gutsy Women

Gutsy Mamas

A Mother's World

A Woman's Europe

A Woman's Asia

50 Best Girlfriends Getaways in North America